STUBBORN FOR LIBERTY

the Dutch in New York

A NEW YORK STATE STUDY

STUBBORN

Published for the New York State American Revolution Bicentennial Commission

FOR LIBERTY

the Dutch in New York

ALICE P. KENNEY

SYRACUSE UNIVERSITY PRESS   1975

Library of Congress Cataloging in Publication Data

Kenney, Alice P., 1937-
    Stubborn for liberty.

    (A New York State study)
    Includes bibliographical references.
    1. Dutch Americans — New York (State) — Hudson
Valley — History. 2. Hudson Valley — History.
I. New York State American Revolution Bicentennial
Commission. II. Title.
F127.H8K4   974.7'004'3931   75-16403
ISBN 0-8156-0113-1

FOREWORD

THE HUDSON VALLEY DUTCH have never received the attention due
them in American history. There were comparatively few of them, they did
not call attention to themselves, and therefore most people are hardly aware
of their existence. Yet their contributions to the American way of life and
particularly to the American Revolution have been significant out of all
proportion to their numbers. This book attempts to restore them to their
proper place in the American heritage.

For this purpose the book presents a general account which does not
pretend to be either exhaustive or definitive. In fact an exhaustive, definitive
history is not yet possible. Many essential sources lie buried in untranslated
documents, uncataloged local archives, and unexplored — sometimes even
unknown — family records. In the last fifteen years, scholars have exploited
many such materials, but their investigations still leave important regions,
periods, people, and areas of human experience untouched. A number of
Bicentennial projects now in process, some for the translation of Dutch
records and others for the publication of local research, will certainly add
many new insights and probably new perspectives to the story here
presented.

This book should be useful to scholars as a summary of what is now
known about the Hudson Valley Dutch, as the first coherent account of the
development of their way of life over the three and a half centuries from
their first settlements to the present, and for its suggestion of numerous
topics on which further research is needed. But it has become evident during
the writing of it that it is inevitably one-sided. Generally available information
about the Dutch tends to overemphasize urban and mercantile aspects of
their way of life, traditions transplanted from the towns of the province of
Holland, and the Hudson Valley settlements of New York City and Albany.
The development of this "Dutch" tradition, which is the only one familiar to
most readers, is the principal subject of this book. But it should be clearly

recognized that the way of life of the Netherlands is exceedingly diverse, and that many of its diverse elements were transplanted to the Hudson Valley. When research now in progress, or published only locally, becomes better known, there will be a very different but equally "Dutch" story to be told, emphasizing the ways of life of the independent farmers from the rural Netherlands, who settled in the middle and lower Hudson Valley, on Long and Staten Islands, and in New Jersey.

In the meantime this book was written primarily for general readers, ordinary people who are curious about how their home towns and their country have come to be as they are. Students of New York State history and their teachers will be interested in learning more about this very important part of that subject. Descendants of Dutch families will want to become more fully aware of their forebears' accomplishments. Hudson Valley residents will discover many unfamiliar facts about their own communities, and residents of other parts of the state may be surprised to realize the part played by Hudson Valley Dutchmen in their development. Americans anxious to learn more about the heritage the Bicentennial is celebrating will find that the Dutch not only played a crucial part in the founding of the nation, but created enduring qualities and values in the American heritage.

The materials for this book are extremely varied and widely scattered and have been accumulated over two decades, often by chance discoveries outside the normal framework of research. It is therefore impossible to list by name everyone who has contributed. The individuals and institutions which follow have made extensive or sustained contributions, but appreciation is hereby expressed to the many others who have offered information or insights.

At various times the staffs of the New York Public Library, the New-York Historical Society, and the New York State Library have helped with research in their collections of manuscripts and rare books. Kenneth McFarlane, formerly Librarian of the Albany Institute of History and Art, has repeatedly gone far beyond the call of duty in locating materials and in many other ways. The library staff of Cedar Crest College also went out of their way to secure quantities of items on interlibrary loan, often on very short notice.

Museums have also gone out of their way to provide pictures and interpretive information about objects in their collections which illustrate Dutch material culture. Friends on the staffs of the Albany Institute of History and Art, the New-York Historical Society, and the Henry F. duPont Winterthur Museum have been particularly helpful. Other materials were contributed by the Brooklyn Museum, the Museum of the City of New York, the Metropolitan Museum, and Sleepy Hollow Restorations. So many Hudson Valley historic houses could be mentioned that it is hardly fair to single out any to the exclusion of others; some are named in the text and the rest are most gratefully remembered.

Individual scholars have been most generous of their time in responding to queries and sharing their unpublished research. Historians who have helped in this way include David A. Armour, Van Cleaf Bachman, James Tanis, Dr. Lawrence G. Van Loon, and George Olin Zabriskie. Students of Dutch artifacts in museums include Mary C. Black, Norman S. Rice, Dr. Th. Lunsingh Scheurleer, and Bruce T. Sherwood. Permission to use unpublished research is most gratefully acknowledged to Roderick Blackburn, Kristin L. Gibbons, Joseph W. Hammond, Paul R. Huey, and Robin Michel.

The production of any book requires concerted effort by many people. William A. Polf suggested that this one be written, and Vivian M. Hutchins edited the manuscript. Ruth Hewett assembled the illustrations, and Frances Johansson drew the maps. The invisible staff efficiency of the Office of State History and Syracuse University Press smoothed away many difficulties. The New York State Bicentennial Commission were generous with their support. Ralph B. Kenney and Leslie J. Workman made it possible to visit many of the museums. Henry A. Way, Jr., contributed essential research and secretarial assistance.

Perhaps most important of all are the numerous descendants of Dutch settlers who have preserved documents, relics, and memories of the Dutch tradition. Of the many who could be named, Morris Douw Ferris and Dorothy R. McNeilly must be mentioned for their generosity in sharing memorabilia of the Douw family, and Mr. and Mrs. Peter G. D. Ten Eyck and Mr. and Mrs. Robert Ten Eyck for making available their Gansevoort heirlooms. The late Huybertje Pruyn Hamlin and Charles K. Winne remembered many interesting facets of the last days of Dutch traditions in Albany.

A group of descendants who must be singled out for special mention is the Holland Society of New York. Richard H. Amerman, Frederick W. Bogert, Wilfrid B. Talman, and George Olin Zabriskie have forwarded this project in many ways, finally by reading the manuscript in the light of their particular expertise. But far more important even than these immediate contributions is the work of the Holland Society as a whole in preserving the Dutch heritage, maintaining the Dutch way of life, and promoting amity between the Netherlands and the United States. It is in appreciative recognition of their continuing contribution to the survival of the Dutch tradition in America that this book is dedicated to the members of the Holland Society.

Alice P. Kenney

Allentown, Pennsylvania
March 1975

PREFACE

"It is well known," wrote the eighteenth-century international traveler, Anne Grant, "that the Province of New-York . . . was originally settled by a Dutch colony, which came from Holland." "Well known" in the eighteenth century perhaps; but what do modern Americans really know about the Dutch people in American history? School children no doubt think of the blustering, one-legged Peter Stuyvesant, stumping about Manhattan tyrannizing his subjects, and everyone is familiar with the mythical Rip Van Winkle, who literally slept through the American Revolution. Reason alone would suggest that there is much more to the story of the Dutch role in American history than is suggested by the stereotypes of a dictatorial governor or an indolent ne'er-do-well.

It is appropriate during a period of revived interest in the ethnic, racial, and national backgrounds of the American people that the American Revolution Bicentennial celebration in New York should include a special tribute to the first major European group to settle in what is now New York. We are pleased to sponsor this book by Professor Alice P. Kenney, a distinguished scholar of the early period of American history and of the Dutch contribution to American society. This book is another in a series of jointly produced works by the New York State American Revolution Bicentennial Commission and a number of the university presses in the state.

This book is for the people of America and of New York State, particularly those who believe that the diverse character of the American population constitutes one of the strengths of American society.

John H. G. Pell, *Chairman*

New York State American Revolution
Bicentennial Commission

Map of New England, New Netherland, and Virginia, by Johannes Janssonius,

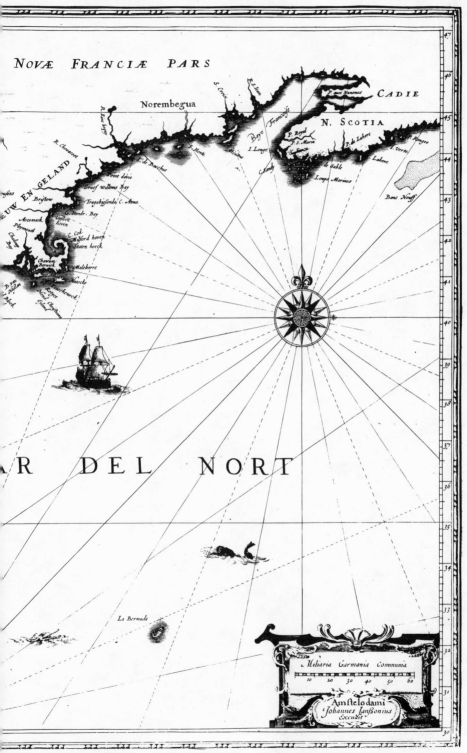

NOVÆ FRANCIÆ PARS

Norembegua

CADIE

N. SCOTIA

NIEUW ENGELAND

AR DEL NORT

La Bermuda

Miliaria Garmania Communia

10 20 30 40 50 60

Amstelodami
Johannes Janßonius
excudit

Amsterdam (1630?). *Courtesy of the New York State Library*

CONTENTS

ILLUSTRATIONS

MAPS

STUBBORN FOR LIBERTY

the Dutch in New York

INTRODUCTION

Silence Is Golden

"DUTCH" means many things to many people. Students of Americana think at once of Rip Van Winkle and the Headless Horseman. Lovers of art recall the age of Rembrandt and Vermeer. Tourists remember cheeses, tulips, windmills, and wooden shoes. American history textbooks recognize a brief "Dutch period" beginning with Henry Hudson's discovery of the Hudson River in 1609 and ending with Peter Stuyvesant's surrender of New Amsterdam to the English in 1664. Most Americans do not even realize that descendants of the Dutch colonists lived on in the Hudson Valley, speaking the Dutch language and maintaining a distinctively Dutch cultural tradition until well after the Revolution. The language and most Dutch customs have all but died out in the twentieth century, but families of Dutch descent still cherish heirlooms made or used by their ancestors, mute relics which remind us that silence is itself a distinctive characteristic of the people whose preeminent hero was William the Silent.

The Dutch settlers came from the Netherlands in its Golden Age, and gold in various forms was also distinctively characteristic of their culture. The West India Company hoped to surpass the spectacular harvest of dividends reaped by its rival the East India Company; the colonists were attracted by the hope of quick profits from the fur trade. After the English conquest of New York, enterprising Dutch burghers branched out into all sorts of commerce, importing manufactured goods from England and exporting New York's produce to others of the Thirteen Colonies and to the West Indies. Farmers — *boers* in Hudson Valley Dutch as in South

Africa — thus found profitable markets for their crops, especially golden wheat. As burghers and boers accumulated fortunes, often over several generations, they expended their wealth upon substantial homes, furnishings, and works of gold- and silversmiths which reveal their taste for solid construction and splendid decoration.

"Dutch" culture in America, like that of the Netherlands, has been further characterized by great diversity. New Netherlanders came from France, Germany, Scandinavia, and the British Isles, as well as Belgium and Holland, which last was in the seventeenth century a melting pot of religious refugees from all over Europe. Merchants in the Netherlands learned the many languages of their customers, and New Amsterdam was likewise from the first a polyglot community. After the conquest by the English, the burghers of New York quickly learned the language and assimilated the customs of the English ruling class, but stubbornly retained many Dutch attitudes and values. Netherlanders directed their loyalty primarily toward their local communities rather than, as did the English, toward their nation personified by the king; for the Netherlands had no king, and the strongest bond among its towns and provinces, traditionally commercial rivals, was the common threat of invasion by ruthless Spanish armies. Similar local loyalties among the Hudson Valley Dutch appeared in continuing jealousy between such towns as New York, Albany, and Schenectady.

The achievement of unity while preserving the benefits of this diversity is the principal theme of the story of the Dutch tradition in the Netherlands and America. It is also an important theme in American history in general, but there is a significant difference between the two. Americans usually think of diversity — as of liberty, which is diversity in action — as a characteristic of individuals. In the Dutch tradition it is primarily an attribute of local communities, protected by their communal privileges and therefore extended to individuals within the framework of those privileges. Since liberty is a communal possession, its defense is the fundamental common activity of the group which possesses it. Liberty for individuals falls primarily within the conception of tolerance, for the very strength of stubborn Dutch loyalty to convictions breeds respect for similar loyalty in others, so long as it does not disrupt the community as a whole. And in practice most

Dutchmen find it possible to express their convictions in actions for the material benefit of the community rather than in divisive controversies about abstract issues.

This tradition, of course, has not been created easily, either in the Netherlands or in America. The history of the medieval Netherlands reveals constant conflicts between jealous and competitive localities, until foreign rulers took advantage of their disunity and provoked the Dutch Revolt in 1565 by one of the most violent instances of intolerant repression in the history of Europe. The Golden Age of Dutch commerce, agriculture, and art grew directly from the response of the Dutch people to this threat to their liberties. During this Golden Age, Dutch traders and colonists founded New Netherland, whose history demonstrates how disruptive diversity could be when it was not restrained by the unwritten customs of generations. The colonists learned this the hard way before Peter Stuyvesant restored order by military force, which in the Netherlands was the customary last resort to maintain the existence of a community and its liberties. Two generations later, the descendants of the first settlers reverted to this tradition during what came to be called Leisler's Rebellion.

After an initial period of adjustment, the English conquest did not interfere with Dutch cultural identity, but rather offered both burghers and boers the unexpected advantage of admission to the rapidly expanding commerce of the British Empire. Imperial conflicts played a far greater part in the history of New York than of the rest of the colonies, largely because of its geographical position. The French and Indian War in particular brought a friendly invasion by the largest British army ever to set foot in the colonies. The Dutch welcomed the defense and the market provided by these troops, but saw all too clearly how they might be used as instruments of tyranny.

The Revolutionary War in the Hudson Valley was likewise unique, for a combination of geography and British strategy subjected it to an extended siege far longer than that endured by any other colony. For the Dutch, therefore, the war was perforce the enlistment of the entire population in a gruelling campaign of fighting invasion, resisting subversion, and enduring privation every day and every night for seven years. In this struggle the traditional Dutch values of individual endurance, communal loyalty, and patience with differences of opinion were as indispensable in women and children as in the fighting men, and the heroism of ordinary people who did not think of themselves as in the least heroic was a necessary element of everyday life.

After succeeding in this conflict, the Dutch helped to establish workable governments on the local and state level in New York, devising machinery to permit the common man to share in the process of governing as well as merely to select his governors; then they contributed this machinery to the American national party system. Dutch entrepreneurs helped to develop nationwide networks of transportation, communication, and finance, and Dutch reformers advocated practical steps to improve the lot of less fortunate members of the national community. But this silent strength was so overlooked by outsiders that it did not appear in nineteenth-century literary interpretations of the Dutch. Even Washington Irving, who loved the Dutch even as he laughed at them, saw their way of life as a conglomeration of picturesque characteristics with no discernable unity. Historian John L. Motley sensed that the endurance of the Dutch people in defense of their liberties was the unifying factor in a period of great diversity, but could communicate that insight only in the context of the not entirely accurate literary conventions of English drama and fiction.

Americans have customarily thought of their colonial experience as founded upon English tradition. Even when they know that certain groups of colonists came from some other country, they know so little about the way of life of their homeland that they tend to assume unconsciously that these colonists thought and behaved like the English. Since this is one of the main reasons why the Dutch have been overlooked in American history, it is important to give some further attention to the tradition the Dutch colonists brought with them. Perhaps its most important aspects are its diversity, its continuity, and its conception of liberty, as shaped by the experience of the Dutch Revolt against Spain in 1565.

First, however, it is necessary to clear up some common confusion about the names "Holland," "Dutch," and "Netherlands." "Holland," which is often used to designate the country from which the Dutch come, refers more precisely to the wealthiest and most important of its seven provinces, in which Amsterdam is located, and will be so used in this book. The official name of the entire country, informally known as the Dutch Republic, is the "United Provinces of the Netherlands," or "Netherlands" for short, which will be so used here. But traditionally the Netherlands also included ten additional provinces (now Belgium), which were culturally akin to the rest but which were reconquered by Spain during the Dutch Revolt and thereafter went a different way. This traditional cultural entity of the Seventeen Provinces will be referred to as the "Low Countries." "Dutch" was originally derived from "Deutsch," a general term including all Germanic peoples, and is still used in that sense in the expression "Pennsylvania Dutch" for colonists from Germany and their descendants. More usually, however, "Dutch" refers to the people of the Netherlands and to the language they speak; in this book it will also denote New Netherland colonists from the French-speaking Low Countries and descendants of settlers of any nationality who chose to identify themselves with and participate in the Hudson Valley Dutch way of life.

The Dutch tradition is inseparable from the geography of the Low Countries, for they owe much of their unity to three great rivers, the Scheldt, the Meuse (or Maas), and the Rhine. These rivers have created the Low Countries, for the land is the rich soil deposited in their deltas, and their streams have been the highways — and sometimes the defenses — of a people who learned to make the most of the advantages of their unusual situation between land and water. Political boundaries within this region have been drawn and redrawn by the accidents of history. Besides the division between the Netherlands and Belgium, diplomatic adjustments have located close kin of the Netherlanders across the borders of France and West Germany. These political boundaries ignore those of language, particularly the frontier between the French and Germanic tongues that runs through Belgium, so that that country still maintains an uneasy balance between its citizens who speak French and those who speak Flemish, which is essentially Dutch. The national language of the Netherlands is Dutch, in which there is a considerable literature, although people from other countries have seldom taken the trouble of learning to read it. The independent, individualistic Frisian people in the northeast also speak a distinct but related language among themselves, although they use Dutch to communicate with the rest of their countrymen.

The economic diversity of the Low Countries is also closely related to their geography. The hills along the border between

The Low Countries at the Time of
the Settlement of New Netherland

━━·━·━ Present-day national boundaries
·········· Boundaries of the Seven Provinces
+++++ The linguistic frontier

N

GRONINGEN
• Groningen

FRIESLAND

DRENTHE

ZUIDER
ZEE

HOLLAND

OVERIJSEL

• Haarlem
Amsterdam

• Leyden

• The Hague   UTRECHT
• Delft
Rotterdam

GELDERLAND

N E T H E R L A N D S

Dordrecht

MAAS RIVER

RHINE
RIVER

ZEELAND

• Breda

Bruges •

• Antwerp

B E L G I U M

Ghent •   SCHELDT
RIVER

• Brussels

Flemish (Dutch)
French (Walloon)

MEUSE
RIVER

• Meuse

LUXEMBURG

Belgium and France contain numerous mines. The cities of Flanders, in the Meuse and Scheldt valleys, have long been centers of the textile industry and of other highly skilled manufacturing. Holland and Zeeland, at the mouth of the Rhine, are the homes of traders, fishermen, and the famous dairy farmers who have made an art of draining and cultivating land reclaimed from below sea level and protected by dikes. Friesland in the northeast, the saltiest and sandiest of all, includes some farmland and many islands whose inhabitants have lived primarily by fishing and seafaring.

Religious diversities criss-cross all the rest. Since the seventeenth century Belgium has been officially Catholic and the Netherlands officially Dutch Reformed, but convinced Calvinists have probably never been more than a strategically placed minority in the Dutch population. A considerable proportion of the people remained — and remain — loyal to the Roman Catholic faith while resisting the excesses committed in its name by the King of Spain. Another substantial group, particularly near the borders of Germany, preferred the doctrines of Luther and those of various local sects such as the Mennonites.

All of these diversities have been reinforced by the fact that Netherlanders have been primarily loyal to their local communities, for they have gained everything they value most as a people by working together on the local level. Merchants won civic privileges for their towns by joining together to secure them from feudal lords and to defend them against competition by neighboring towns. Farmers worked together to build and maintain dikes. Fishermen and sailors knew the intelligent obedience essential to survival at sea and the camaraderie of a ship's company. When they were forced to do so, therefore, Dutchmen fought together to the end in defense of their local traditions as the surest protection for their individual and national independence.

Another conspicuous characteristic of the Dutch tradition is its continuity, both in its historical development and in its emphasis on accomplishing long-term aims by the cumulative effect of many small steps. Netherlanders were defending their liberty in their very first appearance in recorded history, the revolt of the tribe of Batavii against the Romans in A.D. 69, under their high-minded leader Civilis. Likewise, the Frisi along the coast of the North Sea, alone among the tribes of northwestern Europe, saved themselves from being overrun by barbarian migrations and Viking raids by retreating to their marshes and islands and taking to the sea as pirates.

After the Viking raids ceased in the eleventh century — about the time of William the Conqueror — towns sprang up like mushrooms all over the southern Low Countries. Usually located at natural sites favorable for trade — harbors, fords, or the head of navigation of streams — they all had in common a population of busy artisans and merchants eager to make money by selling the artisans' wares and the peasants' surplus produce, and by procuring luxuries from far lands for the nobles. Then these merchants put together a good round sum of gold and gave it to their local lord in return for various privileges of self-government, which, confirmed from time to time in return for further payments, became the cherished traditional "liberties" of the town. Merchant families were therefore recognized in Dutch society as a "patrician" class entrusted with the responsibility of exercising political as well as economic power for the benefit of the whole community.

While the towns of the southern Low Countries were advancing to the economic leadership of northern Europe, the people of the northern provinces were fighting a stubborn battle against the sea. The soil of the river deltas was very fertile, but marshy and subject to frequent floods, such as those in the thirteenth century which created the Zuider Zee. To control the waters, the farmers built dikes; first small local levees, then larger projects organized by lords or merchants, and finally the great reclamation programs made possible by modern capitalism and technology. The invention of the windmill in the thirteenth century provided a source of power for pumping dry the land behind the dikes, and after farmers learned to leach the salt from the soil, their polders (reclaimed land) became rich market gardens and pastures for dairy herds. Meanwhile, the sea brought wealth to Dutch fishermen. In the fourteenth century, discovery of a more effective method of curing herring greatly expanded the markets available to the Hollanders and Frisians. The population of Europe was growing, meat was expensive and often of poor quality even when it was available, and Catholic clergy were emphasizing the conscientious observance of fast days and Lent. Amsterdam and many smaller towns of Holland and Zeeland based a secure prosperity on the herring fishery.

The great wealth of the cities of the Low Countries, and the jealousy and commercial competition which made it hard for them to work together, created an apparent political vacuum which tempted ambitious foreign rulers to interfere. During the Hundred Years' War (1340-1453) the Dukes of Burgundy, a branch of the French royal family who took their name from the home of Burgundy wine in east central France, gained control of the Low Countries and soon rivalled kings with the splendor of their court at Brussels. The 50-year reign of Philip the Good (1418-68) was the high point of a cultural development in Flanders that may be compared in many ways to the contemporaneous early Italian Renaissance, particularly in its contributions to painting, architecture, and music. The less wealthy burghers of the northern provinces shared in these accomplishments to a certain extent, but concentrated more attention on the arts of domestic comfort, such as cabinetmaking. They also devoted themselves to the practice of a religious tradition combining the mystical insight of Thomas à Kempis, the practical charity of Gerhard Groot and the Brethren of the Common Life, and the broadly tolerant humanism of Erasmus.

The Dukes of Burgundy thus won the respect of the Netherlanders in spite of their French origin. But when the domains of Burgundy descended to Charles V (1500-56), who by a series of dynastic accidents inherited also the crowns of Spain and Germany, the Low Countries were not at all sure they wanted to be merged into an empire incorporating half of Europe and all of recently discovered America. They were ready enough to reap the profits of its commerce, as Antwerp became the central point of exchange for the carrying trade which supplied Spain with grain, lumber, fish, and other everyday necessities from the Baltic region in exchange for gold and silver from the New World. But they were not nearly as anxious to pay taxes for far-flung imperial wars, to surrender their cherished civic privileges to the administrative reforms of an absolute monarch, or to sacrifice their religious convictions to Counter-Reformation Catholic uniformity. In the reign of Charles' son Philip II (1556-98) — who regarded the Low Countries merely as a convenient source of funds and was despised in return as a foreigner — tension over these issues burst into violence as the Dutch Revolt.

Matters came to a head at Antwerp in 1565 with an outbreak of violence by the Calvinists, the organized militants of the Reformation, whose effectively demagogic preachers frequently incited their followers to riot. As was customary in Low Countries civic disorders, Philip sent troops to restore order. But the troops were foreigners — thoroughly disciplined Spanish infantry commanded by the ruthless Duke of Alva — and many nobles and burghers, outraged at foreign interference with their liberties, joined the Calvinists in revolt. The terror imposed by Alva's army, his "Council of Blood," and the Spanish Inquisition eventually reduced the 10 southern provinces to submission, but only after a considerable proportion of their population fled to the north — many with much of their wealth.

In Holland and Zeeland a group of Calvinist militants called the "Sea Beggars" ignited rebellion in the summer of 1572, and the widely respected William of Orange (William the Silent) organized it into sustained resistance capable of withstanding the immediate Spanish retaliation. For the first time geography put the war on something like an equal footing, for the Spanish infantry, invincible wherever it could march, was at a distinct disadvantage in a country whose roads were waterways. It was difficult indeed to starve out a city under siege when supplies sailed up to the gates in specially designed shallow-draft boats which, with the sailors who knew how to navigate them, were enlisted on the side of the defenders. Furthermore, when the situation became really desperate, the Dutch could cut their dikes and let the waters fight for them — a great sacrifice for the boers who lost everything, but preferable to starvation or massacre for boers and burghers together.

After seven years this desperate battle was won, and in 1579 the seven provinces north of the Rhine formed the Union of Utrecht, which became the cornerstone of the Dutch Republic. But neither side was ready to give up the other 10 provinces, even after William the Silent was assassinated in 1584. His son Maurice proved to be a brilliant general, and the war continued as a succession of sieges until 1609, when it was suspended by the Twelve Years' Truce. In 1621, when the truce ran out, the rest of Europe was already involved in the Thirty Years' War; the fighting in the Low Countries was again a succession of sieges. Not until the end of the Thirty Years' War in 1648, 80 years after Alva's invasion, did Spain finally acknowledge the independence of the United Netherlands. The southern provinces remained in the hands of various foreign rulers until 1831, when they rebelled and a few years later were finally recognized by the European powers as the Kingdom of Belgium.

Nevertheless, by the time of the Twelve Years' Truce, the Dutch Republic had for practical purposes won its struggle for liberty. Its "constitution," such as it was, was the Union of Utrecht, an offensive and defensive alliance among seven independent provinces fiercely protective of their traditional privileges; it did not describe the powers and limitations of the central government as does the American Constitution. Local loyalties remained paramount, and local jealousies had always to be considered in determining national policy — which meant that most controversial issues were left to local option. The principal activity of this new nation was commerce, which was booming. The fortunes of war had transferred to Amsterdam the primacy of Antwerp in world trade and finance, an addition to Amsterdam's growing prosperity based on fishing, shipping, and shipbuilding. This far-flung mercantile activity made the city a center for processing raw materials from the ends of the earth — sugar, tobacco, and furs from the New World; spices from the East Indies — and of highly skilled specialized crafts such as diamond-cutting, making precision instruments for navigation and science, engraving maps and illustrations, and printing and publishing. The wealth and skills of the city also provided the basis for a Golden Age of creativity in literature, science, and especially painting.

But Amsterdam was merely the focus of this Golden Age, being to the nation very much what New York City is to New York State today — the metropolis, and the center of commerce and culture, but not the capital and by no means overwhelmingly dominant over the numerous smaller cities and rural localities. The fishermen of Friesland and Zeeland, the farmers of Gelderland and Overyssel, the sailors of Rotterdam and Brill, the artisans of Haarlem and Delft, and the scholars of Utrecht and Leyden were as important to it as the merchants and artists of Amsterdam. And though Amsterdam was their market, their prosperity came quite as much from the soil or sea of their own districts, the work of their own hands, and the maintenance of their own communal privileges and customs. It was this local consciousness of a Golden Age that most of the Dutch colonists brought to the Hudson Valley.

1

Beaver Skins and Wild Men

THE HUDSON VALLEY is beautiful at every season, but
perhaps it is most beautiful in the fall. The traveler today notices
the cumulative effects of three and a half centuries of occupation
by Western men with their irresistible urge to make over the
environment — snug stone farmhouses surrounded by fruitful
fields overlook an abandoned railroad track and traffic on the
Thruway. The original inhabitants of the land are seldom visible;
the Indians have gone and the deer and bear, the sturgeon and
shad, and above all the beaver, have grown too wise and too shy
to trust themselves within range of the hunter. But the greatest
beauty of all is little changed — the colorful foliage which attracts
crowds of city-dwellers to the Catskills every autumn weekend. As
they admire crimson branches against the towering grey ramparts
of the Palisades or Storm King, or view the three blue humps of
the highest Catskills across a rolling carpet of scarlet and gold
accented with patches of evergreen, or follow in the footsteps of
Rip Van Winkle up the orange and russet chasm to the silver veil
of Kaaterskill Falls, most of them never think of those who have
marveled over these scenes before them. Yet nineteenth-century
tourists, particularly those from England, were overwhelmed by
the breathtaking spectacle of the Catskills in the fall, and emphasized that this was utterly unlike anything they had ever seen
in their homeland.

Some of these reactions were so intense that it is rather
surprising to contrast them with those of the first visitor to the
Hudson Valley known to have recorded his impressions, who

apparently never noticed the autumn beauty at all, although he was there at the height of the proper season. Robert Juet was mate on the *Half Moon*, a Dutch ship commanded by an English mariner, Henry Hudson, which explored the river in September 1609. Hudson, who had already made two voyages to the Arctic for English employers, had been hired by the Dutch East India Company to explore the possibility of a route around Siberia to the Orient. But when the *Half Moon* encountered impassable ice near Novaya Zemlya, Hudson ignored his instructions to return to the Netherlands and turned his ship westward to investigate the possibility of a passage through North America somewhere north of Chesapeake Bay. After sighting the Virginia Capes and discovering Delaware Bay, he arrived off Sandy Hook on September 3. Here Hudson hove to for a couple of days while his crew fished and bartered with the Indians who, Juet recorded, "brought Tobacco and Indian Wheat [corn], to exchange for Knives and Beades, and offered us no violence."[1] Another group, however, perhaps from another tribe, pursued one of Hudson's boat crews and killed one of his sailors. After that the mariners weighed anchor and set out to explore the great tidal inlet that led into the mountains — would it be another Strait of Magellan?

The flat islands at the mouth of the river would have looked familiar enough to Hudson's Dutch sailors, but almost immediately they passed the towering Palisades and entered the rugged Highlands, which must have been startling unless they had chanced to make a river voyage through the similar scenery of the upper Rhine. Then they came to the Catskills, higher than any mountains in northwestern Europe except the very different-appearing ranges of Norway. But all this time the force of the tide was lessening and that of the current growing stronger, and above the site of present-day Newburgh the water no longer tasted salt. As the mountains fell away to a forested plain through which the river had cut a deep channel, low islands and treacherous sand bars began to slow the explorers. Finally, at a sand bar just below the site of Albany (which was to endanger ships until the channel was dredged over three centuries later), Hudson decided it was unsafe to sail farther. He anchored the *Half Moon* while boat crews explored further — probably to the confluence of the Mohawk, though Juet's journal does not state that they discovered majestic Cohoes Falls — and proved conclusively that this promising "strait" was just another river after all.

In the meantime, Hudson and his crew responded to the proffered hospitality of the upriver Indians, trading with them (with due precautions against treacherous attack) and plying some chiefs who visited the ship with liquor to see what would happen. They became "all merrie" and one passed out, "and that was strange to them [the Indians]; for they could not tell how to take it," but he "slept all night quietly"[2] and recovered the next day. On the way back down the river there were a few untoward incidents, in which Indians tried to steal or apparently threatened to attack and the sailors shot first and asked questions afterward. Juet's diary — the only surviving account — records all these incidents. He described in some detail the Indians and the fruitfulness of the valley in fish and furs, but said little about the land itself and not a word about the colorful foliage, which must have been vivid by the time they left the river in early October. (Should two brief observations of discolored trees, which Juet hopefully attributed to valuable mineral deposits, be ascribed to this cause?) Then the *Half Moon* sailed for the Netherlands, but put in at an English port under stress of bad weather and discontent among the crew. English authorities promptly impounded the ship and refused to allow Hudson to depart or to report his discoveries to his employers. (The following year, while commanding an English vessel searching again for the Northwest Passage, Hudson discovered the strait and bay which bear his name, but was cast adrift in a small boat in the latter by his mutinous crew.)

Hudson was therefore prevented from making a complete report of his discoveries to the Dutch East India Company, although he did write them a brief letter and more details later filtered back when his Dutch sailors got home. The log, charts, and specimens of potential resources for trade which the Company had asked him to bring back were confiscated by the English and have never come to light. Probably the Company did not particularly care, since it would seem to have employed Hudson in the first place primarily to prevent him from discovering a shortcut to the treasure-house of the Orient for its English competitors. The Company, which had been organized in 1602 with the then enormous capital of six million guilders, had its hands more than full exploiting the trade with the East Indies that Portugal, temporarily united with Spain, could no longer monopolize.

In the East India Company's efficient hands, this trade revolutionized the diet of Europe, transforming pepper from a luxury to the common companion of salt; putting cinnamon, cloves, nutmeg, and ginger within reach of every household; and incidentally making Chinese silks and porcelains available to purchasers of moderate means. It was enormously profitable. East India Company stock was the blue chip of its day, increasing rapidly in market value as the Company paid a few spectacular special dividends and gave steady regular returns that made fortunes for capitalists and brought comfortable incomes to the many ordinary investors who owned a few shares. It was also an extremely complicated business, for the voyage halfway around the world took from six months to a year each way, and the great ships which could carry enough spices to make this trip worthwhile had to be supplied not only with trade goods and everything they would need on the way, but with the means of defense against pirates, hostile natives, and warships of competing European powers. The Company also had to maintain posts — "factories" — in the Indies, where spices could be collected and ships loaded, defend them against intruders, and administer the government of native peoples to insure that local disorder would not interrupt the steady flow of spices. With all these matters to attend to, it is hardly surprising that the East India Company had little interest in exploiting Hudson's discoveries in North America.

But the East India Company, for all its wealth, power, and prestige, was only a small part of the booming commerce of Amsterdam in the Golden Age. Even larger, though less spectacular in their operations, were the joint-stock companies engaged in buying grain, fish, and lumber in the Baltic and transporting them to Spain and southern Europe, where they exchanged them for wine, fruit, and gold and silver from America. At the height of the Dutch Revolt, Spain tried two or three times to forbid this trade, but discovered that economic survival was impossible without it. The Dutch turned the situation to advantage by charging merchants fat fees for licenses to trade with the enemy, then used the money to help pay for the war effort. Other Dutch investors were developing the timber resources and the iron and copper mines of Sweden, until in time their foundries and powder mills came to supply munitions for all the wars of Europe — including wars against the Netherlands! Dutch bankers and financiers provided capital for enterprises in many countries, for interest rates were lower in the Netherlands than anywhere else and Amsterdam was, and remained until the Napoleonic Wars, the Wall Street of the

western world. To these early capitalists, concerned with the financing of nations and the expensive ambitions of kings, and to
merchants attempting to supply the established needs and new-
found wants of the growing population of Europe, there were no
obvious attractions in the sketchy report of a beautiful river and a
few curious wild men brought back by Hudson's sailors.

But not all the merchants of Amsterdam were financial magnates, and some of the smaller entrepreneurs who were already
engaged in voyages to the Grand Banks of Newfoundland to
purchase fish from the fishermen of other nations were well aware
that French explorers on the Saint Lawrence River had discovered
a profitable commodity in the pelts of fur-bearing animals,
especially beaver. In Europe furs were prized for their warmth,
especially in the frigid territories of the northeast. Thus far the
French had maintained a monopoly of the furs by permitting no
one else to trade in the Saint Lawrence Valley, but the Dutch,
with their existing commerce in the Baltic, were in a far better
position to exploit the markets of Germany, Poland, and Russia.
Russian nobles, in particular, seized upon the rich, shining pelts of
North American beaver for luxurious cloaks. (When these had been
worn awhile, the lustrous outer hairs fell off and the inner fur
became matted and shabby. The practical Dutch merchants then
bought them back and returned them to the Netherlands, where
the salvaged fur was made into felt for the broad-brimmed hats
fashionable in this period and familiar to us today from numerous
portraits, such as Frans Hals' "Laughing Cavalier.")

The discovery of sources of abundant beaver outside of New
France offered the Dutch the opportunity to engross the first as
well as the later steps of this commerce. Enterprising skippers explored not only the Hudson but also the Connecticut, the Delaware, and the smaller rivers and creeks between them. Soon they
began to leave members of their crews behind over the winter to
assemble a stock of furs against their return — the first to be
recorded was a mulatto from San Domingo who stayed in 1613.
They also built small vessels in America. The first was constructed
in 1614 by Captain Adriaen Block and his crew after their ship
burned.* It was not long before the sailors who remained to trade

---

*Charred timbers believed to be those of the unfortunate *Tiger* were
unearthed in a New York City building excavation in 1916. Block Island
perpetuates the captain's name in spite of his misfortune.

had similar yachts, sometimes brought piecemeal from the Netherlands, to explore the creeks and inlets. Some of these sailors also
explored inland, like the three who in 1616 walked from the upper
Hudson to the upper Delaware, where they were captured by the
Indians but ransomed by a skipper in Delaware Bay. Dutch maps
of this part of North America therefore showed very early a
remarkable knowledge of its geography.

All these skippers soon began to cross each other's tracks, and
even to try to trade with the same Indians at the same time. The
cutthroat competition which resulted was so obviously to no one's
advantage that skippers on the spot quickly made informal agreements among themselves to permit all to share a reasonable
profit. Their merchant employers in the Netherlands, equally
alarmed, joined together as the New Netherland Company, which
in 1614 secured from the Dutch government a monopoly to make
four trading voyages in three years to North America between 40°
and 45° north latitude — approximately from Barnegat Bay to
Eastport, Maine. Their charter was the first to name this territory
"New Netherland" and the first official Dutch claim to it based
upon Hudson's voyage. It is now known that the first European to
visit the Hudson river was Verrazano in 1524, and that occasional
French and Dutch traders certainly came there, perhaps as early as
1598. Nevertheless, Hudson's "discovery" was the first to be
publicized, and the English named the river after him. The Dutch
called it the Mauritius, for Prince Maurice, or later, into the nineteenth and in some localities even the twentieth century, the
North River; the Delaware was the South River and the Connecticut the Fresh River.

The New Netherland Company immediately established at the
head of navigation of the Hudson a year-round trading post, Fort
Nassau, on Castle Island, now included in the Port of Albany.
"This little fort was built in the form of a redoubt, surrounded by
a moat eighteen feet wide; it was mounted with two cast iron
pieces and eleven light cannon, and the garrison consisted of ten
or twelve men."[3] It was well situated for access to the ships and
defense against the Indians, but not for protection against the
floods which rushed down the Hudson every spring when the ice
went out. In 1617, just as the Company's monopoly was about to
expire, this annual freshet swept the little fort away. There is a
tradition that the factor, Jacob Eelkins, rebuilt it on the nearby
banks of the Normanskill, then called the Tawasentha, and that in

this fort or somewhere along the banks of the kill he concluded the first treaty between the Dutch and the Mohawk Indians. The treaty is an unfounded legend; there is no evidence of Dutch treaty relations with the Mohawks for another quarter-century. Although no archeological remains of the fort have been discovered, it seems likely that another post was built, probably on the west bank of the river near the Normanskill.

In the meantime, a powerful group of merchants in the Netherlands were agitating for the formation of a great West India Company to exploit the commercial opportunities of the Western Hemisphere as the East India Company had those of the Orient. Since most of the proven resources of this part of the world were in Spanish possession, organization of such a company clearly depended upon renewal of the war with Spain. When the Twelve Years' Truce ran out in 1621, the West India Company was accordingly chartered as a combined mercantile and patriotic venture. Its 24-year monopolies included trade with West Africa, all of America, the islands on either side of America, and the coast of Australia. The most obvious commerce in this vast area was in the gold, ivory, and slaves of West Africa, the sugar of Brazil, the salt of Venezuela, and whatever trade or gold and silver could be filched from the Spanish in the West Indies; New Netherland with its fur trade was comparatively so unimportant that it was not even named in the charter. The Company's tremendous capitalization of 7.5 million guilders, well beyond that of the East India Company, was intended to support the armed forces necessary to seize and hold this commerce from the Portuguese and Spanish, and the Company could call on the Dutch government for additional warships if it needed them for a naval expedition. In 1625 the Company accordingly commenced the conquest of Brazil, which proved to be much more difficult and less profitable than that of Indonesia. Brazil consumed more resources than it produced for 30 years until the Portuguese, having regained their independence from Spain, finally took it back in 1654.

It was in this context of patriotic piracy that the West India Company made its first settlement in New Netherland in 1624. Its principal purpose was to forestall poaching on the Company monopoly by other traders by reestablishing the year-round trading post at the head of navigation of the Hudson and founding others at the corresponding locations on the Delaware and the Connecticut. The availability of a group of volunteer colonists —

Walloons or French-speaking Calvinist refugees from the southern
Low Countries — probably suggested that it would be desirable to
settle a few farmers at each of these posts to grow food for them.
The loss of most of the West India Company records makes it
impossible to recover many details concerning this first settlement,
but scholars have very recently reconstructed the sequence of
events from the confused and often conflicting accounts which
remain.

It now seems probable that a small advance party of Walloon
families sailed in January 1624 aboard the *Unity* with Captain
Adriaen J. Thienpont. The main body then followed at the end of
March aboard Captain Cornelis J. May's *New Netherland*, which
was long believed to have been the first ship to carry settlers to
the Hudson Valley. Early in May, the *New Netherland* arrived in
the Hudson, where it met another Dutch vessel, and the two joined
to drive away a French interloper. Then the *New Netherland* left
eight traders to construct a fort on Governor's Island in New York
Harbor, sent men to the Connecticut and Delaware, and conveyed
the remaining 18 families and men up the river to the site of
Albany, where they met other Dutch ships including the *Unity*.
The settlers lived on the ships until they built bark huts, and
"forthwith put the spade in the ground and began to plant, and
before the yacht *Mackereel* sailed, the grain was nearly as high as a
man, so they are bravely advanced."[4] In the meantime, the traders
laid out a new fort, this time on the west bank of the river, which
they named Fort Orange. For many years it was believed that all
traces of this fort had vanished in the repeated rebuilding of downtown Albany. Then in the late 1960s, its foundations were discovered during excavation for the Riverfront Arterial. Archaeological exploration uncovered one of the walls of the fort, some
cellars, and numerous artifacts before the site was finally
destroyed by the construction of an approach for the new Dunn
Memorial Bridge.

But it is by no means certain that Fort Orange was intended
to be the center of the new colony. The next contingent of
Walloons was sent to form a similar settlement on an island at the
head of navigation of the Delaware, near the present site of
Trenton, N.J., which post may have been designated the headquarters of the first governor. In 1625 an elaborate plan was
drawn up in the Netherlands for a fort and town whose destined
location is uncertain, and no less than six ships were sent out in

MOHAWK R.

Schenectady

Fort Orange
(Beverwyck)

RENSSELAERSWYCK

Catskill

Esopus
(Wiltwyck)

Fort Good Hope

NORTH R. (MAURITIUS)

(HUDSON)

FRESH R.
(CONNECTICUT)

Pahaquarry

PASSAIC R.

HACKENSACK R.

New Amsterdam
Five Dutch Towns
Breucklyn

PAVONIA

RARITAN R.

STATEN ISLAND

N

High Island
(Walloon settlement)

SOUTH R.
(DELAWARE)

Fort Nassau

Fort Christina
(New Amstel)

Settlement in New Netherland
1624-1664

—··— Present-day state lines

+++++ Boundary established by Treaty
of Hartford, 1650

----- Old mine road

·········· Manor boundaries

SWANENDAEL

that year with additional colonists and livestock. But many things went wrong with these plans, including capture of some of the vessels by pirates, mysterious mortality among the livestock, and revelation of the incompetence of Director-designate Willem Verhulst. The Company therefore decided to reduce expenses by concentrating all the settlers at centrally located Manhattan Island, and sending traders into the outlying regions in ships. In pursuance of this resolution, a settlement was begun on Manhattan in 1625, and Governor Peter Minuit purchased the island from the Indians in 1626 for the famous 60 guilders' worth of trade goods, valued in the nineteenth century at $24. Many myths and traditions have grown up around this event; it is necessary to observe here only that the price does not imply a deliberate attempt to cheat the Indians, who had plenty of land left for their purposes on Long Island and in whose Stone-Age technology the value of manufactured goods was simply not measurable in monetary terms.

The removal from Fort Orange of the eight families who were left there was certainly hastened by the outbreak of war between the Mahican Indians, who lived near the fort, and their fierce traditional enemies to the west, the Mohawks, whose name in Dutch and English is derived from a Mahican word meaning "man-eaters." When hostilities flared up between them in 1626, the Mahicans asked their Dutch friends at Fort Orange for help (as Champlain had assisted the Hurons against the Iroquois in 1609). In spite of strict orders from the Company to avoid any such encounters, the commander of the fort, Daniel Van Krieckebeeck, accompanied a Mahican war party with six of his men. But circumstances had changed since Champlain terrified the Iroquois with their first experience of firearms. The Mohawks laid an ambush at Beaver Falls (a site which has been identified as approximately where Albany's Delaware Avenue passes Lincoln Park) and utterly routed their attackers. Four Dutchmen were killed, including Van Krieckebeeck, while the other three escaped by swimming. Word filtered back later that the Mohawks had roasted and eaten one of their victims, and carried an arm and a leg of another back to their village in triumph. (Anthropologists have suggested that this cannibalism was probably a ritual for assimilating the potency of fallen foes.) Peace was restored a few days later, so far as the Dutch were concerned, by a diplomatic skipper named Pieter Barentsen, who had just performed a similar service after an incident on Long Island. Nevertheless, the Indian war continued until

1628, when the Mohawks defeated the Mahicans decisively and drove them to the east side of the river.

The next few years were a period of transition for both the Company and New Netherland. Under the pressure of its first major setback in Brazil and its first — and only — major success, the capture of the Spanish treasure fleet by Admiral Piet Heyn in 1628, the Company devoted even more of its attention than before to military activities. Those directors particularly interested in New Netherland were sharply divided between some who favored a policy of exploiting the colony for its furs for short-term profits and others who promoted colonization as a form of long-term investment. The latter had already put the Company to considerable expense with little return, and as many — though not all — of the discouraged Walloons drifted back to the Netherlands, it is not surprising that the Company ceased to fund further experiments. But the colonizing group of directors had by no means lost faith in their schemes, and petitioned the Company for grants of land on which they might plant colonies as private investments. In 1629 the Company issued its "Charter of Privileges and Exemptions," setting down the terms on which directors who planted 50 colonists in four years might claim extensive tracts of land, powers of local government, limited participation in the fur trade, and the title of "patroon" or patron — a new title for a new world.

The directors who had urged the charter immediately registered claims for patroonships — so quickly that there was some suspicion of sharp practice, which helped to antagonize some of the other directors and to give the Company second thoughts about these private grants. On some, no settlements were ever attempted, raising the suspicion that their "patroons" only wanted the opportunity to engage in the fur trade for their own benefit. Settlements were begun at Swanendael at the mouth of the Delaware, Pavonia on the New Jersey shore near Staten Island, and Rensselaerswyck around Fort Orange. Of these, Swanendael was intended to exploit the whales which frequented Delaware Bay, but within a year the local Indians massacred the colonists. Pavonia was strategically located where the New Jersey Indians crossed the river to New Amsterdam; it contained two well-stocked farms in 1635 when its patroon, Michiel Pauw, resold it to the Company, but in later years it was repeatedly devastated by Indian attacks.

The only successful patroonship was Rensselaerswyck, founded by Kiliaen Van Rensselaer, an Amsterdam diamond merchant who was a leader from the first among the procolonization directors and who made a hobby as well as an investment of his patroonship. He purchased the land around Fort Orange, including that on which the fort stood, from the Mahicans who, thoroughly defeated by the Mohawks, were now willing to sell and to begin the drift eastward which eventually settled them in the Housatonic Valley as the Stockbridge Indians. Then Van Rensselaer sent hired farmers and a few craftsmen, who were supposed to attend strictly to their own business and leave fur trading to the patroon. They did, however, come by a few skins now and then, by trapping themselves or by selling the Indians dairy products and garden truck — or home-brewed beer or spare cloth and tools — and expectation of this extra profit helped, more than Van Rensselaer really wished, to attract settlers. Although he never sent as many colonists as required and claimed much more land than he was entitled to, Van Rensselaer, by shrewdness, stubbornness, and exploitation of his leading position among the principal stockholders, clung to his patroonship when the directors turned hostile and all the other patroons gave up.

It was also to Van Rensselaer's advantage that the governor of the colony at this time was his nephew, Wouter Van Twiller. Van Twiller, who had been a clerk in the Amsterdam office but had no administrative or overseas experience, has acquired a reputation for incompetence based at least partly on his refusal to write extensive reports to his superiors. Most of the accounts of his nonadministration that have survived — giving Washington Irving the basis for his famous caricature of a Van Twiller whose only accomplishment was drinking — are bitter diatribes by biased opponents, including one whose avowed purpose was to secure the governorship for himself. Kiliaen Van Rensselaer's letters to Van Twiller support the allegation that the young governor was overly fond of the bottle, as indeed were many in New Amsterdam — perhaps, as with other city men assigned to frontier posts, from sheer boredom. But the scanty evidence also shows Van Twiller to have been shrewd enough at milking the Company's assets for his uncle's benefit, as when he bought all its livestock for Rensselaerswyck, and at feathering his own nest by granting himself extensive tracts of land. The "neglect" of which the colonists complained was in accordance with the Company's new policy of concentrating on short-term profits from the fur trade, which Van Twiller increased from an average of 6,500 to 7,500 pelts a year, while winning the good will of the Indians, who remembered him affectionately long after.

In the meantime, the Dutch were eagerly gathering information about the Indians, whom they called the *Wilden*, or wild men. Observations of the Wilden were an important part of every letter and description published about New Netherland. With the fidelity and attention to detail of Dutch painters, these writers described the Indians' persons, clothing, houses, food, domestic habits, and social customs. These descriptions were primarily visual and external, for the traders knew little of the Indian languages beyond the few words needed for trade, and one observer believed that the Indians took good care that they did not learn much more than that. Many traders had casual contacts with Indian women, and a few settled down with Indian wives, as did the French *coureurs de bois*. Somewhat unusual in this respect was enigmatic, amoral Secretary of the Colony Cornelius Van Tienhoven, who seems to have combined with a fondness for Indian women a taste for Indian dress and ways of life and an aptitude for learning several Indian languages, which foreshadows the approach to Indian relations later developed to a fine art by Sir William Johnson — although it did not inhibit Van Tienhoven from leading the Dutch in battle against the Indians when war eventually broke out. More worthy of respect were the efforts of two substantial settlers, David P. deVries and Adriaen Van der Donck, who won the trust of the Indians by their fair dealings, to the point that one party of Indians made a point of sparing deVries when they massacred his neighbors. Van der Donck is particularly noteworthy for the account of the Indians published in his *Description of New Netherland*, which, unlike most Dutch works, focused upon their good qualities as people rather than their usefulness to trade.

Nearly all of these early observations of the Indians concerned the Algonquian tribes of the Hudson Valley with whom the first settlers came into contact. The first description of the Iroquois, who were to play such an important part in the history of New York, was a journal written in the winter of 1634-35, probably by Harmen Myndertse Van den Bogart, the surgeon of Fort Orange.*

*This supposition is based on the author's evident interest in Indian medical practices and descriptions of occasional calls for the exercise of his skill on Indian patients. This journal, rediscovered in 1895, was used effectively by Hendrick Willem Van Loon to create the American dimension of his imaginative study of the Golden Age, *R.v.R.*, republished in paperback as *The Life and Times of Rembrandt*.

He was one of three men sent from Fort Orange to the Iroquois country to verify a rumor that the French were sending traders and missionaries among them. The men and their guides walked over 100 miles up the Mohawk in bitter weather, struggling through the snow, crossing frozen and flooding creeks, and somehow preserving themselves from frostbite and pneumonia while camping out between Indian towns. In the towns they were welcomed to the long houses and hospitably invited to share bear meat, fish, beans, and corn bread. Curious Indians crowded around to stare at them, sometimes almost pushing them into the fire, and Van den Bogart stared back with the keen observation of a trained scientist. When they finally reached the Oneida village that was their destination (and found the rumor about French penetration to be true), the chiefs were polite but critical of Dutch trading practices and prices, which the envoys had no power to adjust on the spot.

In 1639 the fur trade of New Netherland entered a new phase when the Dutch government, fearing that New Netherland (with less than 1,000 people) might be overrun by the colonists of New England, gave the West India Company the choice of populating New Netherland or surrendering it to the nation. The Company thereupon abandoned its cherished monopoly of the fur trade, throwing it open to all comers on payment of a duty and freight charges for trade goods and peltry. This measure achieved its immediate purpose, for the population soon doubled — itself a misleading statement since it does not take many people to double a population of less than 1,000. But this expansion completely upset the internal order of the colony, its trade, and its Indian relations. It soon developed that most of the immigrants, as well as most of the people already in the colony, had no thought in mind but to make a quick fortune in the fur trade and return to the Netherlands. Farmers ceased to farm, craftsmen left their trades, and all of them competed with each other for peltries. Some enticed the Indians by such excessive attentions as seating them at their tables as honored guests and serving them with the best the house afforded; others, especially around Fort Orange, waylaid and sometimes all but kidnapped potential customers. It had become common practice to sell the Indians liquor, in spite of its deleterious effects, and in the late 1630s amateur traders at Rensselaerswyck even began to sell the Mohawks firearms. This trade was forbidden under penalty of death in 1639, but it proved impossible to stop it because the Mohawks were also in a position to purchase arms from the French in Canada and even from the English in New England. Thus the Dutch — already suppliers of munitions for all the wars of Europe — had the dubious honor of providing the Iroquois with the firepower to subdue all their neighbors and achieve a pivotal position in intercolonial affairs.

This disruption of the precarious balance of trade and every-day contacts very soon brought disaster upon New Netherland. The Dutch have a reputation for amicable Indian relations derived largely from their celebrated "chain of friendship" treaty with the Mohawks in 1642, repeatedly "brightened" afterward and never broken until the American Revolution. But this friendship was not altogether innocent or disinterested — its basis in the fire-arms trade has just been mentioned — and the peace which pre-vailed in the upper Hudson Valley until the French Indians invaded in 1690 resulted partly from the distance of the Mohawk villages from the Dutch settlements, which precluded everyday irritations, and partly from the dirty work done for the Dutch when the Mohawks broke the power of the Mahicans in 1628. In the lower Hudson Valley, relations between the Dutch and the Indians of Westchester, New Jersey, Long Island, and eventually the mid-Hudson region were quite as bloody as those of New England, and the atrocities of the Pequot War of 1637 were repeated a few years later in the Dutch wars of the 1640s.

Tensions between Indians and settlers around New Amsterdam were increased by numerous day-to-day provocations, as when the settlers' hogs broke into the Indians' maize fields, or the Indians' fierce dogs attacked the settlers' cattle and hogs. As the number of colonists increased, lands changed hands. The Indians, beginning to feel confined on the tracts they had left, heard of the prices for which farms were sold and, not understanding the value of im-provements, began to feel cheated in the price they had received for the uncleared land. On top of this came the conflict of cultures which construed Indian pride as arrogance, underestimated the importance of revenge for personal or clan injuries, and in general assumed that Indian impassivity indicated a lack of all human feelings whatsoever. The crowning example of this com-plete insensitivity to a different way of life was Governor Kieft's attempt in 1639 to tax the Indians, at a time when the Dutch colonists did not pay regular taxes!

Therefore, when in 1641 an Indian from Westchester murdered

a Manhattan farmer named Claes Swits without apparent provocation, and was supported by his tribe when he claimed that his motive was revenge for the killing of a relative by the Dutch a number of years before, the New Amsterdam colonists reached the edge of panic. When Governor Kieft called upon their representatives — the famous Twelve Men — for advice, they supported the idea of a war of reprisal. In March 1642, therefore, a Dutch force invaded Westchester by night, and though it got lost and made no attack, this narrow escape from vengeance prompted the Indians to conclude an uneasy peace. The following winter, the Mohawks with their guns attacked this tribe, sending a confused crowd of Indian refugees to New Amsterdam and Pavonia on the New Jersey side of the river. At first the Dutch succored them, but when they returned after a second scare, some of the colonists persuaded Kieft to destroy them while opportunity offered. Late in February 1643, accordingly, plans were laid and on the night of February 25 the astonished fugitives, who believed themselves attacked by their northern enemies, were cut to pieces with all the brutality depicted in Breughel's "Slaughter of the Innocents."

The outlying farmers, entirely unprepared for trouble — as deVries had warned Kieft beforehand — were cut off in their fields as the Indians of New Jersey, Westchester, and Long Island took the warpath. (It was at this time that religious exile from Boston Anne Hutchinson and her family were massacred.) The colonists held Governor Kieft solely responsible for this debacle, conveniently forgetting how they had urged him to suppress the Indians; that the Indians might turn the tables seems not to have occurred to them until too late. With the assistance of Pequot War veterans like Captain John Underhill, who with his Dutch wife had settled on Long Island, the Dutch perpetrated two gruesome winter night attacks early in 1644, one on Long Island and one in Westchester. They surrounded sleeping Indian villages, set them on fire, and shot the Indians or drove them back into their burning houses. After the second attack the Indians, who in the lower Hudson Valley did not yet have firearms, sued for peace, which was finally concluded at New Amsterdam in the summer of 1645.

After this war Kieft was succeeded by the bellicose Peter Stuyvesant, under whom there were only two localized outbreaks of Indian hostilities. In 1655, when Stuyvesant and the colony's military force went to the Delaware to conquer New Sweden, some Indians rampaged through New Amsterdam one night, searching for a burgher named Hendrick Van Dyck who had killed a squaw he caught stealing some peaches. They found and wounded Van Dyck and killed a couple of other burghers. The initial damage could have been much worse, but when the incensed burghers assembled to resist, two or three Indians were killed. The rest crossed to Staten Island and Pavonia, which they devastated for the second time, taking numerous prisoners whom they held for ransom, releasing a few at a time over the next three years. The Esopus War, between the mid-Hudson tribe of Esopus Indians and the colonists of present-day Kingston, was longer. Five years of the usual frictions, intermittent hostilities, and a number of provocative incidents by the Dutch finally in 1663 aroused the Indians to attack the settlement of Wiltwyck (Indian-town) destroying much of the town and carrying off numerous women and children. The colonists organized an extensive pursuit, during which they destroyed the Indians' winter supplies, and gradually redeemed the captives. After this, Stuyvesant insisted that the Esopus give up their land near the river and stay away from the settlements, except for carefully controlled opportunities to trade.

The West India Company, therefore, failed to repeat in America the success of the East India Company in trading with and administering native peoples, primarily because it found a totally different situation. The people of the East Indies were numerous, well organized among themselves, accustomed to producing quantities of valuable commodities for trade, and familiar with European civilization and expectations after a century of Portuguese exploitation. The American Indians, by contrast, were few and at a primitive stage of tribal organization; their needs were simple, and the sudden introduction to European commodities disrupted their way of life. Nevertheless, methods that had worked in the East were attempted, and so long as New Netherland was populated only by a few traders, who sold the Indians goods they needed and did not interfere with their way of life, it worked more or less as it was supposed to do, producing generally amicable relations and a measure of profit to both parties. These conditions prevailed at Fort Orange throughout the period of Dutch rule. When free trade introduced unbridled competition in the lower Hudson valley, this commercial balance was upset. Relations between Dutch farmers and Indian hunters and maize-growers in the lower valley were more like those in the English colonies — always precarious and all too often violent.

The question was therefore repeatedly raised whether the profits from the fur trade made the trouble and expense of New Netherland worthwhile. The West India Company, which wanted a commodity comparable to Oriental spices or silks, was bitterly disappointed. So was Kiliaen Van Rensselaer, who wanted a return for a considerable capital outlay. But to smaller traders, who started with small fortunes or none and invested primarily their time and trouble, the reward was much more satisfactory. A number of Dutch colonists made fortunes in the fur trade which secured them leading positions among their neighbors, and some of their descendants continued to find that business profitable until the American Revolution changed its conditions altogether.

2

Many Faces of New Netherland

THE WEST INDIA COMPANY thought of New Netherland primarily as a territory for commercial exploitation, and only secondarily as a field for colonization. This was only to be expected in the 1620s, since the idea of colonization — though familiar today — had only begun to develop. Best known were the Spanish and Portuguese colonies, inhabited by a relatively few conquistadors and missionaries directing the labor of great numbers of conquered natives and imported slaves. When the Dutch encountered this system in the East Indies, they modified it on a commercial basis. The French and especially the English colonies in North America — that were to change the whole meaning of colonization — were struggling to avoid starvation and extermination by the Indians, and in their first years were hardly setting a promising example for anyone else to follow. Nevertheless, New Netherland did develop as a colony of settlement, partly as a result of the West India Company's efforts and partly on its own. Though no one deliberately transplanted the Dutch way of life as such to the New World as the Puritans recreated English culture in Massachusetts Bay, the colony as it grew showed a number of significantly Dutch characteristics which have often been overlooked by historians more familiar with the English colonies.

Misconception has arisen at the very beginning by comparing the Walloon colonists with the Pilgrims, with whom they had little in common beyond their situation as religious refugees. It has been suggested that the Pilgrims themselves, incidentally, narrowly missed being the first settlers of New Netherland, for as they were preparing to leave Leyden they applied for permission to go to the Hudson Valley, but were refused by the Dutch government to avoid antagonizing England. As a matter of fact, the petition to the States-General was a political move by the New Netherland Company, seeking an extension of its charter, while the Pilgrims themselves were attempting to secure permission from the *English* government to settle in the Hudson Valley, which at that time was claimed by both countries. The Pilgrims were an organized congregation, many of whose members had known each other for years in England before they fled. Then they had lived together in exile for 12 years, maintaining their identity in the face of an alien language and culture into which they did not wish their children to become too much assimilated. When the necessities of colonization compelled them to include in their group persons who had not shared these experiences, they promptly drew up the Mayflower Compact setting forth the terms of self-government to which all consented.

By contrast, the Walloons had fled from many places in the French-speaking Low Countries, and became acquainted with each other only after they arrived in the Netherlands. Aside from some difficulty in finding employment where there were so many refugees, they could not have felt themselves altogether in an alien land, since as many as a third of the people of Amsterdam alone were Southern Netherlands refugees like themselves, and their Calvinist religion had just been made the established church of their new homeland. They, and the French-speaking Calvinist refugee merchants who had played an important part in the formation of the West India Company, undoubtedly thought it would be desirable to plant their faith in the New World, but events proved they had no such singleminded conception of a wilderness Zion as motivated the founders of New England. For the Walloons, many of whom had been only part-time farmers who supplemented their incomes by weaving or lace-making, found the New World disappointing. Over half of those settled at Fort Orange in 1624 left even before Minuit called the rest in to Manhattan two years later, and in 1628 it was reported: "A portion of the Walloons are going back to the Fatherland, either because their years here have expired, or else because some are not very serviceable to the Company."[1] Nevertheless, some did stay; the Rapalje, Vigne, and du Trieux (Truax) families are descended from Walloons who came in 1624.

As soon as it knew the settlers had arrived safely and successfully planted their first crops, the West India Company made elaborate and expensive plans to supply them with livestock. It contracted for the preparation of three ships, appropriately named the *Cow*, the *Sheep*, and the *Horse*, with individual stalls deeply floored with sand and with a special water supply for the animals. The men to tend them were carefully selected and well paid. With all this care, all but two animals survived the voyage, and were triumphantly turned out to pasture on Manhattan. It was therefore a bitter disappointment when 20 of them — one-fifth of the entire consignment — immediately died, probably from eating some poisonous plant. Like the Virginia Company, the West India Company also experimented with several types of manufacture. Timber was always at a premium in the Netherlands, which had few large trees, but freight from New Netherland on such a bulky cargo was so high that Swedish timber was still cheaper. Available raw materials suggested attempts to produce less bulky and more valuable commodities, such as tar, potash, salt, bricks, and wine, but all efforts foundered upon the difficulty of inducing really skilled workers to go to New Netherland, stay there, and work diligently at their trades.

This colony was governed at first by mutual agreement among the ship captains who happened to be present, as had been customary on the Hudson River for a number of years. Each year the Company designated one of them to serve as a sort of chairman — in 1624 Cornelis May, skipper of the vessel which brought the Walloons; in 1625 Willem Verhulst, commander of the second Walloon contingent which went to the island in the Delaware. The appointment of Peter Minuit as continuing resident governor in 1626 marked the gathering in of all the scattered colonists to Manhattan, where they could be more easily defended and perhaps form a more cohesive community. But any such hope was frustrated by the circumstances of frontier living. Domine Michaelius, the first pastor, who came in 1628 after service on another frontier in West Africa, was deeply disappointed to find not only that the land did not flow with milk and honey as he had been led to believe, but that the colonists were quite indifferent to their opportunity to make it bring forth these delicacies. No fresh fruits and vegetables or dairy products were available at New Amsterdam, whose inhabitants supplied their tables by traffic with the Indians; Michaelius had not brought trade goods for this purpose, nor could he hire laborers to cultivate the land the Company had promised him.

The next important effort at colonization was that of Kiliaen Van Rensselaer, who had previously engaged in land-reclamation projects on his estates in Gelderland and the Gooi, near Utrecht. A number of his early settlers came from those areas. He sent tools with them, and provided them with the all-important livestock by asking Van Twiller to purchase animals from the Company and send them up to Rensselaerswyck. Van Rensselaer was so interested in his colony that he tried to regulate its everyday activities by long letters full of details which often appear unnecessarily fussy today and certainly seemed so to the colonists. His vivid imagination leaped the Atlantic to visualize the little community of board huts with thatched roofs amid the stumps of the great forest, and he understood its need for something familiar to cling to amid the unknown. To fill this need he established local offices when there were so few colonists that nearly every settler held one, and sent them the traditional habiliments of office — a rapier with a baldric and a hat with a silver plume for the *schout*, or sheriff, and hats with silver bands for the *schepens*, or magistrates. He was well aware that none of the colonists possessed the local social status customarily expected in those chosen for such offices in the Netherlands, but he did not foresee that instead of the offices dignifying their holders, these bumptious young frontiersmen would reduce the offices to objects of ridicule.

For Rensselaerswyck was a young community — younger than New Amsterdam, where there were always a few older leaders including the governor, the domine, and sea captains and traders with experience in many parts of the world. The farmers of Rensselaerswyck were mostly in their twenties, some of them recently married, others with small children, but all — or they would not have come — ambitious and adventurous, stubborn and shrewd, and eager to try something new. In all probability they had lost patience with the tradition-bound way of life of rural Dutch villages, in which important decisions were made by the village elders. Van Rensselaer, back home in his counting-room, was sufficiently in tune with this spirit to appoint some officials even younger than the colonists — Arent Van Curler, his cousin, became *commis*, or manager, at 18 and Adriaen Van der Donck, a brilliant law school graduate, at 21 came out to be legal officer.

These young men, like the only slightly older Van Twiller, then had to learn administration the hard way, and resented it when Van Rensselaer, trying to make himself heard across 3,000 miles, lectured them for their youthful shortcomings. Nevertheless they did learn, and it is a tribute to Van Rensselaer's judgment of character that both Van Curler and Van der Donck became able and public-spirited leaders in New Netherland.

In 1636 Van Rensselaer, wearying of the Company's reluctance to find room in its vessels to transport his settlers and their goods, purchased the ship *Rensselaerswyck* and sent it off with 25 families of settlers — as many as had gone to the colony in the preceding six years. The log of the voyage reveals some of the hazards and discomforts the colonists faced in simply getting to New Netherland. The ship sailed late in September, in company with other vessels until it passed the pirate nest of Dunkirk and the navigational hazards of the English Channel, after which it turned alone toward the Canary Islands. But a late fall storm battered the vessel back into the Bay of Biscay, leaving her damaged and short of provisions, so the captain had to put back to England for repairs. A child born during this tempest was appropriately named Storm Van der Zee; he later became the ancestor of the Van der Zee family still numerous south of Albany.

In England the ship was repaired, but just before she was ready to leave, two of the emigrants quarreled in a tavern and one was killed, which delayed the vessel until the inquest was completed and the culprit arrested. After the *Rensselaerswyck* finally put to sea early in January 1637, it encountered a couple of privateers and pursued a possible prize itself on its way south to the latitude of the steady trade winds, where day after day it sailed westward without further incident. On February 26 it reached the coast of Virginia, and a week later anchored at Manhattan Island. But the river above was still frozen, so the captain had to wait nearly a month at New Amsterdam, where the two children born since the vessel left England were baptized and the manslaughter victim's widow remarried. Then the ice went out and the freshet subsided, and it was finally possible to go to Rensselaerswyck, where the colonists disembarked on April 7, six and a half months after they had left the Netherlands. The vessel departed at the end of May, making a side trip to Virginia for tobacco before sailing uneventfully back from New Amsterdam to the Netherlands on the prevailing westerlies, arriving on November 7. But Van Rensselaer was not satisfied with this long and expensive voyage; he dismissed the captain and sold the ship.

In the meantime, the sudden and spectacular emergence of New England between 1630 and 1640 suggested to the European world the desirability of well-populated colonies of settlement. Massachusetts Bay owed a great measure of its success to the pre-existing organization of its religious congregations, whose members reconstructed a shared tradition of civil government, a pattern followed at second hand by the migrants to Connecticut and used as a basis for free variations by the dissidents of Rhode Island. The Dutch, however, had no way of knowing how much these deliberately transplanted English institutions contributed to their neighbors' astonishing growth. Their own tradition of social, ethnic, and religious diversities united for commercial advantage depended heavily upon the complex structure of local privileges in the Netherlands. Could enough of this tradition be transplanted to the New World to recreate the familiar sanctions necessary for the maintenance of basic order?

The cherished civic privileges or "liberties" of the Netherlands had been acquired one at a time as the wealthiest merchants pooled their resources to purchase them from feudal lords who very often needed extra money. Each town possessed at any given time whatever liberties it had been able to win from its own lord, so the liberties of every town were different. But competition between them was intense, and if one town secured a new liberty its neighbors would not rest until they had secured similar liberties. Therefore, despite myriad local variations, the general structure of government was remarkably similar throughout the Low Countries. Some fundamental liberties included freedom from serfdom for all residents of the town, town courts for the collection of debts and the settlement of disputes among the burghers, and the right to propose two names for each vacancy on the town council, from which the lord appointed one. This procedure, known as "cooptation," became the customary method of selecting officials throughout the Low Countries.

The working of this process of cooptation meant that Dutch communities came to be ruled by a small, self-perpetuating clique of the wealthiest families, called "patricians." Since these families had originally put up the money to purchase the privileges, and since the prosperity of the whole town depended upon their success in supplying its workers and selling their products, this system was not inherently unreasonable or at first unjust. Furthermore, when merchants and fishermen were away for long periods of time and farmers and artisans had to work from dawn to dusk to make a living, none of them had the leisure to keep up on public affairs which citizens take for granted today. Holding office required a scale of living which only the wealthy could afford, and a familiarity with the details of government which young patricians learned from their elders since the art of government was not then taught in schools. Therefore, the ordinary people of most towns were proud to be governed by their patricians, whom they considered as much the embodiment of the town's cherished privileges as the city hall, and glad to see the patricians become wealthy and invest their wealth for the benefit of the community — so long as that prosperity was reflected in their own standard of living. It is important to note that, though this tradition was deeply rooted in the cities of Holland and the southern Netherlands and in the surrounding countryside, the agricultural provinces of the north, particularly Friesland, had a very different tradition in which farmers and fishermen valued their stubborn independence even more than communal loyalty.

But circumstances could arise in which the policies of the patricians did not forward the interests of the rest of the townsmen. Such was the case in fourteenth-century Flanders, when the merchant patricians gave insufficient consideration to the interests of the artisans, particularly the weavers, many of whom worked long hours in ill-paid dead-end jobs. Sometimes the people rebelled violently, rioting through the streets and lynching unpopular officials. When the town council could not restore order, the lord would intervene with military force, putting down the revolt, executing the ringleaders, and sometimes, if the whole town were in rebellion, revoking some of its privileges. But after such an outbreak the patricians would usually do something about the conditions which provoked it — in the Flemish towns, they admitted representatives of the most important craft gilds to the town councils. Therefore, popular revolt and the threat of military repression served as important checks on the power of the patricians, keeping their government from straying too far from the interests of the people or infringing upon their share of the communal liberties.

The transplantation of this highly localized tradition of patri-

cian rule, popular revolt, and military repression to New Netherland was complicated because the colonists came from many
different towns and provinces. Nearly half were not even from
the Netherlands. In 1643 Governor Kieft told Father Isaac Jogues
that 18 languages were spoken in New Amsterdam, which, even if
some of them would now be considered Indian or European
dialects, made it an extraordinarily polyglot community for its
size. Amsterdam was equally heterogeneous, but Amsterdam had
a population of nearly 200,000 and a tradition going back more
than three centuries, in contrast to New Amsterdam's population
of barely 1,000 and history of 18 years. The ruling families of
old Amsterdam had been wealthy and respected patricians for
generations; the leading citizens of New Amsterdam had been
there for a decade or less and had come as poor servants or soldiers
employed by the Company to take orders, not to give them. In
modern American terms these circumstances by no means made
them unfit for community leadership, but in the Dutch context
of their own day, it was unthinkable that they should be qualified
to participate in government.

Therefore, tensions which in Netherlands towns were restrained
by the weight of established custom threatened to tear the communities of New Netherlands apart. Governor Kieft learned this the
hard way. He had impeccable credentials — except, perhaps, for
the fact that he had failed in business. He was of Amsterdam patrician descent, grandson of a heroic leader of the Revolt, and an intelligent and cultured gentleman interested in conversing with
educated visitors like Jogues, and in preparing as his final report a
little book, illustrated with watercolor sketches, which was unfortunately lost at sea with him on his return to the Netherlands. But
in New Amsterdam Kieft was left to stand alone, a patrician with
no other patricians to back him, no town council to consult, and a
population which in this case associated obedience not with civic
loyalty but with the demands of employers who (from the em-
ployes' point of view) had not lived up to their side of the bargain.
It is hardly surprising that Kieft proved unable to cope with the
situation, although he did what he could. When Indian troubles
erupted, since there was no town council, he called together all the
heads of families and asked them to select 12 representatives to
advise him. But Kieft wanted to create an advisory body, not a
governing body, and when the so-called Twelve Men ventured to
offer advice on political subjects on which he had not consulted

them, he dissolved the group. The necessity of continuing the Indian war of 1643, however, compelled him that same year to ask for the election of the group soon known as the Eight Men, who performed as he wished until peace was concluded in 1645.

The war solidified local opposition to Kieft, particularly among those who thought his conduct of it had brought them material loss. Some were members of a group of small patroons, granted lands under a new charter of 1640, who had induced settlers to come to Staten Island and New Jersey. We see these new patroons as public-spirited citizens crying out in anguish after seeing their houses, barns, and crops go up in smoke and the colonists who had trusted them massacred, but the Company, inclined to be distrustful of all patroons, saw them as recent arrivals complaining because their investment had brought them loss instead of quick profits. Nor was it perhaps possible at that time for anyone in the Netherlands to appreciate the tension and fear under which the settlers lived, forced to trust the Indians and to admit them freely to their towns and houses in order to trade, but never knowing when this trust might be abused or betrayed.

The best known of these opponents of Kieft, because he later wrote a book about his experiences, is David P. De Vries. De Vries had more colonial experience and probably more ability than most of the leaders of New Netherland, for he began his career as a sea captain for the East India Company and rose to a responsible position in their organization before tropical disease forced him to resign. Then he offered his services to the patroons of Swanendael, and commanded the expedition which discovered that the colonists had been massacred (and also proved that the whales of Delaware Bay contained insufficient blubber to make whaling profitable). He then bought a farm on Staten Island and suggested himself as a candidate to succeed Van Twiller. But De Vries was not of patrician descent although his brother was an official in the West India Company. The principal qualities he had to offer were his wide experience and knowledge of the colony, which in the 1630s were qualifications far ahead of the Company's thinking. He was also a Frisian and thus a member of a minority group noted for its outspoken independence, a characteristic prominent in his writing, which suggest that he may not have possessed the tact to be desired in the governor of such a heterogeneous and turbulent colony. Despite this disappointment, De Vries became a public-spirited citizen, taking the lead among

David Pietersz de Vries, from his journal, *Korte Historiael*...
Courtesy of the New York State Library

the Twelve Men and urging Kieft not to provoke the Indians, with whom he had developed a relationship of mutual respect. After the Pavonia massacre was committed against his express warning and his own plantation devastated during the reprisal raids, however, he gave up in disgust and returned to the Netherlands.

Others vented their resentment in more direct action. A Long Island farmer named Maryn Adriantz, who had been one of the earliest settlers of Rensselaerswyck and was one of the Twelve Men, became so angry that he tried to assassinate the governor, and when he failed his servant tried and also failed. The servant was killed in the attempt, but Adriantz was sent to Holland for trial, where he was let off with a light sentence. Then two farmers named Cornelius Melyn and Jochem P. Kuyter, both of whom had been burned out in the raids, composed a ringing account of the devastation and an indictment of Kieft, which they sent to the West India Company. Kieft was recalled in 1645, but it was two years before his successor, Peter Stuyvesant, reached the colony. When he arrived, Melyn and Kuyter moved to take legal action against Kieft, collecting depositions attesting to his misgovernment. Stuyvesant, who had no conception of the tension they had been under, saw this as a threat to his authority and arrested them, convicted them of sedition, fined them, and banished them from the colony. Melyn and Kuyter and Kieft all boarded the same ship to return to the Netherlands to plead their respective causes. But the ship was wrecked on the Welsh coast, and the people regarded it as a judgment of God that Kieft was drowned, while Melyn and Kuyter were among the few who escaped.

In the meantime, Peter Stuyvesant was attempting to restore New Netherland to some semblance of order. Learning its lesson after the damage was done, the West India Company had appointed a soldier with administrative experience. Peter Stuyvesant was the son of a Frisian pastor, a university dropout who had joined the Company as a soldier and had served several years in the West Indies where, in an attack on a Spanish island, he lost his right leg. His background was, therefore, military by experience and militant Calvinist by association, a combination which had previously appeared in Dutch history in the person of Prince Maurice. Although Stuyvesant was too young to have served under this great general, his career as governor recalls in many respects Prince Maurice's approach to civil administration.

To appreciate this approach, it is necessary to understand that

Peter Stuyvesant, by an unknown artist. *Courtesy of The New-York Historical Society, New York City*

Prince Maurice was not a king, or even a reigning prince in the Netherlands — his title was personal, derived from the minute territory of Orange in southern France which his family had inherited. His official title in the Netherlands was *Stadholder*, formerly the title of the deputy of the King of Spain, to which his father William the Silent had been elevated during the Revolt. William's prestige and Maurice's military success won great popularity for the Orange family, which gave them an independent base of power, but when some later members of the dynasty tried to use this power for their personal advantage, the States-General quickly reminded them that they were the servants rather than the masters of the nation. The States-General was for most of the seventeenth century the only representative body in Europe that was actually governing a country, for through that century the English Parliament was gaining power by conflict with the Stuart kings. The States-General represented the towns and provinces, its members being chosen by the Estates of the seven provinces, which in turn consisted of representatives from the principal town councils. Members from each province voted as a unit, and no measure could take effect unless all seven provinces approved. This meant that the States-General was pretty much confined to the conduct of war and foreign affairs and the licensing of trade monopolies to prevent ruinous competition, such as the New Netherland and East and West India Companies. Most controversial matters were left to local option.

As a rule local interest (represented in the States-General) and the national interest (represented by the Stadholder) managed to work together, but on occasion they conflicted. The Remonstrant controversy produced the first great constitutional crisis of the Dutch Republic and forced Prince Maurice to intervene with the army to prevent the nation from tearing itself apart. This conflict arose during the Twelve Years' Truce, when the Calvinists turned their fervor from fighting the common enemy to converting their compatriots. Since many Dutchmen did not wish to be converted, what began as a theological dispute quickly became a power struggle which spilled over from the churches into the city councils, and from there into the streets. The Calvinists were still a minority, but they were better organized, strategically located in commerce and civic affairs, and quick to capitalize on their signal contributions to the struggle for independence. In the States-General, the representatives of non-Calvinist localities formed a faction known as the "Remonstrants," led by Johan van Olden-barnevelt, the leading civilian statesman of the day; this faction stubbornly maintained the sanctity of existing local privileges, including religious toleration. The Calvinist members thereupon organized as the "Counter-Remonstrants," and since neither could command the votes of all seven provinces, the States-General was powerless to act in the face of mounting disorder. The government was therefore on the verge of collapse when Prince Maurice intervened with the army in behalf of the Calvinists, whom he directed to call the Synod of Dort (1619) to agree on the basic tenets of a state-supported Dutch Reformed Church. Remonstrant protests were halted by the arrest and execution of Oldenbarnevelt on a trumped-up charge of treason. This was well within the Netherlands tradition for settling irreconcilable internal differences, and Maurice was no Duke of Alva to overstep the limits of tradition. The execution of Oldenbarnevelt introduced no reign of terror, and the Calvinists, entrusted with the religious welfare of the nation, soon discovered that they had to make many compromises on matters of local importance to keep the support of the people.

All this took place when Peter Stuyvesant was a small child, and since he was the son of a Calvinist minister and a soldier by profession, the example of Prince Maurice probably contributed much to his conception of his role as governor of New Netherland. He faced the same situation in which Kieft had failed — a diverse, disorganized colony without stable traditions of its own, with the additional problems of reconstructing after a devastating war, preventing the Indians from starting another, and controlling a few citizens (some public-spirited and some self-seeking) who were making an organized attempt to take the government into their own hands. They were going so far as to propose throwing off altogether the rule of the Company — which was not only the employer to whom Stuyvesant was responsible, but the only source of stability the colony then possessed. All in all, Stuyvesant would have been quite justified in concluding that the situation was not so different from that of the Netherlands during the Remonstrant crisis of 1618-19.

One of the first objects of his effort to impose a measure of unity was Rensselaerswyck. Kiliaen Van Rensselaer had died in 1646, leaving Wouter Van Twiller chief among the guardians of his several minor children. Van Twiller sent out an experienced local administrator named Brant Van Slichtenhorst, who could almost have been one of old Kiliaen's letters come to life. He scrupulously guarded every prerogative, asserted every right, and collected every due which could be claimed by the "infant patroon," and during his four-year term of office the patroon's private court was busier than it ever was before or afterward.

Stuyvesant first clashed with him over the maintenance of a little fort called Rensselaersteyn on an island at the entrance to the patroon's domain, which tried to prevent ships from sailing up to Fort Orange. It is quite probable that the Van Rensselaers' able agent, Arent Van Curler, had aroused their concern lest the unrestricted intrusion of free traders disrupt Indian relations at Fort Orange as it already had at Manhattan. But Stuyvesant saw only over-mighty subjects interfering with commerce, and when he ordered Rensselaersteyn abandoned, Van Slichtenhorst had no choice but to obey. Then possession of Fort Orange itself became an issue, when Van Slichtenhorst moved the patroon's colonists from the east to the west bank of the river for defense against a threatened Indian attack. The free traders at Fort Orange complained to Stuyvesant, who, when Van Slichtenhorst ignored an order to move his settlers away from the fort, sailed up the river in 1652 and declared Fort Orange the independent municipality of Beverwyck (Beavertown). To make all sure, he arrested Van Slichtenhorst and shipped him back to the Netherlands — ostensibly for his own protection from the Patroon's irritated tenants, many of whom quickly seized the opportunity to slip out of their obligations by becoming burghers of Beverwyck.

Stuyvesant's relations with New Amsterdam were very different. That community was rapidly developing a civic identity of its own. Kieft had provided it with its first public buildings, the City Tavern for the entertainment of travelers, and, under prodding from David P. deVries, who was concerned about the town's image in the eyes of New England skippers, a church. Now the burghers thought the Company ought also to provide them with an orphanage, an almshouse, and a school. Kieft had given them their first taste of consultative government; now they wanted more. At first Stuyvesant welcomed their enthusiasm. He permitted them to select nine men to advise him, in the tradition of the Twelve and the Eight, but intended this time as a permanent body, some of whose members would be replaced each year by cooptation. He even invited them to draw up a statement of their

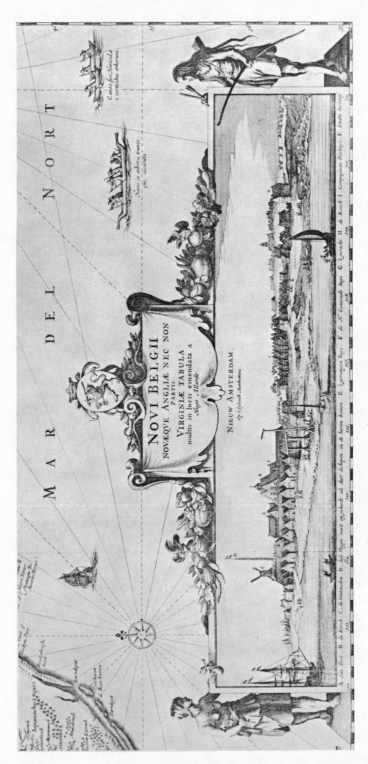

View of New Amsterdam, 1655. *Courtesy of the New York State Library*

grievances to present to the Company, so long as they allowed him to see it before it was sent.

But the Nine Men had other ideas, especially after Adriaen Van der Donck was selected as one of their members. Van der Donck, one of Van Rensselaer's ambitious young men who had turned out to be too ambitious to remain in the patroon's employ, was a patrician by birth with a law degree from the University of Utrecht. As a reward for helping Kieft arrange the Indian peace of 1645, he had been granted an estate of his own at Colen Donck, now Yonkers (for *Jonkheer's* — the young lord's — land). He had married an English girl, the daughter of a dissident pastor named Francis Doughty, who had led a group of secessionists from New England to settle on Long Island. Stuyvesant suspected that Doughty influenced his son-in-law's protest movement, but though Van der Donck may have profited by some tactical suggestions, his part in the history of New Netherland was that of Oldenbarnevelt to Stuyvesant's Prince Maurice, and he very nearly succeeded because the Remonstrant principles of Oldenbarnevelt came into ascendancy at the same time in the Netherlands.

When Stuyvesant discovered — by the summary expedient of raiding Van der Donck's office and seizing his files — that the grievances being collected by the Nine Men included complaints against himself, he abruptly turned against them. When they persisted, he dissolved the group and forbade them ever to meet again. About the same time his fury was fanned by the return of Melyn and Kuyter with a writ from the States-General revoking his sentence of banishment. This they dramatically produced at a public meeting, taking Stuyvesant completely by surprise; he lost his temper and nearly tore the document to pieces before he collected himself and heard it out in stony silence. Such yielding to anger only encouraged Van der Donck and his friends to complete their catalogue of grievances by a house-to-house canvass, and then to embark with the list for the homeland in August 1649.

Within the year after the three-man delegation arrived, the Netherlands underwent a quiet revolution. The Eighty Years' War, which had been a fact of life since before almost everyone then living had been born, had just been concluded by the Peace of Westphalia. About the same time Prince Frederick Henry, another successful general and youngest son of the great William the Silent, had died. His son William II, who succeeded him as Stadholder, had married the eldest daughter of King Charles I of England and was inclined to be a high-handed ruler himself. When he too died in 1650, a week before the birth of a son whose royal grandfather had just been executed by his rebellious subjects, the Dutch were in no hurry to select a new Stadholder. The infant William III obviously could not serve for many years; perhaps, since the war was over, the Dutch Republic could get along without a Stadholder. So began the *Stadhouderlos* (Stadholder-less) period, which lasted for 22 years, until the Netherlands again stood in mortal danger from invasion and the baby had grown up to become a young man whose spirit and ability proved to be a worthy inheritance from his great ancestors. In the meantime, the country was administered by a civilian statesman named Jan de Witt, an Amsterdam patrician who embodied the traditions of toleration, free enterprise, and maintenance of local privileges upheld by Oldenbarnevelt.

In this rapidly changing political climate, Van der Donck and his colleagues presented their petition to the States-General and set about a campaign to arouse public opinion in their favor. The West India Company was already under attack as an unprofitable economic dinosaur, no longer needed now that the war with Spain was over. Someone — perhaps Melyn — had already collaborated with some Portuguese expatriates who wanted to get the Company out of Brazil, in a piece of propaganda called "Broad Counsel" which was so broad in its attack — and its humor — that it was downright scurrilous. Now Van der Donck published a pamphlet entitled "The Remonstrance of New Netherland" — the title itself would have recalled the name of Oldenbarnevelt's Remonstrant party — relating in ruthless detail what he interpreted as the Company's long history of neglect of its colony. These works achieved their purpose; the plight of New Netherland was widely discussed and in 1650 the States-General voted a preliminary resolution granting the colony many liberties. Two of the delegation returned home with this news, while Van der Donck stayed behind to tie up the loose ends.

But the Company, though hard-pressed, was by no means beaten. It had an able advocate from the colony in Cornelis Van Tienhoven — the Secretary of equivocal morals and views on Indians — who now prepared a skillful reply to the "Remonstrance," showing that the Company had not neglected its colony but had on the contrary gone to great expense for it with little return, pointed out that the remonstrants were complaining about matters which by Dutch custom were no affair of theirs, and identified them as ambitious, self-seeking men who were either ungrateful former servants of the Company or its debtors trying to evade their obligations. The Company also had all the resources of a great corporation lobbying in a disunited legislature — with whose front and back stairs it was thoroughly familiar. The reforms of the provisional order were steadily whittled away until, in May 1652, Van der Donck finally secured a letter which recalled Stuyvesant and granted the privilege of municipal government to New Amsterdam.

Then, just as he was about to depart in triumph, the wind changed — war broke out between the Netherlands and Cromwell's England. With only a disputed boundary separating New Netherland from the Puritans of New England, the martial virtues of Prince Maurice suddenly seemed more attractive to the States-General than the civil-government tradition of Oldenbarnevelt. The recall of Stuyvesant was revoked, and the West India Company, deciding that Van der Donck was too shrewd and dangerous to be disrupting the colony in wartime, refused to permit him to return home. Two years later they relented, on condition that he stay out of politics and refrain from the practice of law, but he only enjoyed life at Colen Donck for a year or so before he died about 1655, so obscurely that not even the date and circumstances are known.

While Van der Donck was in exile, he wrote a book entitled *Description of New Netherland*, a combination of a promotion tract to encourage settlement, an expatriate's lyrical reminiscences of his lost home, and a classical scholar's criticism of contemporary civilized morals by depicting an earthly paradise of Noble Savages in the manner of Tacitus' *Germania*. All this he accomplished with the fidelity to observed detail of a Dutch painter and the accuracy of expression attributed by one scholar to the habits of thought of "realistic businessmen who weighed their phrases as they did their grains and cheeses, and the words they used referred to concrete things."[2] From Van der Donck's pen thus came the first systematic description of the natural resources of New Netherland, the first extended attempt to appreciate the Indians as people, and the first projection of the colony's future as a community in its own right. It is regrettable — though under the circumstances understandable — that the West India Company denied Van der Donck access to its records for the history he

wanted to write, which surely would have taken a place beside
Bradford's *History of Plimoth Plantation* as a cornerstone of
American literature.

In the meantime, under the force of the *fait accompli*, the
threat of war, and the grant of municipal government, the opposition to Stuyvesant in New Netherland had subsided. Stuyvesant
himself was able to capitalize on his position as the official
representative of both the States-General and the West India Company, once he learned not to let his Frisian temper get the better
of him in public, and the circumstances of the next 12 years,
furthermore, gave him many opportunities to exercise his considerable military and diplomatic ability. The only dissidents in the
latter part of his administration were religious — Lutherans, Jews,
Quakers — and these he repressed with all the fervor of his militant
Calvinist forebears. But the West India Company, hearing of all
this in tolerant Amsterdam and anxious to promote the population
of its colony, rebuked him severely and ordered him to let people's
consciences alone unless they fomented disorder. Once again the
tradition of Prince Maurice crossed swords with that of Oldenbarnevelt, and this time that of Oldenbarnevelt won.

The history of New Netherland therefore makes sense in terms
of important patterns in the history of the Netherlands. This has
not been recognized because that history is unfamiliar to Americans accustomed to think of colonial history in an English context.
Americans also have difficulty envisioning a national tradition
based not upon homogeneous adherence to a written constitution
but on a heterogeneous, unwritten acceptance of unity arising
from the balance between traditional diversities. Thus "Dutch
tradition" in New Netherland is not one but the interaction of
several — the relentless search for profit of merchants; the venera-
tion for local liberties of Oldenbarnevelt; the imposed military
unity in times of crisis of Prince Maurice, the cosmopolitan
heterogeneity of Amsterdam; the suspicious local jealousy of small
cities and villages; and the independence of farmers, sailors, and
fishermen facing a new world on their own. The balance of these
traditions, like that of the Netherlands, created a type of unity no
less real than, but very different from, that of any of the English
colonies.

3

The Cockpit of America

THE LOW COUNTRIES have long been called the "cockpit of Europe." The same geographical situation at the intersection of many transportation routes that made them a center of commerce also made them a battleground between neighboring powers. Throughout the Middle Ages, their wealth and political disunity tempted both France and England to seek their alliance and to interfere in their local affairs. The Netherlanders, however, were successful in preserving their basic liberties until the Spanish invasion, when both France and England harassed Spain by supporting the Dutch Revolt. The Dutch Republic emerged from the Eighty Years' War a major power, at a time when both England and France were rent by internal dissension. This Dutch position on top of the world was supported by an army and navy drilled to a peak of efficiency by three generations of warfare, and by a mutually profitable relationship between war and commerce which insured that merchants would reap large profits and rich prizes by keeping the troops adequately financed and supplied. But once again Dutch wealth aroused the jealousy of other nations, and throughout the latter half of the seventeenth century the Netherlands were subjected to constant economic pressure and occasional military attack from England, France, or both.

These conflicts of empire extended to the Hudson Valley, which, like the Netherlands, was particularly exposed to them because of the very geographic location which made it such a profitable location for trade. The Dutch came to the Hudson Valley in the first place to outflank the French monopoly on the

furs of the Saint Lawrence, and competition between them became intense as both became familiar with the country and enlisted the various tribes of Indians on their side. Henry Hudson, of
course, had no way of knowing that at the very time he was discovering his river, Samuel de Champlain was exploring the lake
which bears his name. But the Dutch very soon learned that the
Indians of the Saint Lawrence Valley and the Great Lakes could
travel down Lake Champlain to Fort Orange almost as easily as
they could journey to Quebec, and that they particularly valued
the *seawant* (wampum) manufactured by the Indians of Long
Island.

The French immediately countered this competition by exploiting rivalries among the Indians, encouraging the Mohawks —
who were neither so hostile to the French nor so powerful as they
later became — to attack the Mahicans around Fort Orange. It was
in all probability awareness of this French influence which
prompted Van Krieckebeeck to assist the Mahicans, who, until
that incident, appear to have been winning the war. But then the
Mohawks gathered their resources, defeated them, and drove them
east of the Hudson, thus clearing their own path to Fort Orange.
After their victory, the Mohawks played French and Dutch traders
against each other for 10 years, until the Dutch purchased their
lasting alliance by selling them the firearms which enabled the
Mohawks to gain the upper hand over all of their Indian neighbors,
including those of Canada, and even for a time to threaten the
existence of New France itself.

Another conflict of empires developed with the growth of
New England. As early as 1628 a Dutch visitor to Plymouth was
concerned lest the Pilgrims, who were repaying their debt to their
London backers with the fur trade of Maine, should intrude upon
that south of Cape Cod. In 1633 the West India Company founded
a permanent post, Fort Good Hope, at the head of navigation on
the Connecticut, but only three years later Thomas Hooker's first
contingent of dissatisfied colonists came from Massachusetts Bay.
The Fundamental Orders of Connecticut and the Pequot War
followed in quick succession, and the fur trade of Connecticut was
ruined. The Dutch soon ceased to maintain the post at Fort Good
Hope, but they clung to the land it stood on and to their claim
that all this territory was part of New Netherland, although the
English had begun a town at nearby Hartford and were settling all
along the coast and the opposite shore of Long Island.

This dispute over jurisdiction finally prompted Stuyvesant to conclude the Treaty of Hartford in 1650, setting the western boundary of Connecticut approximately where it meets Long Island Sound today and giving Connecticut the eastern half of Long Island. Although Stuyvesant had to give up some territory long claimed by the Dutch, the treaty represented a considerable diplomatic triumph for him, in view of the much larger population of New England. This was made possible by his astute exploitation of the differences between Connecticut and Rhode Island, which were eager to annex Dutch lands, and Massachusetts Bay and Plymouth, which were not at that time interested in expansion. It was concluded just in time, for the next year Cromwell's England passed the first Navigation Acts forbidding foreign — *i.e.*, Dutch — ships to trade with the English colonies, which soon set off the first Anglo-Dutch War (1652-54), in which Admirals Blake and Van Tromp first developed the tactics of modern naval warfare.

In the meantime, some dissidents from the New England Way of Massachusetts discovered that they did not like Connecticut's version of it any better, and migrated once again into the jurisdiction of New Netherland. Anne Hutchinson, Captain John Underhill, and the Rev. Francis Doughty have already been mentioned. Many of these transplanted New Englanders settled on Long Island, until its Dutch population was by and large confined to the five "Dutch towns" at the extreme western end. (Only Brooklyn still retains its Dutch name.) At first these English settlers, grateful to the Dutch for their religious toleration, were loyal to Stuyvesant in his controversies with the Dutch settlers, but later they began to be homesick for association with Englishmen under English institutions. By the 1660s they were quite ready to join with the Connecticut settlers on the east end of Long Island in pressing for annexation to New England.

But before this situation arose, New Netherland sustained and overcame a challenge from an entirely different empire, that of Sweden. Sweden was the leading Protestant military power in the Thirty Years' War and possessed rich resources of timber and minerals, but her economic development was in the hands of Dutch entrepreneurs whose vessels took her lumber to market and whose capital financed her iron and copper mines. A group of Dutch investors, dissatisfied with the West India Company, prompted the Swedish government to found New Sweden on the west bank of the Delaware in 1638, and to appoint as the first governor Peter Minuit, formerly governor of New Netherland. The Swedes founded their principal settlement, Fort Christina, at a key location for trading with Indians coming from the Susquehanna Valley — which the Dutch had overlooked. Stuyvesant rectified this oversight by moving the principal Dutch post from Fort Nassau on the east side of the river to Fort Casimir on the west. When incidents resulted, he invaded New Sweden with all the military force at his disposal. When he besieged Fort Christina, the outnumbered Swedes had no choice but to surrender; it was from this almost comic-opera triumph that Stuyvesant was recalled in haste to deal with the deadly serious massacres of Staten Island and Pavonia. The following year the West India Company sold the Delaware territories (including all of southern New Jersey) to the city of Amsterdam, which operated them for a few years as the separate colony of New Amstel, with its principal settlement, the former Fort Christina, on the site of Newcastle, Delaware.

Tension with New England was in the meantime becoming more severe. Indian wars made common measures of defense advisable, but the more populous New England colonies wanted to direct them — which Stuyvesant would not permit. There were boundary disputes, instances in which fugitives from justice in one colony sought asylum in another, and incidents when authorities on each side protected vessels evading the commercial regulations of the other. Stuyvesant's New England colleagues indulged a grim Yankee sense of humor in allowing him to embarrass himself by belligerent letters, which all concerned knew his underpopulated colony had no force to sustain. Finally, in 1663 an English adventurer named Col. John Scott stirred up revolt among the English colonists on Long Island and then sent insolent challenges to Stuyvesant, who, despite Scott's entire lack of legitimate authority, had no choice but to let the settlers do as they wished.

New Netherland was thus maintaining a precarious existence when in 1664 King Charles II, blithely disregarding the rights of others, granted his brother James, Duke of York, all the territory between the Dealware and Connecticut Rivers. On August 28 four warships under Col. Richard Nicholls anchored before New Amsterdam and demanded its surrender. Instead, Stuyvesant called out the militia, put laborers to work repairing the tumbledown fort, and inventoried available supplies. But the Long Island militia, fearing their English neighbors, refused to assemble; the fort was in hopeless disrepair; and both food and gunpowder were insufficient to sustain a siege. The burghers heard of the generous terms Nicholls had offered. Still, as the British fleet approached, Stuyvesant ordered his gunners to load and stood ready to give the word to fire. The two Domines Megapolensis, father and son, pleaded with him in the name of God and the people to spare them futile bloodshed. The guns remained silent. Then the burghers demanded to see Nicholls' letter, and one from Governor Winthrop of Connecticut urging acceptance of his terms. Stuyvesant tore Winthrop's letter to shreds before their eyes, but the burghers insisted that the terms be accepted. The history of New Netherland was over.

The change of flags over the fort meant very little change at first in the lives of the people. Nicholls granted the garrison surrender with all the honors of war, the municipality the unaltered enjoyment of its civic privileges, and the people maintenance of their customs, particularly those of inheritance. All who wished to return to the Netherlands were given six months to gather their property and go, and trade with the Netherlands was to continue without interruption for the same period — probably to allow for the arrival of ships already on the way. The most important immediate changes were in the names: New Amsterdam became New York, and Fort Orange became Albany, called after two of the new proprietor's dukedoms. The settlements on the Delaware, however, were less fortunate, for Fort Amstel offered resistance and Sir Robert Carr reduced it by force, burned the buildings and scattered the settlers — even though the west bank of the Delaware was not included within the area of the Duke's grant.

This highhanded seizure of New Netherland in time of peace was certainly one of the causes of the Second Anglo-Dutch War, which broke out a few months later. The Duke of York, commanding the navy, blockaded the Dutch coast, capturing some merchantmen but missing the great East India fleet. Then London was struck by the Great Plague and Great Fire of 1666, and England was left in no condition to wage war. In 1667 the Dutch fleet sailed up the Thames, destroyed part of the English fleet at anchor in the Medway, and carried off in triumph the English flagship, the *Royal Charles*. After that the English had little choice but to make the Peace of Breda — but they did not return New Netherland. Instead, five years later the Dutch took it back, in one of their few successes of the Third Anglo-Dutch War. Very little is known of the brief administration of Dutch Governor

Anthony Colve, because its records were thrown overboard to avoid capture when the ship on which he was returning to the Netherlands was taken by the enemy. It has been pointed out that the reconquest went unchallenged because England was preoccupied and New England again divided — and, despite some greed for land, not overanxious to pull the Duke of York's chestnuts out of the fire. Nevertheless, in the diplomatic horse-trading of the Peace of Westminster of 1674, the Dutch exchanged New Netherland for Surinam, and this time surrendered it for good.

New York was the first of several proprietary colonies founded in this period, and New Jersey, which the Duke soon granted to two of his friends, was the second. The proprietary colony, like many other institutions of Restoration England, was an updated version of a longstanding tradition — land development by lords who made a considerable investment, at great risk of loss in the many years before the increased population and productivity of the new land afforded any return. This was the same general European medieval tradition of land development which had produced "patroonships" in New Netherland. The great difficulty in applying it in the English, as in the Dutch, colonies was the distance between Europe and America. Where absentee proprietors took their responsibilities as developers and administrators seriously, as did Kiliaen Van Rensselaer, or settled in their colonies, as did the Lords Baltimore and William Penn, the system worked more or less effectively at first. But other proprietors like the Duke of York, his friends to whom he granted New Jersey, and the friends of King Charles who founded the Carolinas, preferred to maintain their aristocratic life style as courtiers in England, and looked to their colonies merely as sources of revenue to help them do so. This shift in emphasis, similar to that of the Dutch patroons who only wanted short-term profits, was disastrous, particularly in the early stages of colonization when the colonists had all they could do to make a living, and found the "quit rents" they were expected to pay a political as well as economic burden.

Because the Duke's governors administered New York within this quasi-feudal tradition, the necessity of dealing with the English rulers fell first upon families who claimed large tracts of land, such as the Van Rensselaers. As Kiliaen Van Rensselaer's children grew up, one after another of his sons came to America to live for a time in their domain, so that after 1656 there was always at least one member of the family in residence. Jan Baptist and Jeremias came first; Jan Baptist stayed only a few years, but Jeremias married Maria Van Cortlandt, daughter of one of the wealthiest merchants in New Amsterdam, and settled down for the rest of his life. Richard came in 1664 and remained until 1670. Nicholas, the black sheep of the clan, who ironically had performed a service for the exiled Charles II and was therefore the family's friend at court, turned up in 1674 and stayed until his death four years later. The contrast between these wealthy, cultured men and the hardworking farmers and rough traders of their domain is striking. Jeremias, for example, brought a falcon with him and tried to introduce the noble sport of hawking in the American forest, pursuing his quarry amid the stumps and burned-over patches of American clearings — bringing it home not to a castle or even a comfortable manor house but to a rough board cabin with a thatched roof no different from that of the humblest settlers. When he and Jan Baptist built themselves a more suitable brick house, it was swept away (with 40 other settlers' homes) by a particularly devastating spring flood.

After Jeremias' death his widow Maria continued to administer his domain, striving to keep it together for her children although the rest of the family in the Netherlands — distressed by the wars — was ready to sell it. This family situation became very complex as the shares of Kiliaen's nine children were subdivided in the third generation. In the meantime, the Van Rensselaers sought from successive English governors a new patent confirming their political privileges and their possession of all the land they had engrossed, which stretched far beyond their original limits. By combining their influence in England and the Netherlands, they secured such a grant from the Duke of York in 1678. But Governor Nicholls and his successors, faced with the practical problems of ruling the colony, repeatedly made it clear that the family had better be satisfied with title to their land and forego their claims to political privileges, and succeeded in evading the implementation of the 1678 patent. Finally in 1685 Governor Dongan granted them title to their land, and in 1695 the Van Rensselaer heirs in the Netherlands and America agreed to end their many disputes by each retaining the assets in their own country.

The impact of English government on ordinary Dutch colonists was gradual. Nicholls immediately required all who owned land to secure new patents, both to insure the validity of titles and to

"Watervliet," home of Jeremias Van Rensselaer; drawing by Major Francis Pruyn.
Courtesy of the Albany Institute of History and Art

collect generous fees. But enforcement of this policy was slow, especially in outlying areas and where titles were already in dispute, and subsequent governors had to make repeated efforts to put it fully into effect. The British also enforced the Navigation Acts, insisting that all trade be with England, although a number of Dutchmen led by Stuyvesant (who had retired to his farm in New York) petitioned for continued trade with the Netherlands, on the ground, among others, that the Indians were demanding the familiar Dutch goods. Otherwise, the Dutch system of law courts and municipal government was more or less left intact, under the terms of the surrender, except for the promulgation of a fundamental legal code, the Duke's Laws, in 1665. After the return to English rule in 1674, various English practices were gradually introduced, of which the most important was the code approved in 1683 by the first elected assembly ever convened in New York, which divided the province into counties and established English courts and local administration.

Absorption into the British Empire by no means ended friction between New York and New England. Boundary disputes continued, intensified by the carelessness of King Charles in granting his brother lands which had already been settled from Massachusetts and Connecticut. There were also Indian troubles, as during King Philip's War when Philip and his warriors fled to the tributaries of the Connecticut within forty miles of Albany. Later, when Indians raided the Massachusetts frontier, New Englanders, knowing that the Dutch at Albany sold firearms to the Mohawks without asking too many questions, feared that they were conniving at such attacks. (It was later found out that the Indians came from Canada.) This accusation was often repeated during the years which followed, but there is no reason to believe it was well founded. Finally in 1688, after the Duke of York became King James II, he tried to resolve all these difficulties by uniting all the colonies north of the Delaware under one government called the "Dominion of New England," but the colonists never accepted it and broke it up as soon as they heard that James had been driven from his throne by the Glorious Revolution of 1688.

In the meantime, France had become a menace in both Europe and America. King Louis XIV, who in 1643 at the age of five had inherited a throne threatened by rebellion, came of age in 1661 and immediately embarked upon an ambitious policy of making himself first in France and France first in Europe. This soon involved him in a series of wars in the Low Countries which kept him busy the rest of his life and eventually brought France to the verge of collapse. In the first, the War of Devolution (1664-68), he attempted to round out his frontier by annexing part of Belgium, which inevitably created conflict with Dutch interests there. This conflict became open war in 1672, when French armies crossed the Rhine and threatened the Netherlands with extinction. The burghers of Amsterdam revolted, lynched Jan de Witt and his brother, and called upon young William III of Orange to lead them. Then, with their backs to the wall — or rather, the sea — the Dutch rallied, cut the dikes, and called in the waters to fight for them. Gradually they pushed the French back foot by muddy foot, until in 1678 Louis finally acknowledged he could not defeat them and made peace.

At the same time, Louis and his finance minister Colbert were trying to make the French mercantile empire greater than those of the Dutch and the English. In 1666 they ordered the governor or Canada to punish the Iroquois, who had been carrying their war against the Hurons into the very suburbs of Montreal. The French governor accordingly marched a little army on snowshoes from Montreal to the Mohawk Valley in the dead of winter, arriving nearly frozen at the five-year-old Dutch settlement of Schenectady — where the colonists thawed them out and gave the Mohawks an opportunity to escape. A similar force the next year succeeded in destroying the Indians' winter food supply, which compelled them to make peace. One of the terms was that they would admit French missionaries to their villages. During the next 15 years the Jesuit "black robes" made some converts, whom they encouraged to migrate to new villages near Montreal, to separate them from their unconverted kin. To a degree this attempt to conquer the Iroquois by dividing them succeeded; the "Praying Indians" of Caughnawaga remained loyal to France and became a terror to the other Iroquois. But after about 1680 the climate of Iroquois opinion shifted and one by one the missionaries returned to Canada.

French missionaries came to New York at the instance of their government and their Orders; French traders came on their own. *Coureurs de bois*, dissatisfied with their employers among the merchants of Montreal or attracted by the English trade goods that even then were cheaper and better than those supplied from France, found their way to Albany in unknown numbers. Now and then the local magistrates called them in for questioning, but as a rule they seem to have come and gone fairly freely, and some settled near Albany. Among others, the explorer Robert René de la Salle came to Albany in 1678 before he set out on his famous explorations of the Mississippi, and from such *voyageurs* the Albany merchants learned of the wealth of furs in the trans-Appalachian West.

Others were learning of those furs at the same time. When the Iroquois conquered the Susquehannocks in 1677, there was no colony nearer than Maryland and the struggling, fragmented Quaker settlement in West New Jersey, but five years later William Penn received his grant of Pennsylvania and embarked upon an intensive, carefully thought-out plan to attract settlers. He and they were of course interested in profiting by the fur trade, and within the decade of the 1680s the Dutch merchants of Albany found themselves facing not only the expansion of French traders like La Salle into the Great Lakes but efforts by Pennsylvania traders to reach the western furs through the Susquehanna Valley. Therefore, in 1686 the Albanians sent out an expedition to Michilimackinac which made direct contact with the "farr Indians" and returned with a profitable load of furs. But the next year the French were waiting for them; they ambushed this second expedition and imprisoned some Albany Dutchmen in Montreal. After that the Albanians tried a flanking move, sending interpreter Arnout Cornelisz Viele on a mission to the Ohio Valley, where he made friends with the Shawnees and returned in 1692 with much beaver. Then the outbreak of war intervened, and when the fighting was over the Albanians discovered other ways to tap the furs of the interior of the continent.

This delicate international balance was upset in 1689 by the Glorious Revolution in England. The English, always suspicious of James II's Catholicism and fed up with his clumsy attempts to imitate the high-handed rule of his cousin Louis XIV, finally lost patience when he tried to impose the Catholic religion upon England. They compelled him to abdicate and called to the throne his Protestant daughter Mary and her husband William III of Orange. One of William's conditions for accepting the crown was that England join the coalition he was forming to fight Louis XIV, and since Louis supported James by encouraging Catholic rebels in Ireland, the English were quite willing. After the inconclusive War of the League of Augsburg (1689-98), which consisted mostly of sieges of fortresses in the war-weary Spanish Netherlands, William organized the Grand Alliance for the War of the Spanish Succession (1701-14). He died soon after the war began, but his work was continued by the great English general Marlborough, who won a series of famous battles in and near the Low Countries, including Blenheim, Ramillies, Oudenarde, and Fontenoy, after which the road to Paris was open. But the allies decided it would be impolitic to destroy France altogether, and concluded the Peace of Utrecht in 1714, the year before the Grand Monarch died.

The ravages of Louis' armies, like those of Philip of Spain, confirmed the people of the Netherlands in their fear and hatred of Catholicism. The Dutch in New York, who remained in contact with events in the Netherlands through letters from relatives and visits to the homeland, thus had more occasion to be aware of the Catholic menace than most of the British colonists. The reality of that menace was further brought home to them by James's appointment, even before he became king, of a number of Catholic officials in New York, of whom the most important was Governor Dongan. When they heard of the expulsion of James from his throne, they lost no time in expelling his representatives from the colony. The leader they selected for this uprising was a merchant named Jacob Leisler, the son of a Calvinist minister from the Palatinate (which had been forcibly converted to Catholicism by French troops) who had begun his career in New Netherland in 1660 as a soldier under Stuyvesant's command.

Nevertheless, it is important to note that Leisler did not start the "rebellion" which came to bear his name. It seems to have erupted spontaneously, in the Dutch tradition, with a riot provoked by the tactlessness of Lieutenant Governor Nicholson, who in a burst of temper gave the impression that he was about to sell the colony out to the Catholics. Leisler, the captain of one of New York's militia companies, conspicuously avoided participating in this outbreak; his men came to his home and insisted that he lead them. He then served on the ad hoc "Committee of Safety" (which, following the example of Massachusetts, proclaimed the allegiance of the province to William and Mary), and only gradually emerged as the leader of an interim government. His conduct in that position, which has been regarded as enigmatic in the light of later American traditions of government, reflects faithfully the Dutch tradition of turning to military leadership in an emergency, personified in the Netherlands by Prince Maurice and William III, and in the colony by Leisler's first commander, Peter Stuyvesant. Leisler always insisted that this uprising was not a Dutch revolt against English rule — and there were both Dutch and English colonists on each side — but since at this period a large proportion of the colonists were Dutch, any popular movement was bound to have Dutch characteristics.

Leisler, who was about 50 years old, was, like many other New York merchants, a self-made man who had improved his fortune by marrying a rich widow, but he had quarreled with her relatives over her inheritance and they had no use for him. His principal supporters were the lesser merchants and artisans of New York City, particularly those fervent Calvinists who were now clinging to their faith as a symbol of ethnic identity. The greatest merchants, who had obtained commercial privileges and extensive land grants from James' government (and who included Leisler's wife's estranged relatives) opposed him bitterly under the leadership of Stuyvesant's nephew Nicholas Bayard, whom Leisler soon imprisoned. Also opposed were the principal merchants of Albany, who only three years before had secured from Governor Dongan a city charter granting them civic privileges and a monopoly of the fur trade. The humbler burghers of Albany, however, were much more sympathetic to Leisler. When he sent a body of troops to Albany, they welcomed them into their homes, but Mayor Peter Schuyler retired into the fort with the English garrison and called upon the Indians for help. His many years of friendship with the Mohawks were decisive; when Leisler's force prepared to storm the fort, the Indians threatened to intervene and the burghers insisted that the attack be called off.

The Albany leaders then tried to go it alone in preparing defenses against an extension to the colonies of the war with France. They asked Connecticut for help, and Connecticut sent 80 men, who were stationed in Albany, Schenectady, and other outlying settlements. But the residents of Schenectady, resentful of the Albany monopoly which excluded them from the fur trade, were careless about participating in any defense organized by the Albany leaders. Therefore, when on February 8, 1690, a party of French and Praying Indians reached the village (almost as frozen as the expedition of 1666) they found the gates wide open, no one on guard, and the way clear to warm their blood by a massacre. Perhaps a third of the inhabitants were killed, a third carried off prisoners to Canada, and a third escaped to Albany with the lurid tale. The Albanians succored them as best they could and wrote to Connecticut for more help, but Connecticut replied that they should seek aid closer to home this time. So the magistrates swallowed their pride and wrote to Leisler, who appointed a military committee to organize the town for defense, but recognized the necessity of leaving Mayor Schuyler in his position to administer Indian affairs.

Then Leisler turned his attention to retaliation for the massacre, and the steps he took clearly reflected the example of William III, who was then forging the Grand Alliance. He sent all the governors of the colonies from Virginia northward invitations to meet as soon as possible in New York to organize a grand intercolonial expedition against Canada. This made perfect sense in the Dutch tradition, in which independent cities and provinces called upon each other for offensive and defensive aid whenever they were attacked, but the English colonies were accustomed to act either on their own or under orders from the king. Some ignored the summons, some sent delegates but pledged no help, and Connecticut and Massachusetts, who were most directly threatened, offered some. Massachusetts, however, put her efforts into the maritime portion of the expedition, which turned out to be an independent excursion against Quebec under William Phipps (who thereby earned the title of Sir William), so New York and Connecticut were left to fend for themselves.

Leisler was clearly a soldier rather than a diplomat. As a soldier he understood the importance of supplies for an expedition that had to cross 200 miles of wilderness, and he strained the resources and credit of the province to assemble them. But in so doing he made himself unpopular with peace-loving lower Hudson Valley merchants who saw no reason for such an elaborate and expensive venture, and with the Albany leaders whose support was essential but who wanted to organize it their way. The Connecticut contingent would not march until their candidate was given command, and with one delay and another the company did not reach the head of Lake Champlain until too late in the season to make bark canoes. Then smallpox struck the army, and most of it went home in disgust. Only a small Albany Dutch contingent, determined that Schenectady should not go unavenged, dashed over the familiar fur route to Montreal and burned one of its outlying settlements, LaPrairie, in September 1690.

The contrast between the success of this sub-expedition and

the failure of Leisler's grander plan shows some differences between Dutch tradition suitable for the Netherlands and Dutch tradition Americanized by two generations in the wilderness. Leisler evidently thought much and clearly about strategy, and his thinking was not unworthy of the people who fought under William the Silent or the bold trader-raiders of the West India Company. He saw what the French menace threatened, and the war which ensued showed that the cost of his plan was not excessive in view of the damage it might have prevented. But he was neither diplomat to make others see what he saw nor demagogue to make them fear what he feared, and in any case the time at his disposal was too short. He was right; French power had to be eradicated for the safety of New York, but he overlooked a thousand logistical, tactical, and political problems which would have to be solved first. In the meantime, the Albanians' response in kind for Schenectady was more appropriate to American conditions, and perhaps, had Leisler's resources been laid out on a number of such small parties, the French might have been deterred from later attacks.

The failure of this expedition disillusioned many people with Leisler, though the ordinary citizens of New York City still admired him. In any case, the new English governor, Sir Henry Sloughter, delayed for two years by the war, was on the way. When he arrived, Leisler did not turn over the fort quite as quickly as Sloughter thought he should have, and when he did so he and his principal followers were promptly arrested for treason and sentenced to death. Nevertheless, the English hesitated to make a martyr of Leisler; the cry for his blood came from his fellow citizens, the most powerful and most assimilated merchants in the city. Their pressure finally prompted Sloughter to execute Leisler and his son-in-law Jacob Milborne before any reply could be received to appeals lodged in England. They met their end like Calvinist martyrs, making moving speeches in their own behalf and reportedly singing the 79th Psalm, chanted under similar circumstances by Huguenot martyrs in Europe; thus they testified that the tradition they embodied was that of the factional disputes of Netherlands cities.

In the meantime, the French and Indians continued the war, known in America as King William's War. The Praying Indians fought against their brethren with all the fervor of the convert, and the Iroquois fought back with the desperation of the trapped.

It is interesting that at this time — and at no other — the Mohawks were baptized into the Dutch Reformed Churches in Albany and Schenectady in considerable numbers. Some of this was certainly due to the missionary efforts of Domine Godefridus Dellius, a militant Calvinist, but quite possibly the Mohawks themselves were anxious to try the efficacy of Protestant "medicine" against that of the potent "black robes." Nevertheless, this war of kinsmen was as devastating as such wars are likely to be, and the Mohawks admitted that they had met their match. In 1701 they and the Praying Indians buried the hatchet, and beseeched their allies not to ask them to dig it up again at the behest of the Great White Fathers across the Atlantic. Therefore, after the War of the Spanish Succession broke out in the same year, some Albany traders who happened to be in Montreal on business were approached by French authorities who suggested that their respective colonies informally ignore the conflict. The Albany magistrates duly forwarded this proposal to Lieutenant Governor Nanfan (who took no action either way) and in the meantime proceeded to act upon it. The only hitch was that their power, derived entirely from the influence of their trade, did not reach far enough to extend this truce to New England. Yankees viewing the smoking ruins of Deerfield in 1704 quite understandably suspected the Albanians of purchasing their own safety at the expense of their neighbors.

In 1709, however, the English government announced plans for an intercolonial amphibious invasion of Canada. The principal colonial promoters of this scheme were British, although one of them, Samuel Vetch, had married a niece of Peter Schuyler. The land force was to leave from Albany, and was to include the Iroquois; but before it could assemble, the naval force was dispatched elsewhere. In the meantime, the Albanians heard that the French had built a trading post among the Onondagas in western New York, so once again they performed the only positive action of the campaign when Schuyler and a party of Mohawks destroyed it. Then Schuyler went to London to collect the debts owed him by the Crown for his expenses, taking along four Iroquois sachems — the "Indian Kings" — to meet Queen Anne. They made a sensation in London, their visit being reported in Richard Steele's periodical *The Tatler* and inspiring an essay in Joseph Addison's *Spectator* which enshrined them in a classic of English literature. More immediately, their presence aided Schuyler in collecting his debts and helped convince the government that the expedition against Canada should be rescheduled for 1711, when much to the disappointment of the Indians, it never went beyond the head of Lake Champlain.

By this time the war in Europe was almost over and negotiations well under way for the Peace of Utrecht, which ended fighting in the Low Countries until the Napoleonic Wars. The role of the New York Dutch on the front lines of the conflict of empires had also ended; when it was renewed, their part would be much different. But for three generations, they — especially the Albany Dutch — had played as pivotal a part in that conflict in New York as their compatriots did in Europe. Furthermore, their interpretation of that role was typically Dutch: to maintain commerce with both sides; to fight wherever possible by subsidizing and arming allies; but, when finally forced to defend themselves, to hang on with grim determination and make geography fight for them. The application of this tradition to American conditions prompted them to develop some different tactics. The military engagements of this war were not the patiently engineered sieges for which Prince Maurice was famous, or the battles in flooded fields to which both William the Silent and William III were driven, but the lightning descents of small bodies of trader-raiders whose tactics bear more resemblance to those of the Sea Beggars and the West India Company privateers than to the Dutch tradition of land warfare. Such modifications showed that the Dutch colonists, like the English and the French, were learning from their three generations of American experience — but they were still responding to that experience within the fundamental framework of their inherited Dutch tradition.

4

Patricians and Plebeians

THE extent to which many Dutch traditions took root in the Hudson Valley has been underestimated because it has been assumed that the history of the Dutch in America ended with the English conquest, when in fact it was just beginning. As a result of that conquest, those transient traders who came to New Netherland only to make their fortunes finally went back to the homeland, while the Dutch colonists who stayed really cared about making permanent homes in the colony and recreating the way of life that had been familiar in the Netherlands. Although this culture was in many ways diverse, it achieved in New York more homogeneity than was common in the Netherlands, as settlers from many parts of the Low Countries, as well as from France, Germany, and Scandinavia, developed a way of life whose common denominators were the Dutch dialect they spoke, worship in the Dutch Reformed Church, and similar patterns of behavior.

The colonists who settled in towns — particularly New York, Albany, Schenectady, Kingston, Brooklyn, and New Brunswick — recreated the way of life of Dutch burghers. Its distinctive characteristic was the patrician social system, through which the wealthiest merchant families controlled civic activity. The scarcity of land in the Netherlands forced most of these families to remain in the city for many generations, reinvesting their fortunes in commerce and using their leisure for civic service, scholarship, and patronage of the arts, instead of moving out to a country estate as did English merchants. The absence of a king closed off royal preferment as a road to social advancement, unlike the situation in France where wealthy merchants purchased titles of nobility and thenceforth refused to soil their hands with trade. The children of patrician Dutch families usually intermarried, creating a closely woven texture of kinship, in which civic officials considered it a duty to their families to put forward deserving relatives for offices of trust and profit. Children of families with newer wealth also married into the patriciate, so that an ambitious burgher would strive to make a fortune not so much that he might sit on the city council himself but so that his son or daughter might marry a patrician and his grandson might sit there.

The history of Dutch towns in America begins in 1652, with the grant of municipal privileges to New Amsterdam by the States-General and to Beverwyck by Stuyvesant. In each case these privileges were secured by the means traditional in the Netherlands since the early Middle Ages — appealing from the oppression of a local lord to the self-interest or public spirit of his overlord. In accordance with widespread Dutch custom, each town was granted a board of *schepens*, or magistrates, in Beverwyck numbering six, two of whom were replaced each year by cooptation. These magistrates sat as an undifferentiated town council and court of justice, making local ordinances (particularly regulations of trade) punishing infractions of these ordinances and offenses against the peace, and settling routine cases of debt and trespass. In 1657 Stuyvesant attempted to draw a distinction between "great burghers" who paid a generous fee for the privilege of being eligible to sit on this council and "small burghers" who paid a smaller fee for the privilege of doing business in the town, but it was apparently not consistently enforced.

The English conquerors soon changed the government of New York City to the English form of a mayor appointed by the governor and a common council elected by the citizens. Albany continued until 1686 with its Dutch board of magistrates, chosen by cooptation, conducting proceedings and keeping their records in the Dutch language, and following Dutch court procedure as it was understood by ordinary citizens without legal training. In the late 1670s a few English usages began to creep in; juries were empanelled in important criminal and civil causes, and fines came to be stated in pounds sterling instead of guilders, beaver pelts, or *seawant* (wampum), although they were undoubtedly still paid in these commodities. In 1683, when the Assembly established English local administration, the Albany magistrates were constituted justices of the peace.

Then in 1686 Governor Dongan granted Albany a city charter, under circumstances entirely in the Dutch tradition. The Van Rensselaers, who had been trying ever since the conquest to assert their claim to the town, had been granted it in their all-inclusive royal patent of 1678. But Governor Andros evaded implementing this patent, and Governor Dongan flatly refused:

> What reason sir Edmund Andros has given for not putting these orders into execution I know not. The Rensselaers came and brought me the same orders which I thought not convenient to execute, judging it not for his Majesty's interest that the second town in the province and which brings his Majesty so great a revenue should be in the hands of any particular men.[1]

One of his motives was certainly the 700 pounds sterling presented to him by a group of the principal fur traders, led by Peter Schuyler, in return for a charter granting Albany an English form of government by an appointed mayor and elected common council like that of New York. The city limits, which had, in the Dutch tradition, enclosed only the land within and very near the town wall, were extended, in accordance with an English practice, to include 16 miles of the surrounding countryside — which the Dutch burghers wanted because it embraced the path to their trading competitor Schenectady and, until Schenectady protested and the boundaries were changed, Schenectady itself. Some specifically Dutch elements in the charter included the survival of the distinction between great and small burghers, the differing fees to be paid for the freedoms suitable for merchants and for artisans, and a monopoly of the fur trade on the entire New York frontier.

The first mayor of Albany, appointed by the charter, was Peter Schuyler. He was then a young man of thirty, fortunate in being the eldest son of Philip P. Schuyler, a gunstock maker and leader in Indian and civic affairs, whose wife was a daughter of Brant Van Slichtenhorst. From the beginning of his career as a trader, Peter Schuyler had a talent for winning the trust and respect of the Indians which made him indispensable in dealing with them; their pronunciation of his name, "Quidor," came to be their honorific title for the Mayor of Albany, just as "Corlaer," the name of another beloved and respected Dutchman, was their title for the Governor of New York. Schuyler was closely connected by marriage with other officials named in the charter, particularly City Clerk Robert Livingston, who had married Schuyler's sister. Livingston, who was about Schuyler's age, had grown up in the Netherlands, where his father, a Scots minister, had been exiled; he was therefore bilingual — a priceless asset in postconquest Albany. His fortune and his later political career were founded upon his pivotal position as clerk of all the governing bodies in Albany, including the Commissioners of Indian Affairs. He and Schuyler often worked together for mutual advantage, but they detested each other — largely, it may be suspected, because Schuyler's success was founded upon his reputation for fair dealing and Livingston was notoriously more shrewd than scrupulous.

That the Albany Charter reflected the ambitions of the leading fur traders more than the will of the people was demonstrated almost at once by the outbreak of Leisler's Rebellion. Mayor Schuyler and his common council refused to have anything to do with Leisler, although they proclaimed William and Mary as king and queen on their own authority as soon as they were certain of the fact of their accession to the English throne. When Leisler's troops, led by the demagogue Jacob Milborne, came to Albany, they found a considerable proportion of the burghers — perhaps even a majority — in sympathy with their contention that the "Popish plots" of the late administration included the Albany Charter. Leaders among these dissidents were fur traders who were not members of Schuyler's clique, a number of them close relatives of leading Leislerians in New York. Several were substantially older than Schuyler and Livingston, which suggests that the charter may have been a project of a younger generation willing to make more adjustments to English rule than some of their elders. Other Albany Leislerians included artisans, whose interests were substantially ignored by the charter, and members of a small but vocal Lutheran congregation who had been at odds with their Calvinist neighbors for at least a decade. There is some evidence that some of the leaders of the latter group, and perhaps some of the other Leislerians, were fiercely independent Frisians, whose way of life conflicted in some respects with the patrician tradition. Their hopes were frustrated by Leisler's failure, however, after which the Schuyler clique secured a stronger position than ever.

During Leisler's Rebellion and for a generation thereafter, until its monopoly of the fur trade was struck down by the courts in 1726, Albany behaved in many respects like a semi-independent

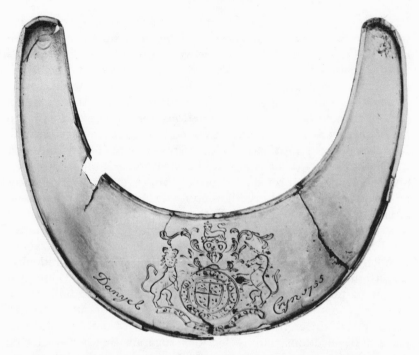

Silver gorget for Indian gift, by Barent Ten Eyck of Albany, 1755. *Courtesy of the Museum of the American Indian, Heye Foundation, New York City*

Dutch city-state. It was administered by magistrates who still spoke Dutch more readily than English, though Robert Livingston kept their records in the latter language. English procedures were finally introduced in the Mayor's Court about 1705 by two English residents who gradually began to act as attorneys for their neighbors. The magistrates were also provincial Commissioners for Indian Affairs, a position inevitable because of their unique knowledge of the Indians and familiarity with their languages. (Provincial governors long complained that the Albanians, who contributed the interpreters, took the conduct of Indian affairs completely out of their hands.) Albany merchants notoriously ignored British restrictions forbidding trade with Canada, particularly after the Peace of Utrecht when they quickly discovered that it was more profitable and less trouble to sell trade goods to the French and let the *coureurs de bois* distribute them to the Indians than it was to compete directly by westward expeditions.

King William's War (1689-98) brought disaster to the fur trade, for while the Indians were on the warpath they of course had little time to hunt for peltries. A quarter of Albany County's 2,000 inhabitants fled from the hostilities. Those who were left intermarried and formed the nucleus of a group of families that dominated Albany until the Revolution. When the complex pattern formed by these family relationships is compared with the list of members of the common council, it reveals a very definite patrician social stratification closely resembling that of cities in the Netherlands. At the top were the fur-trading families, of which Schuyler's clique formed one group whose children frequently intermarried, and the Leislerians another. Marriages between these groups were at first unusual — the most conspicuous exception was the 1695 wedding of Johannes Schuyler, Peter's younger brother and the hero of the raid on LaPrairie, and Elizabeth Wendell, the widow of Leisler's choice for mayor — but gradually, as bitterness subsided, they took place more often. These two groups of families dominated the common council so long as the fur-trading monopoly lasted, particularly in the decade 1710-20, when in two different years they held 11 out of the 12 seats. This pattern of elections and reelections suggests that although the Albany Dutch were learning to vote for representatives to govern them, their candidates were still nominated by what amounted to a form of cooptation.

This pattern was finally broken by the direct intervention of Governor William Cosby, who clashed with the Albany magistrates in 1732 over a land grant in the Mohawk Valley which Cosby had secured from the Indians by tactics of doubtful legality. The outraged Albanians allied with the provincial faction of Lewis Morris, which was opposing Cosby in the Assembly and arousing public opinion with the newspaper of John Peter Zenger, whose famous trial for libel was the Morris group's most notable victory. Cosby fought back by appointing Albany's first English mayor, Edward Holland, a son of a former commandant of the British garrison, which was the town's principal English population. Holland manipulated the next election to secure a common council dominated for the first time by burghers who were not fur traders. Cosby then wooed this group with generous land grants, and by the time the fur traders recaptured the common council after Cosby's death, this new group of burghers had organized into a local faction led by merchants who had made their fortunes in general commerce.

This reflected an important development in the economy of the province. As New Netherland grew, the captains of the river sloops which provided nearly all the colony's transportation began to find it worth their while now and then to take a cargo of fish or flour to the West Indies to trade for sugar and molasses. When they got there they found that, in this period of constant war among the maritime powers, the multinational West Indies were a center of privateering and piracy as well as legitimate trade. Already accustomed to smuggling goods from the Netherlands and to the patriotic piracy of the West India Company, they took full advantage of these opportunities. Throughout the 1690s, when the ruin of the fur trade made the province desperate for both goods and hard money, several of the leading families of New York swelled their fortunes by dealing in pirate loot, and in 1698 Frederick Philipse sent a ship to Africa for slaves and, incidentally, to exchange supplies for pieces of eight at the world pirate capital of Madagascar. "The pirates paid premium prices for lime juice, sugar, salt, peas, shirting, pants material, shoes, hats, tobacco, and tobacco pipes."[2] But none of the most famous American pirates were Dutch, unless tradition is correct in ascribing Dutch ancestry to William Teach (Teachout?), better known as "Blackbeard." Evidently a century of experience had taught Hudson Valley Dutch skippers how to wring the utmost profit from dubious expeditions without flagrantly overstepping the limits of the law. The spectacular fate of Captain Kidd, who turned pirate himself after persuading several prominent Englishmen and New Yorkers (including Governor Bellomont and Robert Livingston) to finance him on a voyage to pursue pirates, ended the direct involvement of New Yorkers with these questionable ventures. Piracy itself soon thereafter declined, as the Peace of Utrecht brought an end for the time to the privateering which had spawned it and aroused public opinion demanded its suppression.

In the meantime, Hudson Valley farmers had begun to grow a surplus of wheat, which was ground into flour and shipped to the West Indies, where sugar planters bought it to feed their slaves. New York City was granted a monopoly of this trade in 1675, but Long Island at once challenged it. The growing number of farm families needed tools, textiles, and other goods not produced in the colonies. The merchants of New York, therefore, established a triangular trade between the West Indies on the one hand and England on the other, developing their own city into a center of sugar refining in imitation of Amsterdam, the world center of this industry in the seventeenth century. Albany merchants profited by a thriving retail trade with nearby farmers, and wholesale dealings with storekeepers in more remote new settlements. Some of them bought their goods in New York but others entered direct correspondence with London factors, and a few, like the Vanderheydens, sent scions of the family to England as their agents. An interesting imaginative interpretation of this is the characters of Jacob Van den Bosch, an Albany merchant in England, and his granddaughter Lydia, in William Makepeace Thackeray's novel *The Virginians.* Allowing for comic exaggeration, the shrewd old merchant and the beautiful heiress, ambitious to exchange her fortune for a title but equally open about her experience behind the counter of the family store, are a very fair depiction of eighteenth-century Dutch colonists; Thackeray had lectured in Albany before this novel was published.

Patrician rule of towns of course implied the existence of a much larger number of plebeians who took little part in civic affairs. In Hudson Valley towns many of these plebeians were not Dutch, partly because the Dutch were there first and so established themselves in positions of leadership, but partly also because most Dutch colonists came to the Hudson Valley to trade rather than to practice crafts. Some Dutch artisans, such as the gold and silversmiths whose traffic in the precious metals involved them in banking, were equal in status to merchants; for example silversmith Jacob C. Ten Eyck became in 1747 the first Dutch mayor of Albany from other than a fur-trading family. Comparable were masters of trades who made fortunes supplying their neighbors with basic commodities, such as brewer Leendert Gansevoort, elected alderman during the upheaval engineered by Edward Holland. Little is known about humbler craftsmen — coopers, blacksmiths, shoemakers, wheelwrights, and the like; as a rule they were content with minor offices such as that of constable. Many of these craftsmen were of other ethnic origins — Walloon and French Huguenot, German and English — for most of the Dutch preferred earning money by commerce to buy the things they needed rather than making them.

Another very important group of Hudson Valley artisans were black slaves, and a few free blacks. The Dutch had been involved in the slave trade since the beginning of the seventeenth century, importing the first slaves to Virginia in 1619 and to New Amsterdam before 1628. As a rule the Hudson Valley Dutch bought their slaves in the West Indies rather than purchasing them directly from Africa, since they needed labor not for plantation gangs but for a variety of purposes which required some familiarity with the language, the culture, and the expectations of masters. The disproportionate emphasis on trade by the colonists of New Netherland produced a chronic shortage of labor which was met by the importation of slaves, so that by 1664 they comprised one tenth of the population of New Netherland, more than in any other northern colony.

Since the Dutch regarded their slaves first and foremost as servants, they seem to have been less distressed by the difference of race than the English. They worked alongside their slaves, training them to do whatever kind of work was needed, and took it for granted that they would eat with the family and share in its life and holidays in the same manner as white servants. They often freed the slaves after a number of years of service, or granted them a condition called "half-freedom" in which they owed certain annual dues and services on the public works — particularly fortifications — and in which their children remained slaves. In New Netherland, freedmen engaged in a variety of trades, employed white servants, and even intermarried with whites. Under English rule, distinctions based on race were more sharply drawn, but Dutch masters still treated their slaves well, taught them a variety of skills, and permitted them to hire themselves out in their spare time and use the money earned to buy their freedom. The considerable proportion of urban slaves, in particular, enjoyed a degree of liberty and responsibility not generally associated with American slavery. On the other hand, in the close contact of the urban environment, slaves who committed crimes which endangered the community, such as arson, were severely and sometimes brutally punished, as in a suspected attempt at revolt in New York City in 1712 for which several slaves were burned at the stake.

As in Dutch towns, Hudson Valley burghers contributed to a wide variety of civic improvements. The first thing the little settlements needed was a wall for defense — a palisade was sufficient for protection against Indians — and a burgher guard to defend it. New Amsterdam's palisade was built in 1653, at the time of the first Anglo-Dutch War, for protection against possible invasion from New England, along the line still marked by Wall Street. Albany waited another twenty years, until King Philip's Indian warriors took refuge nearby in 1676, when the governor replaced Fort Orange with a new fort on the hill near the site of the present State Capitol, and the burghers surrounded their village on the river flats with a palisade. For a generation, whenever attack threatened the magistrates assigned each burgher a number of rods of palisade to repair in proportion to his wealth; in 1680, for example, this assessment ranged from one to five rods, each rod containing a dozen posts 12 inches square and 13 feet long. Next would come some sort of city hall. In New Amsterdam, the City Tavern — built a decade before the burghers were granted civic privileges — was later used for the meetings of the city council, and its cellar for a jail, until gradually it was entirely taken over for civic purposes. Albany built a new three-story Stadt Huys (city hall) in 1742, which was also used for Indian conferences and in 1754 for the intercolonial convention which brought forth the Albany Plan of Union. Commercial improvements such as wharves and ferries were provided, as in the Netherlands, by private enterprise, encouraged by a grant of fees or tolls. New York had such facilities early, but at Albany vessels had to be unloaded by small boats repeatedly because the ice and floods carried away all wharves until the city built three substantial wharves in 1767.

The appearance of these towns was also similar to that of cities in the Netherlands, for the burghers built homes like Dutch city houses. They were one or two stories high, with steep roofs containing one or more lofts. The gable end, which was turned to the street, was built of brick, usually laid in the complex pattern known as "Dutch bond"; although there are many legends concerning bricks brought from Holland as ballast in ships, there were brickyards in the Hudson Valley very early, where bricks were made in traditional Dutch sizes and shapes. Some of the gables showed the familiar "steps," but in at least as many others the steps were filled in by bricks laid at an angle, known as "mouse toothing," to produce a straight parapet gable, which was then topped by an iron or brass weathercock. The roof in the earliest days was of thatch, but very soon the danger of fire prompted the burghers to import tiles from the Netherlands, since the clay in the Hudson Valley did not prove suitable for making them. The

Bronck house museum, Coxsackie, New York, built by Jan Bronck (1633) and Leendert Bronck (1738). *Courtesy of the Green County Historical Society, Coxsackie, New York*

main door of the house, usually a horizontally divided "Dutch door," was in the gable end, flanked by a pair of benches, or "stoep," on which the burghers sat to take the air and greet their friends on summer evenings. But the other three walls were of wood, as was the bearing portion of the gable wall; the bricks were merely a veneer secured to the wooden wall underneath with decorative iron "anchors."

The front room was the shop; the family lived in the back room. The cupboard beds provided a measure of privacy and protection from night air for adults, while children slept on trundle beds or on mattresses spread on top of large chests. In the daytime all the bedding could be put away in the cupboards or chests, and a large trestle table with benches, not unlike a picnic table, was set

Hardenbergh bedroom. *Courtesy of the Henry Francis du Pont Winterthur Museum, Winterthur, Delaware*

in the middle of the room. The fireplace was built flat against the wall, with a Dutch tile or cast iron fireback but no chimney breasts and a free-hanging mantel from which hung a cloth valance that encouraged the smoke to go up the chimney. The principal piece of furniture, the large cupboard, or *kas*, traditionally made with a heavy cornice and ball feet, usually contained drawers or shelves for linen in its lower part and closed cupboards or open shelves for displaying pewter or silverware on the top. As the family grew in size and wealth, the second floor might be used for chambers, but many large families continued to live in very small houses. As in the Netherlands, where houses built on piles had no cellars, the loft was used for the storage of wares, and was equipped with a door and an iron crane for hoisting the goods. The servants, or some of the children, also sometimes slept there. An English traveler from Maryland described these homes in the mid-eighteenth century:

> The Dutch here keep their houses very neat and clean, both without and within. Their chamber floors are generally laid with rough plank, which in time, by constant rubbing and scrubbing, become as smooth as if it had been planed. Their chambers and rooms are large and handsome. They have their beds generally in alcoves, so that you may go through all the rooms of a great house and see never a bed. They affect pictures much, with which they adorn their rooms. They set out their cabinets and buffets much with China, their kitchens are likewise very clean, and there they hang earthen or delft plates and dishes all round the walls, in manner of pictures, having a hole drilled through the edge of the plate or dish, and a loop of ribbon put into it to hang it by; but not withstanding all this nicety and cleanliness in their houses they are in their persons slovenly and dirty. They live here very frugally and plain, for the chief merit among them seems to be riches, which they spare no pains or trouble to acquire, but are a civil and hospitable people in their way, but at best rustic and unpolished.[3]

As the townsmen grew wealthier, they invested in fine furniture made by local or metropolitan craftsmen, samples of which may be seen in many Hudson Valley museums. Some pieces perpetuated Dutch styles, as did numerous *kasten* and some chairs in the Henry F. du Pont Winterthur Museum in Delaware. Others reflected the international style of the late seventeenth century, commonly known as "William and Mary," which derived many of its motifs from the work of the fine cabinetmakers of the Netherlands, and was exported and imitated all over northern Europe. Eighteenth-century burghers purchased fashionable Queen Anne and Chippendale pieces, like those to be seen at Van Cortlandt Manor, Tarrytown, New York, and in the Verplanck Room at the Metropolitan Museum of Art. Of their taste, a visitor to Albany during the French and Indian War observed: "Valuable furniture (though perhaps not very well chosen or assorted) was the favorite luxury of these people, and in all the houses I remember, . . . the mirrors, the paintings, the china, but, above all, the state-bed, were considered as the family Teraphim, secretly worshipped, and only exhibited on very rare occasions."[4]

Both these travelers noticed that the Hudson Valley Dutch shared the love of pictures that was widespread among ordinary Netherlanders as well as wealthy patrons during the Golden Age of Dutch painting. Merchants of New Amsterdam imported pictures, though no works of any of the well-known Old Masters have been, traced to the Hudson Valley, and inventories of seventeenth-century estates often mention more pictures than books, although they rarely describe either. There were at least two families of Dutch painters in colonial New York, Pieter Vanderlyn of Kingston and his descendants and the Duyckinck dynasty of New York City. Neither could make an adequate living solely by painting pictures, however. Other artists who have not been identified were itinerant "limners" who traveled from one community to another, painting portraits and sometimes illustrations of scenes from the Bible. These limners, who have been called "patroon painters" — mistakenly, since their sitters were rarely from the families of manor lords, but rather Albany burghers and some substantial farmers from the nearby countryside — flourished between about 1710 and 1740 and represent the very first "school" of American painting.

The first of these portraits, and the one that seems to have set the fashion for the rest, was that of Peter Schuyler, which still hangs in the office of the Mayor of Albany. It was long believed that Schuyler had this portrait painted on his trip to England; this is now known to be erroneous, but since the Indian Kings were portrayed by English court artists it is quite possible that Schuyler brought the idea home from his travels. Its pose and background were suggested by English mezzotints — engravings of portraits of national heroes and reigning beauties that were widely sold in the colonies — and scholars believe that the artist may have been an Englishman, possibly one of the soldiers in Albany's fort who practiced trades to supplement their scanty pay. This artist has been identified on the basis of his style as the painter of some 60-odd portraits probably executed between about 1715 and 1725, many of which he "signed" with the legend "Aetatis Suae," a number of years, and the date, indicating the age of the subject. His sitters included many of the proudest and wealthiest of Albany's patricians, whom he depicted standing in formal gardens imitated from mezzotints, and wearing rich costumes which they may have owned, or which may have been copied from the same source.

Another limner with a very different style is known as the "Gansevoort limner" from two of his subjects, Leendert and Catarina Gansevoort, a substantial Albany brewer and his wife.

Leendert and Catarina Gansevoort, by an unknown limner, ca. 1730. *Courtesy of Stephen C. Clark, Cooperstown, New York*

These portraits are characterized by still beauty of composition, honesty which depicted their subjects in their own sober, simple Sunday best clothes, and imaginative ingenuity which showed behind Leendert a pond full of geese and behind Catarina a fort at a river ford, the two together forming a clever rebus on the family's name, "Ganse-voort" (goose-ford). Catarina's features, like those of a number of other Albany burghers' wives, are more shrewd than beautiful, bearing out the observation of an English traveler that in Albany "their women in general, both old and young, are the hardest favoured ever I beheld."[5] Besides a number of portraits attributed to the Gansevoort limner, there are also others, including likenesses of some rural families, whose limners were of widely varying ability, some being quite crude in style compared to those who have been discussed.

The other art patronized by Hudson Valley burghers was that of the silversmith. A number of families of Dutch silversmiths have been identified, including the Boelens of New York and the Ten Eycks and Lansings of Albany; others were French Huguenots, like the Le Roux of New York — and Paul Revere of Boston. It is difficult to identify Dutch characteristics in silverware, since here as in furniture Dutch decorative features developed into the international "William and Mary" style at the end of the seventeenth century. Nevertheless, it is known that some objects, such as the beaker, are characteristically Dutch, while others, such as the tankard, are of English origin. Pieces made by Dutch silversmiths often have more splendid and substantial ornament than those made by English or French craftsmen. These silver pieces were made from the family's savings in hard money, and as they were fairly bulky and engraved with the owner's name or monogram, they may have been less attractive to thieves. They were also suitable for display, whether on the top shelves of the *kas* or in use of special occasions.

The most important events were often commemorated by gifts of silverware, frequently spoons, marked with the name of the person honored, the date, and the occasion. Two such spoons inform us that they were given to Leendert Gansevoort in 1757 as New Year's gifts — New Year's rather than Christmas being the principal Dutch holiday for exchanging gifts and ceremonial calls among adults. (Good children found goodies, and bad ones, switches, in their wooden shoes on the feast of Saint Nicholas, December 6.) But even more important occasions for the giving of spoons were christenings, weddings, and funerals. The "apostle spoon" or "monkey spoon" originated in a medieval tradition that a child's godparents should give him as christening gifts spoons with the figure of the saint for whom the child was named modeled at the end of the handle; after the Reformation, this figure was interpreted to be one of the twelve apostles. For wedding and funerals, the apostle was replaced in the Hudson Valley by the figure of a monkey, often drinking from a goblet, symbolizing the festivities customary on such occasions. If the spoon commemorated a wedding, there was a heart on the handle immediately under the monkey, and a picture of a bridal couple engraved in the bowl. If it commemorated a funeral, the bowl showed the single figure of the "inviter" bidding the guests to the obsequies. The name of the couple, or the deceased, and the date were inscribed on the handle.

Funerals could be the most lavish social events in a Dutch community. When a person died he was customarily laid out on the bed in the best room in the house — which, if the family were wealthy enough to spare the space, was never used for any other purpose and was therefore known as the *dood-kamer*. The "inviter"

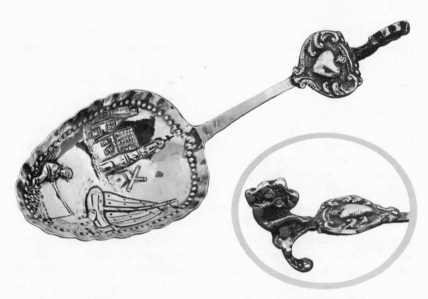

Monkey spoon, perhaps a memento of a wedding. Inset detail, monkey drinking from a goblet.

— often the sexton of the church — bore formal invitations to relatives and friends, who then gathered to follow the body to the grave, which might be in the church for leading citizens, in the churchyard for other burghers, or in a family plot on the farm for boers. It was customary to present the pallbearers, and sometimes other relatives and close friends, with mementoes including scarves, gloves, and rings, as well as monkey spoons. As a rule women, even close relatives, did not follow the dead to the grave. Nor did they participate in the feast which followed, which was usually characterized by excessive drinking — Volkert P. Douw of Albany, for example, insured that his funeral would be memorable by specifying for it in his will a barrel of prime rum which he had aged for many years for the occasion. Some funerals, particularly in the late seventeenth century, were very ostentatious. That given Jacob Leisler and Jacob Milborne by their fellow citizens when they were reburied in the Dutch Church (after the English government decided in 1698 that their executions had been illegal) was particularly so as Leisler's supporters used it as an occasion to celebrate their political triumph. But some did not wish this sort of funeral, and during the eighteenth century an increasing number requested in their wills that they be buried very simply.

Although they did not customarily attend funerals, women had considerably more independence in the Dutch tradition than the English. English tourists in the Netherlands noted with some surprise that girls as well as boys attended the schools which taught reading, writing, and business arithmetic, and the daughters of even the wealthiest Dutch patricians took their turns behind the counter of the family store. Merchants' wives were as familiar with their business as they, and often managed affairs at home when their husbands were away on long business trips. A widow commonly carried on the business until their sons were old enough to take it over. Women in New Netherland were equally active in commerce. Jeremias Van Rensselaer wrote, soon after his marriage to Maria Van Cortland, the 18-year-old daughter of a brewer, "I have taken up brewing, and this for the sake of my wife, as in her father's house she always had the management thereof, to wit, the disposal of the beer and helping to find customers for it."[6] The widows of New York were notable for their acumen in carrying on their husbands' businesses, and many of them, like those who married Frederick Philipse and Jacob Leisler, made the fortunes of their second husbands.

But Dutch women were even more famous as conscientious housewives — a quality which an eighteenth-century Albany Dutchman advised a friend to emphasize in choosing a wife:

> Its not the outward beauty nor Gold, that adorns a woman, but when thou findest Sensibility, Gravity, Discretion, and one that hath innocents in her mind and modesty in her looks her hand seeketh employment, herself delighteth not in gadding abroad Decency in her words and before her Steps Prudence and Virtue attended her right hand, such a one is it that winneth the heart of man to sincere love.[7]

Perhaps their best known characteristic, in both the Old World and the New, was their scrupulous cleanliness, which prompted them to scrub their floors and furniture every Saturday and often several times between. This custom is intelligible in view of the damp climate of the Netherlands, where it was hardly possible to enter a house without tracking in mud, and also in view of the primitive sanitation of preindustrial cities. The Dutch were the first people of northern Europe to live primarily in an urban environment, and in the seventeenth century they were also leaders in the field of medicine; it seems likely that they had perceived in a practical way something of the relationship between cleanliness and health, in which they were ahead of most peoples, including the English.

Dutch women were also famous for their cookery; as a mid-eighteenth century Swedish traveler observed:

> Their food and its preparation is very different from that of the English. Their breakfast is tea, commonly without milk. About thirty or forty years ago, tea was unknown to them, and they breakfasted either upon bread and butter or bread and milk. They never put sugar into the cup, but take a small bit of it into their mouths while they drink. Along with the tea they eat bread and butter, with slices of dried beef. The host himself generally says grace aloud. Coffee is not usual here. They breakfast generally about seven. Their dinner is buttermilk and bread, to which they add sugar on special occasions, when it is a delicious dish for them, or fresh milk and bread, with boiled or roasted meat. They sometimes make use of buttermilk instead of fresh milk, in which to boil a thin kind of porridge that tastes very sour but not disagreeable in hot weather. With each dinner they have a large salad, prepared with an abundance of vinegar, and very little of oil. They frequently drink buttermilk and eat bread and salad, one mouthful after another. Their supper consists generally of bread and butter, and milk with small pieces of bread in it. The butter is very salt. Sometimes too they have chocolate. They occasionally have cheese at breakfast and at dinner; it is not in slices, but scraped or rasped, so as to resemble coarse flour, which they pretend adds to the good taste of cheese. They commonly drink very weak beer, or pure water.[8]

This diet emphasizing dairy products and vegetables exhausted the patience of this writer, who preferred the beef and beer of the English colonists and thought that the thrifty Dutch housewives did not give him enough to eat.

Perhaps because a traveling naturalist was unlikely to attend many ladies' tea parties, he missed the many varieties of pastry and confectionery enjoyed by a Scottish girl who visited Albany during the French and Indian War (1756-63):

> Tea here was a perfect regale, being served up with various sorts of cakes unknown to us, cold pastry, and great quantities of sweetmeats and preserved fruits of various kinds, and plates of hickory and other nuts

ready cracked. In all manner of confectionery and pastry these people excelled; and having fruit in great plenty, which cost them nothing, and getting sugar home at an easy rate, in return for their exports to the West Indies, the quantity of these articles used in families otherwise plain and frugal, was astonishing.[9]

The cookies served at such events and many others contributed a Dutch word to the American language as well as a toothsome delicacy to the American diet. There were special recipes for special occasions — huge molded figures of Saint Nicholas that were far too big to put in a child's wooden shoe, New Year's cakes, and wafers baked in special irons for Communion services and commemorations. Some *doedkoeks* ("dead cakes") made for funerals, bearing the name of the deceased and the date, were meant to be preserved for years as mementoes, in the manner of wedding cake in more recent times.

Dutch burghers were much more likely than most of their cousins in the country to be forced into contact with English culture. In New York City, where the English Governor set the social pace, the Dutch families had to learn the English language very early for business and political reasons. By the middle of the eighteenth century socially ambitious young people of Dutch extraction did not like to be reminded of that heritage. In Albany, where comparatively few Englishmen came until the French and Indian War, the patricians — particularly those who served on the Common Council — were bilingual throughout the eighteenth century. They continued to speak Dutch in their homes, however, as a traveler observed in 1749: "the inhabitants of Albany and its environs are almost all Dutchmen. They speak Dutch, have Dutch preachers, and the divine service is performed in that language. Their manners are likewise quite Dutch; their dress is however like that of the English [colonists]."[10] In smaller towns — Schenectady, Kingston, Poughkeepsie, New Brunswick, N.J. — there was still less reason to learn English, and surviving records indicate that the burghers of Schenectady, for example, were still insecure in that language at the time of the Revolution. This stubborn insistence upon maintaining their own medium of communication often isolated the Dutch from their neighbors of other ethnic groups, reinforcing the Dutch tendency toward local loyalty which sometimes made them exclusive even with respect to each other. The traveler just quoted noticed this in New Brunswick, where the burghers who had come from Albany lived together on a certain street and avoided contact with their Jersey Dutch neighbors.

Hudson Valley burghers therefore retained throughout the colonial period important features of the urban tradition of the Netherlands. Although their institutions of civic government were soon Anglicized by the conquerors, they continued to carry out civic functions in the context of Dutch tradition. The social and economic organization of Hudson Valley towns — of which Albany was the largest outside of the British capital at New York, the most fully developed, and the best recorded — make sense only in the context of the Dutch patrician system. Some wealthy and ambitious patricians, especially in New York, left their Dutch ethnic identity behind and adapted to English culture, but many others, particularly plebeians, stubbornly retained their language as long as possible — and Dutch customs, patterns of behavior, and standards of values still longer. Their customs and way of life were reflected in the Dutch architecture of their houses, most of which have not survived to the present day and are known only from nineteenth-century pictures, and in the style of their furniture and silverware, some of which has been preserved in museums. The interest in owning pictures among people of very ordinary origins, rather than the style of paintings they collected, continued another important Dutch tradition. The Dutch also continued to enjoy many customary festivals, such as New Year's and weddings and funerals, by gatherings of family and friends and consumption of substantial amounts of food and drink. Women were valued as helpmates in commerce and in domestic affairs, and took particular pride in their conscientious housekeeping. These traditions continued in urban Dutch families until well after the American Revolution, and some of them are still maintained by their descendants today.

5

Golden Fields

DUTCH farmers in the seventeenth century were the best in Europe. The nature of their agriculture was determined partly by the geography of the Low Countries, with their flat, fertile delta soils, and partly by the commerce of Netherlands cities, which supported a far larger population than the nearby farms could feed. The Baltic trade brought in great quantities of grain at such low prices that it was not profitable for Dutch farmers to attempt to compete. Instead, they used their fields, especially the muck lands left behind after polders were drained, for the crops for which they were best suited — vegetables and fruits, for which prosperous city dwellers were willing to pay generously enough to make the extra labor worthwhile. Meat and dairy products were likewise in demand, so the farmers fed cows and fattened beef cattle on the clover which by the sixteenth century they had learned was a valuable crop for restoring the fertility of their soil. The livestock also provided manure which was used to fertilize the vegetable fields, as were organic wastes and refuse from the cities.

The Dutch themselves did not publicize their innovations, being more interested in the practice of farming than in writing books about husbandry. Dutch methods became known in other countries, such as England, when transplanted by Flemish refugees, observed by travelers, or eventually described in books by foreign authors. This was particularly the case after seventeenth-century Dutch engineers directed projects for draining marshes in England, France, and many parts of eastern Europe, and interest was aroused in those countries concerning the best methods of working these new lands. In England, historians consider the principal impact of Dutch agriculture to have been the development of market gardening and orchard fruits, experimentation with a variety of crops — clover, turnips, carrots — which restored the fertility of the soil and provided nutritious winter fodder for livestock, and the introduction of tools designed to meet the needs of the light soils of former marshland, particularly the "Dutch plow"; in sum, the application of the techniques of gardening to arable farming. It was this tradition which Dutch farmers transplanted to the Hudson Valley, although American historians of agriculture have for the most part been too unfamiliar with it to understand its influence upon the often observed fact that the golden fields of Hudson Valley Dutch farmers brought them fuller garners and a more abundant way of life than did those of their neighbors.

The fundamental difference between agriculture in the Netherlands and that of the Hudson Valley was that the latter concentrated on the growing of grain, first for subsistence and then for market. The first thing the Walloon colonists at Fort Orange did was to "put the spade in the ground" and prepare it for sowing grain. Spading — as for a garden — was necessary because they had as yet no horses to pull plows and probably no plow, but it was also a normal and most efficient means of preparing fields in the lowlands of Flanders. The observation that the crop was "almost as high as a man" is startling to modern eyes — even though people were shorter in the seventeenth century than they are today, as visitors to Plimoth Plantation learn by encountering low doorways, so that the height of a man could have been nearer five feet than six. Nevertheless, a later seventeenth-century observer, Adriaen van der Donck, remarked that oats and barley, in particular, often attained a height of six feet in the virgin soil. Such thriving crops spared New Netherland any such "starving time" as those which nearly wiped out both Jamestown and Plymouth.

Nevertheless, the labors of market gardening and dairying were far less attractive in thinly populated New Netherland than in the homeland, where produce was in great and continuous demand. The West India Company intended much of its first shipment of livestock for a half-dozen farms of its own, to be worked by its servants. Once there farms were set up, however, the men hired to cultivate them (like everyone else who came to New Netherland) proved to be much more interested in the fur trade than in the painstaking practice of Dutch agriculture. The Company farms were so neglected that Domine Michaelius could find no fresh produce for sale, the other colonists apparently being content to subsist on the diet of corn, beans, squash, game, fish, and especially shellfish — Long Island oysters and clams — that they could buy from the Indians. In the light of this, Kiliaen Van Rensselaer's purchase of the Company's livestock may have had advantages for the animals themselves as well as for Van Rensselaer and his colony, for the colonists of Rensselaerswyck came to found permanent farms, and in all probability used the animals more and cared for them better than the Company's notoriously negligent servants.

At first the farmers clustered around Fort Amsterdam, but soon they began to spread out to land as much as possible like that of the Netherlands. The Rensselaerswyck settlers preferred the low, fertile islands of the upper Hudson, even though they were more often than not submerged in the spring floods. The lowlands of Long Island also quickly attracted farmers, who settled in the "Five Dutch Towns," where their culture soon took on a unique character from their association with English settlers who preferred Dutch government to the rule of the "saints" in New England. Staten Island and the Jersey flats were equally attractive; settlements there were repeatedly rebuilt after being destroyed by the Indians. In the mid-Hudson region, settlers found their way into isolated fertile creek bottoms, as at Esopus (Kingston) and Catskill, where they possessed themselves of some abandoned Indian fields. In general, the Dutch selected land already cleared by the forces of nature or the Indians; only after such lands were gone did they begin cutting new fields little by little out of the forest.

The first depiction of agriculture in the Hudson Valley is in Adriaen Van der Donck's *Description of New Netherland.* By the time he wrote, only three decades after the first settlement, farmers had introduced many field crops and a considerable variety of livestock. Van der Donck was astonished at the amazing fertility of the soil, which would grow grain year after year without manure, and was actually *too* rich for some crops, such as field peas. He observed that Dutch horses and cattle throve without diminishing in size in the New World, as some scientists feared, although cows accustomed to the salt hay of the Netherlands sometimes became ill on fresh fodder until the farmers learned to feed them extra salt. Some settlers kept sheep, but there were few weavers in the colony and bushes in the pastures combed out a good deal of wool, so goats were much more popular, and hogs very numerous. Perhaps the most unexpected crop was tobacco, which was extensively grown in New Netherland (as it is still grown in the Connecticut Valley), although after the English conquest this competition with the Chesapeake colonies was gradually abandoned.

The English conquest had even less effect on Dutch boers than on Dutch burghers, once they met the English government's requirement that they secure new patents for their land. But Peter Stuyvesant's 1667 petition for the restoration of trade with the Netherlands reveals that they did encounter some difficulty because they could not use English farm tools. Recent research has revealed that the tools in question were probably the plow and the scythe, distinctive versions of which remained in use in the Hudson Valley until all hand farm tools were replaced by mechanized equipment in the nineteenth and twentieth centuries. There were two types of Dutch plow, one originating in Flanders and the other in the northern Netherlands, both drawn by horses — traditionally a team of three — rather than oxen, and both particularly suitable for low-lying alluvial soils in river deltas or islands like those where the Dutch colonists first chose to settle. The Dutch scythe, or "sith," was introduced while most of the farmers of Europe were still reaping grain by the backbreaking process of cutting it with a sickle. The "sith," which had a long blade and a short handle set at a right angle to it, was wielded by a standing worker with his right hand, while he steadied the grain with a "mathook" in his left. Although these tools made it possible to reap three times as much grain in a day as with the sickle, they never became popular among the English, who in the eighteenth century developed the more familiar two-handed scythe and then the cradle.

Hudson Valley farmers began growing wheat for their own subsistence and that of the townsmen, and for most of the seventeenth century they, like the English colonies, produced little for export. But after the English conquest Dutch merchants, supplying slaves for the West Indies in exchange for sugar, discovered that the sugar planters would gladly pay good prices for grain and flour to feed their slaves so that they could concentrate on sugar production. As early as 1676 the export of flour had become so considerable that New York City secured a monopoly on the process of "bolting" (sifting flour through fine cloth to remove chaff, bran, and foreign bodies such as fragments of the millstones) ostensibly in the interests of maintaining a high standard of quality. This monopoly, however, was at once successfully challenged by the Yankee towns of Long Island, which like their compatriots in Connecticut, shipped their produce in locally owned vessels.

Nevertheless, New York merchants, such as Frederick Philipse, invested some of their profits in large tracts of land on which they settled tenant farmers who paid rent in grain. The rest of their crop was sold through the landlord who, by his ownership of the mills where the grain was ground and the ships which carried it to market, reaped all the middleman's profit on its sale. Wheat thus became the cash crop of boers who, like their counterparts in the Netherlands, thought of farming as a profitable form of activity within a complex economic system. Other crops, mostly for their own use, included field peas (a nitrogen-fixing legume like clover) until they were destroyed by an insect pest; hops for brewing Dutch beer (still a cash crop around Catskill); flax, garden vegetables, and orchard fruits, especially apples and pears. Peter Kalm, a Swedish naturalist, observing Hudson Valley farms with the eye of a trained botanist, remarked in 1749:

> Wheat is sown in the neighborhood of Albany to great advantage. From one bushel they get twelve sometimes; if the soil is good, they get twenty bushels . . . The wheat flour from Albany is reckoned the best in all America, except that from Sopus [Esopus] or King's Town [Kingston], a place between Albany and New York. All the bread of Albany is made of wheat. At New York they pay for the Albany flour with a few shillings more per hundred weight than for that of other places. Rye is likewise sown here, but not so generally as wheat. They do not sow much barley, because they do not reckon the profits very great. Wheat is so plentiful that they make malt of that. In the neighborhood of New York, I saw great fields sown with barley. They do not sow more oats than are necessary for their horses.[1]

The Hudson Valley Dutch also transmitted to America the Dutch tradition of kitchen and ornamental gardening, in which in the seventeenth century they were far and away the leaders of Europe. Van der Donck mentioned a wide variety of flowers, fruits, and vegetables which had been successfully transplanted from the Netherlands, but devoted most of his space to describing the delicious flavor and many uses of the native pumpkins, squash, melons, gourds, and Indian beans. About the same time, Jeremias Van Rensselaer imported numerous plants from the family estates in the Netherlands — no mean task at a time when the voyage could take up to six months. During this time seeds had to be kept secure against the damp, premature germination, and the ship's rats; growing plants, often planted in wooden tubs, had to be watered, exposed to light and air, and protected from cold by the captain or a passenger charged with this task. After Van Rensselaer's garden was swept away in the flood of 1666 (which also destroyed his house, storehouses, and much of the community), he apparently did not repeat the effort to start another. In the next century, gardening shifted from a traditionally male activity to an occupation of women:

> I think I yet see what I have so often beheld both in town and country, a respectable mistress of a family going out to her garden, in an April morning, with her great calash, her little painted basket of seeds, and her rake over her shoulder to her garden labors. All day long a woman, in very easy circumstances and abundantly gentle in form and manners, would sow, and plant, and rake, incessantly. These fair gardeners were also great florists; their emulation and solicitude in these pleasing employment did indeed produce "flowers worthy of Paradise."[2]

The farmers also followed Dutch traditions in the construction of their buildings. Many farm houses, especially in the upper Hudson Valley, were built in the same manner as Dutch city houses, and therefore resembled them in style; the Bronck House in West Coxsackie and the Van Alen House in Kinderhook (both museums) are examples of such houses which are still standing. In New Jersey and Long Island, however, another type of house developed, with the graceful double-gambrel roof now known as "Dutch colonial." Some scholars believe that these houses were derived from peasant homes in the southern Netherlands and northern France, and others that they were an original invention by the eighteenth-century Dutch in America; the subject awaits further research. Inside these houses the more substantial boers maintained a standard of comfort not so different from that of burghers of comparable wealth, as is suggested by the rooms from

South room, Jan Martinse Schenck house, ca. 1675.

Courtesy of the Brooklyn Museum

the Schenck House on Long Island at the Brooklyn Museum and those from the Hardenbergh House in Ulster County at Winterthur. They maintained traditional Dutch styles in furnishings much longer than many burghers, however, partly because they passed down many items as the farmstead changed hands by inheritance, and partly because they had few English neighbors to emulate.

Even more typically Dutch were the barns on these farms — in which, in the earliest years, the farm family sometimes lived in accordance with a tradition of the Netherlands and North Germany in which people and livestock customarily lived under the same roof. These barns were divided into a "nave" and "aisles" resembling those of a Gothic cathedral. The family lived in one "aisle," set off by partitions; the livestock had stalls in the other, and the great central space under the soaring loft was used in season for a threshing floor and on occasion for community meetings and church services. This construction, which resembled Gothic architecture not only in its division of space but also in the complex diagonal bracing of its sturdy posts and huge crossbeams, remained characteristic of "Dutch" barns well into the nineteenth century. Such barns, numbers of which are still standing and some of which are still in use, are unmistakable because they are wider than they are long, with very low walls and a great expanse of roof, and have doors in both ends so that wagons can be driven in one door, stopped in the middle of the floor while their loads are pitched up into the loft, and driven out the other door without turning around.

But not all the harvest was stored in the loft. An equally important feature of Dutch farms was a structure called a "barrack," which consisted of a pyramidal roof mounted on tall poles so that it could be slid up or down from ground level to the top of the poles, which might be forty or fifty feet high. Under this shelter the boer stored hay or grain, which was carefully packed in with a pitchfork in a process called "layering." Each forkful of hay was rolled and laid beside the rest, very much as if they were bricks, first around the edge and then in toward the center until the layer was complete. When the stack was finished it was protected from the weather by the roof, and the barrack could serve the purpose of a silo whose walls were bundles of hay. Another nearby barrack was sometimes built with a floor a few feet off the ground, under which the cattle could shelter, serving themselves from the hay that they could reach while the heavy roof kept it pressed down to their level. It was necessary, however, to be sure the hay was thoroughly dry or it might set itself on fire by spontaneous combustion; many destructive farm fires started in this way.

The way of life on a substantial Dutch farm is vividly illustrated by a remarkable folk painting known as the Van Bergen Overmantel, which is now at the New York State Historical Association at Cooperstown, New York. This picture of a Hudson Valley Dutch farm with all its buildings, people, and livestock, was probably painted between 1730 and 1735 by an itinerant limner. Its peculiar size and shape — 18 inches by 7 feet — reflect the fact that it was intended to be hung over the fireplace of the house shown in the picture, where it remained until the house was torn down in the nineteenth century. The farm depicted is that of Martin G. Van Bergen at Old Catskill (now Leeds). Van Bergen's

Van Bergen overmantel, by an anonymous limner, ca. 1735.
Courtesy of the New York State Historical Association,
Cooperstown, New York

father had purchased five clearings from the Catskill Indians when they moved away, and in the 1720s his sons, having come of age and married, settled there. Gerrit, the elder, took over the homestead his father had built on the hill in 1680; the barn, dating from that year, stood until very recently, and the "new" house Gerrit built in 1729 is standing yet. Its gable may be seen in the upper righthand corner of the picture. The buildings shown include Martin's house (a rural version of an urban Dutch house), his Dutch barn, and two hay barracks filled with the harvest, one with and one without a shelter for animals. The fence and the wagon are also typically Dutch in construction.

Martin, the younger son, built a quarter-mile down the hill the house that is the center of the painting. Outside the house stand Martin and his wife Catarina, in their Sunday best. Their four young daughters are near them, the elder two trying hard to be young ladies but the younger running away to play. The three sons, in their early teens, evidently have no patience with such posing for they are racing their horses around the farmyard. Up the road from the lower right-hand corner come Uncle Gerrit and his two elder sons, also in their Sunday best, for a visit. Meanwhile, the necessary work of the farm goes on in the capable hands of two white laborers and four black slaves. One laborer has just returned from the mill with a wagon-load of flour in sacks while the other hastens to bring water to the horses. Slave girls feed the

Detail, house and family of Martin G. Van Bergen.

chickens and go to milk the cows, while a slave boy plays with a dog and a man sets off for the field, either to care for the sheep or to separate two fighting stallions. An Indian brave and squaw have also stopped by, perhaps to visit but more likely to trade.

The Van Bergen Overmantel therefore shows the way of life of a boer family substantial enough to own several slaves — when Uncle Gerrit died he left ten to his heirs — one of the leading families of Catskill. Catarina Van Bergen was the daughter of a Kingston merchant, and the family's social level was perhaps comparable to that of the Gansevoorts, who were leaders among the artisans and general merchants but by no means the equals of the fur-trading patricians. Such families, the Dutch counterparts of the English "yeomanry," who were not too proud to work in

Detail, black servant feeding hens.

their own fields alongside their slaves, were the mainstay of the Dutch rural tradition. The Van Bergens, who had acquired their land early in the English period, perhaps had more than most, but their way of life did not differ substantially from that of their neighbors who had somewhat less wealth. The number of Martin Van Bergen's slaves — half as many as there were members of the family — was also about that of other substantial farm families, particularly in the counties around New York City, where both the colony's Dutch population and its slaves were concentrated. In Queen's County, where a high proportion of the white people were Dutch, a third of the entire population was black — twice the percentage of King's County, Staten Island, and New York City. Nor was the Van Bergen's entire fortune made by farming, for like many sons of the soil they had also served apprenticeships in crafts, although it is unknown to what extent they practiced them. It has been suggested that the small outbuilding in the over-mantel may have been a smithy. Like many other families whose lands included a suitable waterfall, they owned a little mill which ground the harvests of the entire community. A similar mill may be seen in operation today at Philipsburg Manor, Sleepy Hollow Restorations, Tarrytown, New York.

The Philipse family living quarters at Philipsburg Manor illus-trate the standard of living of the manor lords who were the rural counterpart of the urban patricians. There were three kinds of manor lords in colonial New York: those who regarded their land primarily as an investment, profiting not only by the rents they collected from their tenants but from the tolls they were paid for services, such as the mill, and from the mercantile profits derived from selling their produce; those who looked upon land primarily as a source of social status and a basis for the way of life of the landed gentry; and those who saw land as a speculation to be held for profit by sale after settlement spread and land increased in value.

The first type of manor was particularly characteristic of the Dutch, being represented by Rensselaerswyck under Kiliaen Van Rensselaer and Philipsburg Manor under Frederick Philipse. These men were primarily merchants who directed the development of their estates from their city counting-rooms and rarely if ever visited them; when they did so they were content to live, as did the Philipses, somewhat more comfortably but not in essence differently from their more prosperous tenants.

The second attitude toward landed estates was essentially English, and was introduced into the Hudson Valley by ambitious Englishmen who secured large grants from early governors — particularly Benjamin Fletcher in the 1690s, whose grants were so excessively large that a number of them were later revoked by the authorities in London. As leading Dutch families associated with these men politically and socially, and sometimes permitted their daughters to marry them, they began to share in a way of life similar to that of English "county families." Van Cortlandt Manor illustrates this tradition, in which the manor house was as much the center of the community as a private residence. Here manorial and civic business was transacted, meetings of gentry involved in public affairs were held, and important guests, visitors from other

Restored dam and mill at Philipsburg Manor, North Tarrytown, New York.
Courtesy of Sleepy Hollow Restorations, Tarrytown, New York

colonies, and foreign tourists were entertained as a matter of course in preference to the often inadequate lodging available at country inns. The mistress of such a house had to be a chatelaine rather than a housewife, and its furnishings were selected for display, which was expected of a family of manorial status, as much as for use. Families like the Van Cortlandts purchased furnishings in the latest English styles by leading New York and Philadelphia craftsmen for the public reception rooms and relegated their inherited Dutch pieces to the family living quarters, the servants' rooms, or the attic, when they did not discard them altogether.

An example of a colonial grant of the third type, exploited by a Dutchman, was the Hardenbergh Patent in the Catskills near

Kingston. Johannis Hardenbergh was an ambitious Dutch merchant from Kingston, who joined with several greedy English officials to register a claim for a supposedly small parcel near Kingston in 1708. The officials, who were not supposed to participate in land grants at all, hid behind dummy shareholders and other ingenious devices, meanwhile manipulating the boundaries of the patent to take in much more land than originally appeared to be intended — an operation very easy, and often performed, where land claims were based on vague phrases in Indian deeds. But several of these hidden proprietors died before it was safe to acknowledge their ownership, and Johannis Hardenbergh became the agent for their heirs — in effect the only resident, visible proprietor of the land.

Enough rumors leaked out to call the title of the patent in question, and eventually the Livingston family secured a large part of it by buying up the rights of some of the absentee heirs. Nevertheless, the Hardenbergh family clung tenaciously to their share — the seventh part of a million and a half acres — although their efforts to assert their rights as landlords made some of them very unpopular and led to the murder of Gerardus Hardenbergh in the early nineteenth century. Although many tenants were known to have expressed their hatred for him openly, even going so far as to wish him a bad end, no murderer could be brought to trial because no one in the community where the crime took place would testify.

This third type of landholding, practiced throughout the colonial period, became particularly important after the Revolution, when wealthy Patriots bought up confiscated Tory holdings and tracts recently vacated by the Indians, and sold them to settlers from New England, in whose experience leaseholding was unknown. They were uneasy as tenants from the beginning and were responsible for much of the tenant unrest which eventually led to the abolition of perpetual leasehold tenure in New York by the Constitution of 1846.

Beyond such instances of tenant unrest, there is very little information about the way of life of tenants and other poor farmers. Their homes were less solidly built than the farmhouses which have survived, their furniture was rudely constructed and usually used until it wore out, and even if they were sufficiently literate to sign their names and laboriously spell out passages in their big Dutch Bibles, they did not leave letters, diaries, accounts, or other written records. Since practically all that is known about them is the discontent of some with what they considered the unreasonable exactions of their landlords, it is important to note that not all tenants were dissatisfied, and that for some boers, especially indentured servants who had served out their time and poor immigrants who had exhausted their resources paying their passage to America, tenancy had some positive advantages. The American idea of "free land" developed in the trans-Appalachian West in the nineteenth century — and even then land that was "free" was always on the far frontier, remote from markets and covered with huge trees, requiring several years of backbreaking labor to turn it into profitable farmland. The purchase of cleared land suitable for the type of farming familiar to the immigrant; the building of house, barn, and barracks; and investment in tools, livestock, and seed required an amount of capital far beyond his reach.

Tenancy provided a framework within which the landlord made these investments, and the tenant paid in return an annual rent and a portion of the price he received should he transfer his lease to someone else, which permitted the landlord to share in the increase in the value of his property created by the tenant's improvements. The tenants might also be required to use such facilities as the landlord's mill, to contribute a few days' work a year — usually for public works, at a time when money for the payment of taxes was scarce — and token levies such as the "two fat fowls" of Rensselaerswyck, which reflected the original provision that the increase of livestock provided by the landlord should be shared. This means of organizing and financing frontier development had been normal in Europe throughout the Middle Ages — during which a tremendous work of clearing forests, cultivating wastelands, and draining marshes had been accomplished by the efforts of feudal lords — and was therefore quite familiar to immigrant settlers, especially those from the continent of Europe. The New England colonists had modified it by vesting the traditional functions of the lord in the town, which hastened to give unrestricted titles to its "freeholders." But the Dutch, French, German, Scots, and Irish settlers who came to the Hudson Valley were quite familiar with tenancy and were not unwilling to accept it as a way of getting started in a new country; some of them, like the Van Rensselaers' Dutch tenants, remained satisfied with it for several generations.

In the eighteenth century, tenant unrest arose primarily from two sources. One was the exactions of landlords who deliberately cheated or otherwise exploited their tenants, among whom the Livingstons were particularly notorious. Robert Livingston's mistreatment of a group of Palatine German refugees whom he invited to settle on his manor in 1710 was so flagrant that most of the settlers migrated to Pennsylvania, and warned their relatives and friends in Germany to avoid the Hudson Valley altogether. In the 1750s and 1760s, Robert Livingston III had endemic difficulties with tenants who resented his harsh policies, which came back to haunt his family when it needed their support during the Revolution. Part of his problem, however, was the other reason for tenant unrest, the appearance among the tenants of land-hungry settlers from New England who were not really comfortable with the leasehold system, and who communicated their discomfort to their Dutch and German neighbors. Such, for example, was the point of view of a half-dozen tenants high in the Berkshires on the Massachusetts border, who petitioned that colony to accept them as citizens though geography isolated them almost completely from it; the terrain was so difficult that Livingston, who was much closer, was not able to enforce his claim, and in time the boundary between the states was fixed to include them in the town of Mount Washington, Massachusetts.

All these rural areas were held together by the great highway of the river, with its "Landings" every 10 or 15 miles, wherever a tributary creek entered. These landings were ports of call for the river sloops, traditionally owned in Albany, which plied from one to another carrying away flour and bringing in manufactured goods, passengers, and mail. The sloops were sturdy little craft of 70 to 100 tons burden, capable of a voyage to the West Indies — or even China — if profit beckoned, but normally confining their druising to the fourteen broad and beautiful "reaches" of the Hudson River. In the "Landings" also lived the fisher folk who made their living seining for the sturgeon and shad which crowded up the river to spawn in the spring; sturgeon in particular was so plentiful that it was called "Albany beef." In the winter the frozen river was closed to shipping, but it was more than ever a highway for the people who lived near it, for the Dutch were then as later a nation of skaters, and for longer journeys there were sleighs and ice boats.

As boer families had large numbers of healthy children — six to 12 were normal — the population along the river grew denser,

"Sleigh Riding on the Hudson River," print by Benson J. Lossing.

and some of these young people sought land on newer frontiers. Those from Long Island, New York City, and Westchester, finding the good land in their neighborhoods taken up by New Englanders, moved west into New Jersey. The valleys of the Hackensack and Passaic Rivers, where colonies were twice begun, and twice devastated during the Dutch period, were finally permanently colonized after the English conquest, largely by children of Dutch families from Long Island and Staten Island. Their children pushed up the Raritan and its tributaries, and the third generation penetrated into the mountains of western New Jersey. Some went on into Bucks County, Pennsylvania, soon after 1700, and well before the Revolution there was a considerable Dutch settlement at Conewago, near Gettysburg. Their paths may be traced by their characteristic gambrel-roofed houses and their Dutch barns, which stand out conspicuously among the English and New England houses and the English and German barns built by other New Jersey settlers. The

few books and articles that have been published about the New
Jersey Dutch and their neighbors in Orange and Rockland
Counties reveal that their way of life was different in some very
important respects from that of the Dutch in the upper Hudson
Valley. Perhaps most significant was their rugged, even stubborn,
individual independence, which prompted them to settle by choice
at some distance from their neighbors, on tracts of land large
enough to provide an adequate inheritance for each when divided
equally among the numerous children they anticipated. The
staunch communal loyalty so conspicuous in Albany, Schenectady,
and some of the surrounding rural areas was far less important in
the lower Hudson Valley than loyalty to various subgroups, about
which little is yet known. This loyalty often tore communities
apart and was sometimes handed down for generations in the
form of grudges which have not totally disappeared in the twentieth century. As has been suggested, it is possible that regional
differences between settlers from Belgium and others from the
northern part of the Netherlands contributed to this bitterness.
Certainly the presence of a considerable number of Frisian
families, particularly noted for their fierce individualism, their
sharp tongues, and their long memories for an injury, did nothing
to decrease it. It is clear, even from the little that is known, that
this Dutch tradition is very different from that which has
previously been described — which is one reason that perplexed
historians may have neglected it — and that a great deal of
detailed research into the abundant local records of the lower
Valley is urgently needed.

A second region of Dutch settlement was the mid-Hudson area,
centering upon Kingston, Newburgh, and Poughkeepsie. This was
the mountainous territory of the Highlands and the Catskills, in
which early settlement was confined to the occasional creek
bottoms. The Dutch at Kingston very soon explored the route to
the Delaware by way of the Esopus and Neversink Valleys, and in
time settled all the way to Port Jervis. Among their other discoveries was a copper mine at Pahaquarry in the Kittatinny Mountains of western New Jersey, which they are reported to have
worked at a very early date. The copper was supposed to have
been brought up the Delaware and over the mountains to Kingston
by the "Old Mine Road." Documentation of this venture, however, has not yet been discovered. There were also a few Dutch
settlements along the Delaware in Pennsylvania, of which Bushkill

Demarest house, River Edge, New Jersey, built by David Demarest, ca. 1698.
Courtesy of Adrian C. Leiby

Falls still preserves its Dutch name, and perhaps a settlement in northwestern Lehigh County still known to the Pennsylvania Germans of that area as "Albany Eck" (Albany corner or district), of which nothing further is yet known.

The upper Hudson region of Dutch settlement consisted primarily of the fertile bottom of an ancient glacial lake, in the middle of which Albany is situated. This basin begins to spread west of the Hudson above Coxsackie, and is dissected by several creeks in whose valleys boers quickly settled. By the time of the American Revolution this "West District of Rensselaerswyck" contained about 270 tenant families, nearly all of them located in the triangular tract between the Hudson and Mohawk Rivers and the steep Helderberg escarpment. The "East District" contained about 240 families, most of them concentrated on the river and the first slope of hills to the eastward, and only a few penetrating into the rugged Taconic Mountains along the Massachusetts border. Dutch settlers from Kinderhook and Claverack, however, early found their way to the valley of the Housatonic, which they called the Westenhook, and a significant proportion of the early settlers of Great Barrington were Dutch — who acquired such a substantial position in the community that when they quarreled with the Congregational minister in 1764 and withdrew from his church, the church collapsed and did not revive for a generation. The northernmost settlements of this region were Schagticoke and Hoosac on the east side of the river and Saratoga (now Schuylerville) on the west, which were raw frontier when the French and Indians devastated them in 1745.

West of Albany, Schenectady was the gateway to the Mohawk Valley. That town was founded in 1661, ostensibly for agriculture, but its farmers were always eager to take advantage of their location fifteen miles nearer the Indians than Albany, and it was a Schenectady trader, Johannes Myndertse, who eventually succeeded in challenging the Albany monopoly in the courts. The destruction of Schenectady by the French and Indians in 1690 proved to be only a temporary interruption, for as soon as the war was over the settlers returned and many more came after them. Some of the houses they built are still homes in its "Stockade" district. From Schenectady the farmers pressed up the Mohawk, taking over its flats as the Indians abandoned them. Settlement reached the Schoharie Valley before the 1730s, and in the 1740s and 1750s Sir William Johnson and the Albany merchants competed for lands all the way to Little Falls. Dutch farmers then settled on the merchants' lands — Johnson preferred Scots and Irish tenants — so by the time of the Revolution there was a thin line of farms all the way up the Mohawk to the site of Rome, where the river crossed the boundary of Indian lands set by the Fort Stanwix Treaty of 1768.

A fifth region which must be mentioned, although very little is known about it, is the area of Dutch settlement in Delaware and South Jersey. Although the Dutch claimed this territory on the basis of Hudson's discovery and built Fort Nassau on the east side of the river in 1626, they sent few permanent settlers there until after the conquest of New Sweden. The Swedes thus colonized this region for twenty years, the Dutch for only ten. Furthermore, hardly any descendants of Dutch families from New Jersey found their way that far south before the Delaware Valley was inundated by the Quaker colonists of West Jersey and Pennsylvania. Nevertheless, Peter Kalm observed that settlers in this region had widely

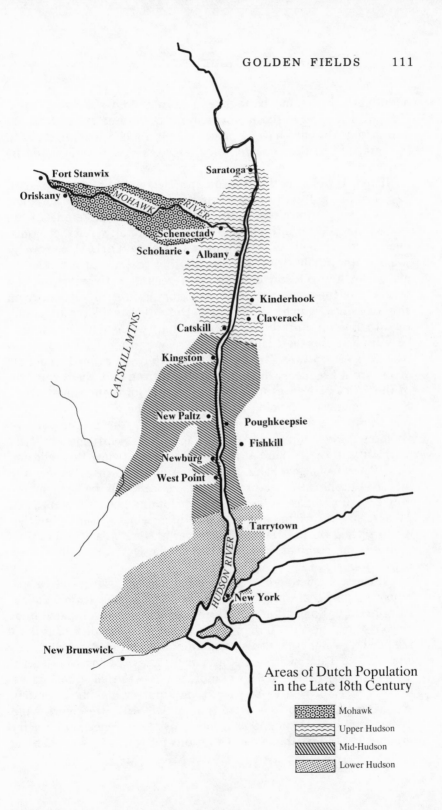

Areas of Dutch Population
in the Late 18th Century

Mohawk
Upper Hudson
Mid-Hudson
Lower Hudson

adopted the Dutch hay barrack, and a few buildings showing Dutch characteristics have been located in Delaware; students from Winterthur Museum have learned enough about these buildings to indicate that further research on the Dutch in this area would be worthwhile.

These regions in the Hudson and Delaware Valleys appear to have been as culturally distinct as the regions of the Netherlands. Their styles of houses are quite different, and boer families from one region seldom intermarried with those of any other, although many burgher families had branches in New York, Albany, and some of the smaller river towns. Another factor which tended to make the mid-Hudson and Mohawk regions different from the others was the presence of considerable groups of settlers from ethnic groups which, though not Dutch, were closer to Dutch than to English culture and who adapted to the Dutch, particularly by learning their language, before they found it necessary to adopt English culture. The first of these groups were the Huguenots driven from France by the persecutions surrounding the revocation of the Edict of Nantes in 1685. Only some of them came to New York — many more going to England and the English colonies — but those who did were made welcome by the descendants of Walloons, and soon found places among the craftsmen of New York City or on the land at their settlements of New Rochelle and New Paltz. At New Paltz their stone houses, which reflect the medieval stone architecture of France, can still be seen in the only museum village in the country maintained by an organization of descendants of an ethnic group of original settlers. Another group settled on the Hackensack River in New Jersey, and in time they became completely assimilated to the Dutch culture of their neighbors.

The other such group was composed of Palatine Germans, refugees from the conquests of Louis XIV in the Rhine Valley, who fled to England in 1709 and aroused the compassion of Queen Anne and the "Indian Kings" — and the cupidity of Robert Livingston. When the British government organized a project to employ the Palatines in making naval stores, Livingston eagerly invited them to settle on his manor, which was rich in pine trees. But the pines proved to be the wrong kind for making tar, pitch, and resin, the Palatines were unfamiliar with the work, and Livingston cheated them outrageously by issuing cheap and scanty supplies instead of the generous rations for which he was charging the government. By 1712 the Palatines were thoroughly disgusted, and most of them left Livingston's land for the Schoharie Valley, which they understood the "Indian kings" had offered them for their home; a few remained on Livingston Manor in the area still known as Germantown. But after a few years of building up fat farms in their seven little settlements at Schoharie, their titles were challenged by New York City speculators. Some of the Palatines gave in and paid the speculators for their lands, and some moved west on the Mohawk frontier, but many shook the dust of New York from their feet and moved to Pennsylvania, where the great bulk of German immigration began to follow them. The Germans who remained in the Mohawk Valley intermarried with the Dutch, and created a composite culture which funneled west along the river, but did not attempt to clear the steep hills on either side.

Dutch farmers therefore spread throughout the Hudson and Mohawk Valleys in the eighteenth century, carrying with them their Dutch dialect, their tools and techniques, and their styles of building. The dialect has died out almost completely, as a medium of communication, although some words are still in use in rural localities, Dutch Reformed churches in numerous communities indicate where it once was spoken. The tools and techniques continued to be used by descendants of the Dutch colonists until all farming was revolutionized by mechanized equipment. In accordance with the Dutch tradition of farming for the market rather than for subsistence, Hudson Valley boers early developed grain as a cash crop. The material culture of the boer way of life, particularly its houses and barns, is most visible today, because some of these buildings are still standing and a number of them have been opened to the public as museums. It is to be hoped that further study of all these aspects of the boer way of life will restore them, the most silent of all the silent Dutchmen, to their rightful place in the American tradition.

6

Faiths of Their Fathers

LONG before the Protestant Reformation, the religious tradition of the Low Countries embraced such diversities as the mysticism of Thomas à Kempis, the practical charity of the Brethren of the Common Life, the humanist tolerance of Erasmus, and the rigid particularism of local churches which considered doctrinal orthodoxy as aspect of civic loyalty and regarded the religious ideas current among their neighbors with the same jealous suspicion they directed toward their commercial competition. The Reformation itself reflected these diversities, for some Netherlanders responded to the teachings of Luther, others to the preaching of Anabaptist sects, others to the doctrines of Calvin, and still others to the revitalization of the Catholic Church that followed the Council of Trent (1545-63). As a result of the close association between resistance to religious persecution and defense of civic liberties during the Revolt, the Dutch came to regard religious doctrines much in the way that the English regarded political issues. Therefore, when religious controversy threatened to tear the Dutch Republic apart in the early seventeenth century, there seemed no way to preserve the unity of the nation but to establish the Dutch Reformed Church. The Synod of Dort (1619), however, by no means ended religious disputes; it merely brought them within the framework of the established church. Although the history of these disputes is usually written in terms of theological arguments among the clergy, it seems open to question how much of these debates were understood by, or even of interest to, most churchgoers — especially in America where few of them were educated and most of the polemical pamphlets current in the Netherlands never circulated. At least as important, but seldom considered, are the various folk religious traditions which conditioned the people's response to their preachers.

Calvinism originally embodied folk traditions familiar to French-speaking Netherlanders. Calvin, who came from the part of northern France adjoining the Low Countries, was a burgher and a lawyer before he became a theologian, and spent most of his career devising religious sanctions for maintaining public order in Geneva. His doctrines emphasized God's role as judge, and the importance of obedience to a moral code of social behavior. Calvinists in France — the Huguenots — and Walloons in the Netherlands emphasized these aspects of their faith, using it as the basis for organizing as a local and national political faction. In the Netherlands this point of view was very often, though not exclusively, found among the numerous, wealthy, powerful refugees from Belgium and their descendants.

The burghers of Holland and Zeeland shared a rather different tradition descended from that of Thomas à Kempis, Gerhard Groot, and Erasmus. It emphasized practical good works in the community and toleration of others' beliefs so long as they did not stir up civic disorder. In a tradition inherited from the late medieval church, it considered orthodoxy of doctrine a form of communal loyalty and heresy the most dangerous kind of sedition. But orthodoxy was likely to be broadly defined, for the burghers were practical businessmen, unwilling to let religious disputes interfere with commerce. In these cities, religion, whose zeal must be restrained within the civic structure, was very much an aspect of communal life. Such towns were racked by civil strife while the Calvinists were struggling for supremacy; after they attained it, Calvinism in practice soon bore far more resemblance to this existing tradition of civic orthodoxy than to its original militant sectarianism.

The third important religious tradition of the Netherlands came from the agricultural provinces of the northeast, particularly Friesland and Gelderland, which had been united with the Seventeen Provinces only a generation before the Dutch Revolt against Spain and were still culturally close to North Germany. The distinctive language, way of life, and independent character of this people have already been mentioned. From this region came a significant proportion of Dutch Lutherans. Even more important, however, was an indigenous movement called Pietism, which had some affiliation with similar movements in Germany but in the main followed preachers of local origin such as Menno Simons, and French refugee Jan Labadie. They stressed withdrawal from the wickedness of the world to cultivate mystical experience, and both advocated the formation of quasi-monastic communities within which the faithful could sustain themselves independently and encourage each other on their spiritual pilgrimage. They also shared some doctrines with the Anabaptists, the radicals of the 1530s, and therefore seemed subversive to both Protestants and Catholics, so that Mennonites and Labadists were persecuted even in the tolerant Netherlands. Similar beliefs in the importance of an emotional experience of God's grace, however, were widespread within Reformed congregations in this region.

Since the settlers of New Netherland came from all parts of the Netherlands, all these traditions were likely to be represented in any given community, and many religious controversies in America arose from conflict at close quarters among beliefs which in the Netherlands were sanctioned by local custom and kept separate by distance. The West India Company's initial requirement that all emigrants be Calvinists was not, in 1621, sectarian bigotry, but acknowledgment of the national establishment defined by the Synod of Dort and — in view of the preceding sectarian violence — a very necessary provision for the preservation of basic order in the colony. The fact that the Company's directors included a number of French-speaking Calvinist refugees, and that the first settlers were the Walloons, has somewhat obscured this, but as has been pointed out, religious zeal was nowhere near the moving spirit for either of these groups that it was to the colonists of New England.

The provision made by the Company for meeting the spiritual needs of these settlers followed a pattern already developed out of Dutch experience in providing such services in crowded city parishes, ships at sea, and colonies in other parts of the world, particularly the East Indies. Where worshipers were on the one hand too numerous or on the other hand too few for the effective ministry of a university-educated domine, they were reached by specially prepared laymen called "comforters of the sick," who were trained to offer spiritual consolation to those in danger of death and also to assist the ailing poor. It also became customary to assign such lay readers to ships' companies, particularly those going on long voyages, and to the "factories" established in the East Indies. In such circumstances, their function shifted its emphasis from consoling the dying to sustaining the faith of the living by informal services consisting of the reading of prayers and Scripture and the singing of Psalms, by the reading of published sermons on special occasions, and, in the colonies, by missionary work among the natives. In colonies where there were too few settlers to justify the sending of a minister, it was also possible for "comforters of the sick" to be specially licensed to solemnize baptisms and marriages, as was Bastiaen Jansz. Krol, who accompanied the Walloons to New Netherland. But the requirement that "comforters of the sick" be literate — Krol seems to have been self-taught as an adult — may have tempted the Company to employ them in secular administrative positions; after the Walloons left Fort Orange, Krol was appointed to command the fort, which position he retained for two decades.

Perhaps in an attempt to satisfy the Walloons, who had been petitioning for a qualified minister ever since their arrival in the New World, the Company employed Domine Johannes Michaelius in 1628, after which the colony was never without at least one ordained domine. "Comforters of the sick" and other lay leaders such as catechists and schoolmasters continued to provide many spiritual services, particularly in outlying areas. Michaelius quickly assembled a heterogeneous congregation of Netherlanders and Walloons, to whom he preached in Dutch, which they all understood more or less, but whom he encouraged to sing the Psalms each in their own language, to the common Genevan tunes. The worshipers met temporarily in a large room over the horsemill until a church building was constructed in 1633; it is not recorded where they hung New Amsterdam's civic carillon, nine little church bells which were presented to the city by the Company after one of its ships captured them in a raid on Puerto Rico in 1625. But Michaelius fell out with Governor Minuit, whom the domine considered insufficiently zealous in enforcing the discipline of Christian behavior in this rough frontier town, and when his three-year term was over he returned to the Netherlands to complain to the Company of Minuit's self-seeking administration.

Nor could Michaelius' two immediate successors agree with the governors concerning the role of the church in the community. Both the colorful Domine Everardus Bogardus, who was constantly in controversy with Van Twiller and Kieft, and Johannes

Backerus, who served temporarily under Stuyvesant after Bogardus' death, seem to have been militant Calvinists of the sort whose intolerant zeal had roused their followers to civic disorder during the Remonstrant controversy. Bogardus, who was a young man in his first pastorate when he came to New Amsterdam in 1633, was a lusty individual subject to the temptation of intemperance in food, drink, and words, so that there was always a new and juicy tale of his latest indiscretion for wagging tongues to relish. His running battle with Kieft — castigating him in his sermons by racy epithets, while the governor tried to drown him out by ordering soldiers to drill outside the church with drums beating, trumpets blaring, and cannon firing — ended only when both were drowned in the same shipwreck while returning to the Netherlands to carry their dispute before higher authorities.

In the meantime, Kiliaen Van Rensselaer was taking his responsibility to provide pastoral care for his colonists with his customary seriousness. Until 1636 there were too few of them to justify sending a minister, although Van Rensselaer directed various officials to conduct informal services by reading prayers, Scripture, and Psalms, and Krol was still available at Fort Orange to solemnize baptisms and marriages. But after the voyage of the *Rensselaerswyck* in 1637, the patroon bestirred himself promptly to employ a minister and send instructions — including a plan — for the building of a little octagonal church, in a style popular in the rural Netherlands because it made it easier to hear the preacher. But the colonists neglected to carry it out, as they did so many of Van Rensselaer's directions, and when Domine Johannes Megapolensis arrived in 1642 he was, like Michaelius, appalled at their abandonment of the fundamental standards of Christian behavior. He was further disappointed by the poor response from the Indians to his missionary efforts. These, despite his efforts to learn their language and teach them in it, were more impressed by the indifference of his white auditors to the practice of the doctrines he preached. He was therefore quite ready to leave when his contract expired in 1648 — particularly since Kiliaen's executors had fallen behind in the payment of his salary.

Megapolensis was finally succeeded by Domine Gideon Schaets in 1656. By this time, Beverwyck had been set off as an independent community and the younger Van Rensselaers had begun to reside on their domain. The town promptly built a little square church, for which the burghers imported a handsome carved oak

Pulpit made in the Netherlands for the original Albany Dutch Reformed Church, 1656. *Courtesy of the First Church in Albany, Reformed*

pulpit from the Netherlands and commissioned stained glass windows bearing the donors' coats of arms — some of which were invented for the occasion — from glazier Evert Duyckinck, who had just completed a similar set for the New York church. The deacons of this congregation administered a considerable fund of contributions made for the poor, and someone, perhaps the Van Rensselaer brothers, built a poorhouse, but since there were no poor to live in it, Domine Schaets took it over for a parsonage — probably considering that he had as much right to live there as any of the poor, since the congregation was habitually in arrears with his salary.

In the meantime, Megapolensis had stopped in New Amsterdam on his way back to the Netherlands, and was promptly drafted by Stuyvesant to fill the pulpit vacated by Backerus, whom he had driven back to the Netherlands for supporting the Nine Men. Megapolensis, who had been born a Catholic but had converted to Calvinism in adulthood after his birthplace in the southern Netherlands was reconquered by the Dutch, saw eye to eye with Stuyvesant on the importance of preserving religious orthodoxy as an aspect of maintaining order in the community. His approach to the New Amsterdam charge was therefore in the spirit of the doctrine of supporting the powers that be, which was entirely satisfactory to Stuyvesant both as a zealous Calvinist and as a public administrator, and there is no record of Megapolensis taking a stand on any political issue until he finally beseeched Stuyvesant not to open hostilities with the English conquerors.

Concerning religious dissidence, however, Megapolensis, with the zeal of the convert, was even more inflexible than Stuyvesant, encouraging and even prompting the governor in his policy of excluding all other organized religious groups from the colony. New Netherland had long contained almost as many religions as languages; as Father Isaac Jogues observed in 1643: "No religion is publicly exercised but the Calvinist, and orders are to admit none but Calvinists, but this is not observed, for besides the Calvinists there are in the colony Catholics, English Puritans, Lutherans, Anabaptists, here called Mnistes [Mennonites], etc."[1] In the 1650s the Lutherans and the Jews, both of whom could count on support from their coreligionists in Amsterdam, attempted to assert the same right to meet for worship without interference at which authorities in the Netherlands had long been conniving. Megapolensis preached against both groups, fear-

ing that they would disrupt the community, and Stuyvesant succeeded in shipping the Lutheran pastor back to the Netherlands,
but was compelled by the Company — under pressure from its
Jewish stockholders — to extend full civil rights to Jewish refugees
from Brazil.

Quakers, who in the 1650s were militants who called attention
to their beliefs by deliberately disturbing the peace, Stuyvesant
shipped off summarily to Rhode Island, then regarded as a nest of
cranks and fanatics. Things went so far that one young Quaker
submitted to brutal punishment rather than acknowledge his
error, and a group of substantial English settlers on Long Island
presented the "Flushing Remonstrance" in support of their right
to welcome members of any religious persuasion to their community. Perhaps alarmed by the title of this document, with its
overtones of Dutch civic controversy, Stuyvesant suppressed the
petitioners ruthlessly and exiled one of their leaders to the Netherlands, where the staunch Quaker won so much sympathy — and
publicity — for his cause that the Company rebuked Stuyvesant:

> Although we heartily desire that these and other sectarians remained
> away from there, yet as they do not, we doubt very much whether we
> can proceed against them rigorously without diminishing the population
> and stopping immigration which must be favored at so tender a stage of
> the country's existence. You may therefore shut your eyes, at least not
> force people's consciences, but allow everyone to have his own belief, as
> long as he behaves quietly and legally, gives no offense to his neighbors
> and does not oppose the government. As the government of this city has
> always practiced this maxim of moderation and consequently has often
> had a considerable influx of people, we do not doubt that your
> Province too would be benefitted by it.[2]

In the last decade of New Netherland's existence several communities reached the point of wishing for ministers, although not
all of them were as willing as they thought they were to accept the
burden of their support. Brooklyn, for example, complained in
1661 that it could not afford the 1,200 guilders a year promised to
Domine Hendrick Selyns, to which Stuyvesant retorted that they
should have thought of that before they extended him a call.
Nevertheless, by 1664 there were seven pastors in New Netherland,
two at New Amsterdam, two on Long Island, one at Beverwyck,
one at Esopus, and one on the Delaware. The conquest disestab-

lished the Dutch Church, relieving the West India Company of any responsibility for its support and removing the power of communities to tax the burghers for that purpose. Forced to rely entirely on voluntary contributions, the churches soon fell into arrears on the ministers' salaries, and when the New York City domine died in 1681 there were only three ministers within the former bounds of New Netherland, at Albany, Long Island, and the Delaware.

For the first 10 years after the conquest, the English respected the surrender agreement to refrain from interference with Dutch religion, but after the reconquest of 1674, Governor Andros appointed the Reverend Nicholas Van Rensselaer as a colleague to Domine Schaets at Albany. Nicholas Van Rensselaer, a brilliant but erratic younger son of Kiliaen, was somewhat of a trial to his family, which did not know quite what to do with him; he had, however, paradoxically made himself the family's friend at court by a service performed for Charles II during his exile. When he accepted ordination in England after studying theology in the Netherlands, there were many reasons why the Albany appointment seemed highly suitable — to everyone except the burghers of Albany and Jacob Leisler.

Surviving documents give no indication of the reason why it was Leisler — a zealous Calvinist to be sure, but at this period an

Silver beaker made in 1678 for the Albany Dutch Reformed Church by Ahasuerus Hendricks of New York. *Courtesy of the First Church in Albany, Reformed*

ambitious New York merchant of 35 with no apparent contact with Albany — who brought suit in the Albany municipal court to bar Van Rensselaer's installation of the ground that his ordination was invalid in the Dutch Reformed Church. The suit was long and hard-fought, being one of the few in seventeenth-century Albany in which reference was made to Dutch legal textbooks as well as to the facts before the court, but Leisler eventually won his case, and Van Rensselaer was not installed. It seems probable that the Albanians, who were not only suspicious of Van Rensselaer's character but were fighting desperately to keep the family from taking over the city, sought Leisler's help because they were unsure of their capacity to defeat the Van Rensselaers in a legal battle. Nevertheless, Leisler's participation in this controversy helps to explain the resistance of those Albanians, who had in the meantime made their peace with the Van Rensselaers, to his assumption of the provincial government 15 years later.

In the meantime, Calvinism became the principal symbol of Dutch ethnic identity, very largely as a result of the work of Domine Hendricus Selyns. Selyns, who had returned to the Netherlands for family reasons in 1664 after a brief and ill-paid pastorate on Long Island, was recalled to the New York City charge in 1681. Brilliant, personable, and persuasive in the pulpit, he was also one of New Netherland's few poets, writing in the tradition of Dutch civic rhetorical competitions. Two other authors in this tradition who worked in New Netherland were Nicasius de Sille and Jacob Steendam. Politically, Selyns was an extreme conservative, expressing his opinions during his stay in the Netherlands by a poem bitterly attacking Jan de Witt as well as by his inflexible opposition to Leisler's Rebellion in New York. His principal concern in the New York church was establishing its legal existence, in the face of English governors' attempts to impose an Anglican establishment. At the time of Leisler's Rebellion the right of the Reformed Church to hold property — whether its own church building or a substantial legacy which had been willed to it — was uncertain, and Selyn was anxious not to jeopardize his congregation's position with the British government. After many delays and efforts to bring political pressure to bear in the colony, in England, and on King William III through the Dutch ecclesiastical organization, Selyns' persistence was finally rewarded in 1696 by the granting of a charter to the church. This gave it legal identity and the right to hold property, conduct business, choose its own officers, and collect funds. This victory was marred, however, by a split in the congregation, for the Leislerian members had from the time of the Rebellion ceased to attend services or contribute to the domine's salary.

Selyns' efforts to build up religious faith as a defense of ethnic identity were also directed toward the instruction of the young people in the congregation. In 1698 these efforts bore fruit in a remarkable display by the catechism students, of whom 65 between the ages of nine and 14 recited the entire versified Psalter; the feat was repeated 18 months later by 50 more. When Selyns reported this accomplishment to the Classis of Amsterdam, the governing body in the Dutch Church which had jurisdiction over the American congregations, it replied in astonishment that it had never heard of such zeal. But barely 20 years later the younger brothers and sisters of these young people were demanding services in English, to the great distress of their elders who feared that the doctrinal purity of the liturgy would be impaired by translation. These young people had learned English for business and public purposes; some, who had married English spouses, spoke it in their homes as well; and some of the more ambitious families were transferring their membership to the Anglican Church. In spite of this pressure, the Dutch tradition was so strong that English services were not instituted in the Dutch Reformed Church in New York until 1763.

In Albany the language problem did not even arise until the American Revolution. In 1712 the burghers enlarged their church to seat 800 people by the ingenious expedient of building the new church around the old one and then removing the old building from inside, so that services were only interrupted for three weeks. Such beloved furnishings of the old church as the stained-glass windows, the weathercock, and the pulpit were installed in the new edifice, along with rich Communion silver donated by the wealthy new generation. This church was described in the nineteenth century by someone who remembered it:

Many of the present day recollect the small, square, stone building, with its peaked roof and small windows. Those who never looked upon that curious pile may have seen the life-like picture of it in various show-windows in our city. The internal arrangement of this church was in keeping with its external appearance; and those of the present day, who

Dutch Reformed Church, Albany, 1712-1806; engraving after a drawing by Philip Hooker (1766-1836). *Courtesy of the Albany Institute of History and Art*

object to gaudy places of worship, would probably be startled with the announcement that it was a gaily painted and richly ornamented church. The pulpit was of an octagon form, constructed of dark oak, resembling black walnut, richly varnished and polished. The ceiling and the front of the gallery were painted sky-blue, and the windows covered with richly colored glass, bearing the insignia of the coat of arms of the most influential members of the church. The pews on the ground floor, with the exception of three, were for the exclusive use of the female members of the congregation; and of the reserved three, one was appropriated for the governor of the state, the second for the judges and clerks of the court, and the third for the infirm male members of the congregation. All the male members, except those for whom special provisions were made, were compelled to sit in the gallery.

In those days stoves and furnaces were unknown in churches, and those who desired to be kept warm during the service by artificial means, were obliged to provide themselves with portable stoves or warm bricks. Foot stoves were then in vogue, and it was not an uncommon occurance to see, on a Sunday, from fifty to seventy-five colored servants or slaves, at the church door, awaiting the arrival of master or mistress, with two or more foot stoves in hand, filled with live hickory coals taken from an old Dutch fire-place . . . In those days it was no laughable matter to sit in a cold church for three long hours to listen to the preaching of the gospel, when the thermometer was below zero.[3]

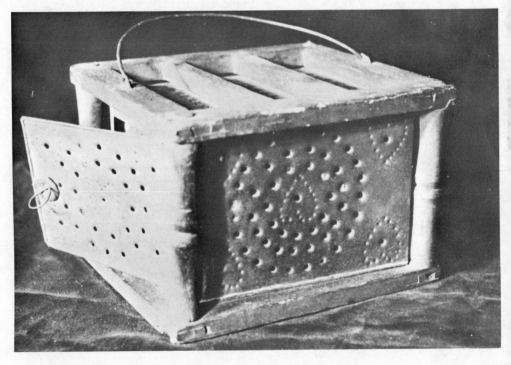

Foot-warmer used by Douw family.
Courtesy of Mrs. J. Stewart McNeilly, Chatham, New Jersey

Worship in the Dutch churches consisted of the traditional liturgy, an hour-long sermon, and the singing of the Psalms. These Psalms, translated into Dutch by Petrus Dathenus and sung to the tunes composed for the French version by Louis Bourgeois, were one of the best-loved parts of the Calvinist tradition. According to Calvin's precepts, they were sung unaccompanied when used in worship, the singing being led by the *voorsanger*, or precentor, who usually also performed the functions of *voorlezer*, or clerk, catechist, schoolmaster, and sometimes even sexton. In 1727 Governor Burnet, whose wife was from a Dutch family, gave the New York Reformed Church a small organ. In the Netherlands, the Calvinists had gradually accepted the great civic organs they found in existing churches, using them to accompany the Psalms but relegating all other music to concerts after the service. Likewise, the New York congregation gave their organist minute instructions in his contract governing the playing of the Psalms, which were still to be sung unaccompanied during the solemn quarterly celebrations of the Lord's Supper. John Peter Zenger, the first organist's blower, was taught by him to play and served as organist himself for a time, but after his imprisonment the instrument seems to have fallen into disuse for 20 years. No other Hudson Valley Dutch church had an organ during most of the colonial period, although Albany was using one at the end of the Revolution.

Private devotions were also important to many of the Dutch, especially the elderly. For this purpose they used manuals imported from the Netherlands, as well as their huge family Bibles and small Testament-Psalters that could be carried to church. They also hung in their homes numerous religious paintings, executed by the limners, which were closely modeled upon the illustrations in Dutch Bibles. This aspect of their tradition differs from that of Calvinism in the Netherlands, where depiction of religious subjects was associated with the forbidden superstitions of Catholic iconography, but its possible derivation from some folk religious custom more closely related to Lutheranism might be investigated. It is interesting that the subjects of the paintings which have survived deal primarily with the family relations of the Old Testament patriarchs or with persecutions. One favorite theme was Isaac's blessing of Jacob, who impersonated his hairy brother Esau by covering himself with skins. One wonders if the Albany fur traders made any connection between Jacob's sleight-of-hand with pelts and their own.

The Pietist tradition did not become important in the Hudson Valley until the eighteenth century. There had been a Dutch Mennonite settlement at the site of Swanendael in 1663, but it was almost immediately dispersed by the English conquest; its leader, Peter C. Plockhoy, eventually found a home among the Germans in Pennsylvania. A pair of Labadists looking for a place to found a New-World community visited New York in 1680, but received such a discouraging reception that they located their colony in Maryland, where it soon failed. One of these Labadists, Peter Sluyter, returned to New York in 1683, and supported his missionary work by practicing medicine, but members of Domine Selyns' congregation soon ran him out of town by suing him for malpractice. It has also been suggested that Leisler's son-in-law Jacob Milborne had a brother who had a reputation as an Anabaptist agitator in London, but possible Labadist influences in Leisler's Rebellion have not been further explored. So far as is now known, pietism was effectively introduced into the Hudson Valley about 1720 by Theodorus Jacobus Frelinghuysen, a young domine from Westphalia whose pastoral experience had been in a village in adjoining East Friesland. His father was a Reformed minister, but his grandfather was Lutheran, and in his homeland the two churches coexisted within a common tradition of popular piety, which was at least as important in his appeal to American worshipers as the doctrines of the Pietist theologians whose works he had studied.

In 1717 Frelinghuysen was called to be pastor of the Raritans, the newly settled area west of New Brunswick. New Jersey finally had been colonized in earnest after the English conquest when Dutch farmers crossed the Hudson to Bergen County and their children and the children of farmers on Staten Island and Long Island cleared lands farther west in the Raritan Valley. At this time they had no religious organization at all other than the infrequent visits of Bergen County pastor Guiliam Bartholf, who had begun as a comforter-of-the-sick but had eventually, as the earnest request of his flock, gone to the Netherlands for ordination. Bartholf was thus the first minister actually produced by the Hudson Valley Dutch, and his point of view was very different from that of the pastors recruited in the Netherlands by the Classis of Amsterdam. He understood how the spiritual needs of frontier farmers differed from those of city burghers, and supported Frelinghuysen unreservedly in the controversies which followed.

For Frelinghuysen was controversial from the beginning. He

was zealous and blunt, criticizing his colleagues before they had a chance to get acquainted, and sometimes gave offense by using Pietist technical language for describing religious experiences to persons not familiar with it. Thus he antagonized the ministers of New York City even before he reached his parish by his impatience with what has been called their "calcified orthodoxy."[4] As a matter of fact, the tradition built up by Selyns was far from calcified, but it was the very different urban tradition which identified doctrinal orthodoxy with civic — now ethnic — identity and discouraged excessive zeal which threatened to disrupt the community.

Frelinghuysen's pietistic ardor immediately disrupted his new parish for, in an effort to create church discipline where none existed, he set up strict standards for admission to the Lord's Supper and applied them to exclude some substantial farmers whose neighbors considered them pillars of the congregation. The resulting controversy, which created lasting local bitterness and ranged most of the lower Hudson Valley ministers on one side or the other in a pamphlet war, earned Frelinghuysen a rebuke for contentiousness from the Classis of Amsterdam. It would be interesting to know the ethnic origins and community status of those who supported and opposed Frelinghuysen; it appears that his backers were the more numerous small farmers, but no genealogical evidence has yet been assembled to suggest what folk religious traditions they may have inherited.

In the meantime, Frelinghuysen's supporters responded to his powerful preaching. The traditional Dutch urban sermon was a carefully reasoned piece of Biblical exegesis with little direct practical application, intended for townsmen with a fair amount of education and strong unwritten standards of social behavior. Frelinghuysen, speaking to a heterogeneous rural audience, many of whom were barely literate, started off with a text and promptly applied it explicitly to his hearers' everyday experience. He went beyond right behavior to the emotional motivation of morality, and used every device of rhetoric to arouse his hearers to an over-whelming awareness of their sinful condition, so that they might be even more overwhelmed by the power of God's grace. This technique, part of the German folk tradition and quite familiar in the eastern Netherlands, had been particularly appropriate to circumstances in Frelinghuysen's former parish near the North Sea, which during his pastorate had been struck by the hand of God in the form of a devastating flood. The farmers of New Jersey no longer feared Indian massacre, but sermons derived from such experiences were certainly closer to the hardships they still suffered than the exercises in logic suitable for city worshipers.

Frelinghuysen's success with this approach soon attracted the attention of his English-speaking colleagues in New Jersey, particularly a fiery young Presbyterian named Gilbert Tennant. Tennant's father, William Tennant, was training candidates for the ministry at his famous "Log College" in Neshaminy, Pennsylvania, at a time when most denominations insisted that seekers after ordination make the lengthy, costly, and dangerous trip back to their homelands. Frelinghuysen, seeing the great need of the Dutch Reformed for pastors, entirely agreed with the Tennants that pastors for America should be trained in America for American conditions, and went so far as to participate in ordinations later declared illegal by the Classis of Amsterdam — which embroiled him in yet another controversy. In the meantime, Gilbert Tennant borrowed Frelinghuysen's preaching technique of direct emotional appeal, and succeeded in arousing great enthusiasm in his own congregation. When the evangelist George Whitefield, who had learned a similar approach from the Moravians in Georgia, toured the colonies in 1740, the fire already kindled in New Jersey exploded into the movement known as the Great Awakening, the first of the major American revivals.

These developments shocked and alarmed members of Frelinghuysen's congregations who, having inherited the urban Dutch tradition, feared the disruptive effects of excessive religious ardor; as a result, some of these churches split outright. Most of the controversy concerned the wider issue of the organization of the American church. Had it reached the point at which it needed an American governing body, as Frelinghuysen and his supporters contended, or should the purity of its doctrines be protected by continued subjection to the Classis of Amsterdam? The American faction wanted to form an informal governing body called a *Coetus*, following a tradition which had succeeded in the Pietist wing of the Frisian Reformed Church; the faction supporting the authority of the Classis of Amsterdam took the name of *Conferentie*. The Coetus was finally formed in 1747 and organized itself as a governing body in 1754, but the Conferentie refused to accept its existence for another generation.

Frelinghuysen spread his influence not only by his own preaching and writing — he was one of a few Dutch preachers who, like the New England divines, published their sermons in both the

Netherlands and America — but by training candidates for the ministry and by siring what should have been a pastoral dynasty. All five of his sons became ministers and both of his daughters married domines. Unluckily for this hope, two of the sons died at sea while returning from the Netherlands after being ordained — a circumstance which turned the family even more in favor of American ordination — and two others died all too soon after assuming their pastoral duties. It is from one of these sons that the still prominent Frelinghuysen family of New Jersey is descended.

The eldest son, Theodorus Jr., became pastor at Albany in 1745; he remained there for 14 years and proved to be as much a son of thunder as his father. His predecessor in Albany, Petrus Van Driessen, had personified the tradition of urban orthodoxy, and the call to young Frelinghuysen coincided with the coming to power in the city of that new faction of affluent burghers created by Governor Cosby and supported by the general merchants and master artisans. It is interesting that among the leaders of this faction were at least two families — the doubly intermarried Douws and Gansevoorts — whose grandparents had been moving spirits in the stubborn little Lutheran congregation of the 1680s. Young Volkert Douw, later to be Mayor and to hold offices in the new State of New York, was so pious that in 1744 he quite disgusted gentlemanly tourist Dr. Alexander Hamilton. It is easy to see why he and others like him became staunch supporters of the younger Frelinghuysen, and also why the fur-trading patricians, already at odds with these ambitious new-comers in civic affairs, would have found it difficult to stomach their new minister's enthusiasm.

This tension finally erupted in open schism during the French and Indian War, when Frelinghuysen's zeal manifested itself in opposition to all things Anglican (always excepting his Anglican wife) and in attempts to maintain strict moral discipline among young people attracted by English ways. The dispute was marked by practical jokes of the sort that had punctuated Everardus Bogardus' compaign against Kieft and the elder Frelinghuysen's controversies; one of these, reported and misunderstood by a British visitor, gave rise to an erroneous tradition that Freling-huysen was driven away from his Albany charge and died of a broken heart. In fact, like his father, he was too stubborn to take even a broad hint too seriously, but he did go to the Netherlands on business for the Coetus, and was drowned in a shipwreck while returning in 1759. His successor, Domine Eilardus Westerlo, a brilliant young divine from the University of Groningen, was a diplomat in the tradition of Grotius and managed to reconcile the factions within a year of his arrival; the community was so grateful that the Common Council presented him with the freedom of the city in 1762.

Changes brought by the same war finally convinced the New York City consistory that it was necessary to give way on the question of English services. In 1763 a call was accordingly extended to the Reverend Archibald Laidlie, a Scot who had been serving a Dutch Reformed congregation at Flushing in the Netherlands; he was to preach in English on Sunday afternoons. The consistory also voted to have prepared and published English translations of the liturgy, the Heidelberg Catechism, and the Psalter. The last was undertaken by Evert Byvank, a member of the congregation, but when he could not complete the complex task of fitting an English translation of Dathenus' not-always-literary Dutch translation of the French version of Marot and Beza to the beloved but metrically difficult Genevan tunes, the consistory called in a professional church musician, Francis Hopkinson of Philadelphia. He adapted the standard Anglican Psalter of Tate and Brady to the tunes, adjusting them a bit where necessary, and the resulting volume was published in 1767. The consistory went to great lengths and expense to have it look as much as possible like the Psalters the Hudson Valley Dutch had been using, even importing music type from the Netherlands and retaining the archaic but familiar diamond-shaped notes and clef system of these volumes. But after all this effort they found it difficult to sell the edition of 2,000 copies, partly because the price was high but also because outside of New York City the language problem was only beginning to arise and most of the numerous rural churches founded during the eighteenth century continued to have Dutch services for at least another generation. In 1774 the consistory used the precious music type again to print a volume of four-part settings of the Psalm tunes, arranged by a now unknown musician in imitation of a 1759 harmonization from the Netherlands. This hints of a persistent tradition of musical sophistication among the New York City Dutch, the existence of which has not even been suspected.

In 1771 the warring factions of Coetus and Conferentie finally came to an accommodation. Much of the credit must go to the diplomacy of John H. Livingston (a great-grandson of Robert

Livingston), who went to the Netherlands to study for the ministry — the last American candidaté to do so. He discussed the
situation in the Hudson Valley, which had been much misunderstood, with members of the Classis of Amsterdam and helped to
devise a compromise proposal which he brought back to America
after his ordination. Then he engineered its passage by a special
convention at which both sides and the "Neutral Brethren" — now
including Albany — were represented. The final settlement established an American governing body, but accepted without change
the traditional statements of doctrine and Church government.
The outbreak of the Revolution four years later, and of the
French Revolution several years after that, then cut off regular
communication with the Netherlands for a generation, leaving
Livingston, Westerlo, and Frelinghuysen's grandson Dirck Romeyn
on their own to lead the transition into the Reformed Church in
America. Their task was made harder by the fact that the compromise was very reluctantly accepted where bitterness had run
deep, particularly in New Jersey, for that bitterness continued to
be a factor in local disputes — and has not been entirely forgotten
in the twentieth century.

Thus the Dutch Reformed Church, which after the English
conquest became the principal institution embodying Dutch ethnic identity, was anything but homogeneous. It reflected the
theological controversies imported from the homeland, but far
more the diversity of folk religious traditions that the settlers
brought with them. Incompatible traditions of how to behave in
and out of church and how to respond to the pastor's message
probably created more tension than did controversies over points
of theology. Factional differences within the community were
also reflected in the church, and vice versa, for the Church was
simply one embodiment of the commune to whose traditions,
customs, and privileges all Dutchmen were preeminently loyal. It
is therefore especially important that the religious history of the
Dutch, like that of early Americans generally, be studied not only
from the pulpit but also from the pews which were its focal point.
This shift in the center of gravity has been considered evidence of
the adjustment of the Dutch, as of the colonists in general, to
American conditions. But it was also a tradition brought from the
Netherlands, where wealthy burghers and pious boers alike allowed
the Calvinist national establishment to go only so far in changing
their fathers' traditions of duty to God.

7

The Dutch Revolt

THE DUTCH tradition of revolt was first and foremost a tradition of fighting in defense of communal privileges, or "liberties." This, of course, determined the Dutch understanding of the meaning of liberty, which was primarily a common possession of the people of a community, and only by extension the particular share of those common privileges exercised by individuals. The "liberties of Englishmen" — defined by Magna Carta, denied by the Stuart kings, and fought for by seventeenth-century Parliaments — were entirely outside the Dutch frame of reference. Parliament itself, like the States-General, was a representative body, but there the resemblance ended, for their High Mightinesses were as a group the sovereigns of the Netherlands, while Parliament was still defining its own identity by striving to limit the sovereignty of the king. Such documents as the English Bill of Rights of 1691 could have little meaning for Netherlanders, whose existing local traditions were customarily altered by a grant of new privileges or by force — exerted either from below in the form of riots or from above in the form of revocation of privileges. Invasion of their liberties by foreign military power was more likely than anything else to drive the Dutch to fight; when it included intrusion upon those particular liberties protecting their religion, the Eighty Years' War proved it was almost impossible to get them to stop fighting.

In this context, it becomes clear that the Dutch colonists were unlikely to react strongly to many of the infringements upon their liberty which provoked the English colonists to revolt, but that there were other forms of interference which could drive them to dogged resistance. And so it proved. With a few exceptions, Dutch colonists were conspicuous by their absence from the long chain of events by which the New York Assembly developed into a provincial Parliament by opposing the King's governors. Dutchmen, of course, sat in the Assembly — Albany County's representatives throughout the colonial period were Albany Dutchmen, with five Dutchmen from Schenectady — and supported whichever faction seemed most likely to back their local interests, but they did not become leaders. The only issue that particularly exercised them, over which they waged a long and ultimately successful delaying action, was Governor Burnet's 1721 attempt to tax their illegal trade with Canada out of existence.

Since many of the wealthiest and most powerful merchants and landowners in the colony were Dutch, it was to be expected that some of them would be appointed to the Governor's Council. As the eighteenth century progressed, the persons so chosen were among the most assimilated Dutchmen in the colony, and they never represented a coherent "Dutch interest" because no such interest existed. Nevertheless, their behavior as individuals shows some Dutch characteristics, particularly their preeminent concern with their own commercial interests. Peter Schuyler's power in the province, as in Albany, was derived from his unique position in Indian affairs. When, as President of the Council, he became acting governor in 1719 between Governor Hunter's departure and Governor Burnet's arrival, he immediately appointed his relatives Mayors of New York and Albany and was suspected of intending to dissolve the Assembly, which the authorities in London quickly forbade him to do. Adolph Philipse, the leader of the faction of which Schuyler was a member, was a Dutch merchant-landowner who saw the government primarily as an instrument to be used in the interests of his class, which prompted Governor Burnet to remove both him and Schuyler from the Council. Rip Van Dam, a New York merchant who similarly served as acting governor in 1731, between the death of Governor Montgomerie and the arrival of Governor Cosby, became entangled with the latter in a lawsuit over the perquisites of office which developed into a major conflict between the governor and the faction headed by Lewis Morris. Finally, Cosby suspended Van Dam from the Council so that he should not be eligible to be acting governor again.

Direct conflict arose between a considerable group of Dutch colonists and an English governor during King George's War. The

War of the Austrian Succession broke out in Europe in 1740, but France and England were drawn into it only at second hand by their alliances with Austria and Prussia respectively, and it did not spread to the colonies until 1744. The Albany fur traders wanted to continue their policy of neutrality, but after French Indians massacred the settlers at Saratoga and Hoosac, neutrality became decidedly unpopular. Governor George Clinton (the first of that name), who believed that the Albany fur traders were using their influence with the Iroquois to hamper his efforts to get them to take up the war hatchet against the French, decided that their role in Indian affairs must be ended and they must be removed from power in the city.

For the first time in a century it was possible even to consider excluding the "old patrician" Albany traders from the official conduct of Indian affairs. Their trade monopoly had been ended for a generation, and the founding of Oswego in 1727 had permitted others to compete with them, although the Albanians themselves promptly sent agents to the new post. Furthermore, a young Irishman named William Johnson, who had settled in the Mohawk Valley, had developed a talent for meeting the Indians on their own ground, which secured him influence with them comparable only to that of Arent Van Curler and Peter Schuyler. Johnson was a nephew of Admiral Peter Warren, a British naval hero whose marriage to an heiress of the powerful De Lancey family made him important in provincial affairs. Johnson came to the Mohawk Valley as agent for Warren's lands, but he soon acquired a vast estate of his own from the Indians and, after the death of the mother of his three white children, he cemented his relations with them further by making Mohawk Molly Brant the mistress of his household. This developing confidence incensed the Albany merchants, who were taken aback indeed when in 1746 Clinton removed them from their time-honored position as Indian Commissioners and installed Johnson in their place.

But this was only the beginning of Clinton's attack on the Albany traders. In 1747 he replaced Mayor Cornelis Cuyler, whose family were leaders in the Montreal trade, with silversmith Jacob C. Ten Eyck. In the same year, no less than three other Ten Eycks were elected to the Common Council, and the "new patrician" faction created by Cosby swept into power, not to be ejected until 1770. Clinton also appointed members of this faction to administrative offices, such as the combined clerkship of Albany city and Indian affairs created by Robert Livingston. But Clinton's appointee, Albany merchant and alderman Harme Gansevoort, was soon challenged in the courts by Peter Wraxall, who had been appointed to the same offices by authorities in London. Wraxall claimed that Gansevoort had purchased the office illegally, but since this was universal eighteenth-century practice it did not prevent the judges from finding in Gansevoort's favor. An eventual compromise left Gansevoort as city clerk and Wraxall, who had become a friend of Johnson's, as Indian secretary, but the whole incident increased friction between Johnson and the Albany Dutch.

In the meantime, King George's War had given way to a breathing spell rather than a peace, for incidents between French and English in North America (and India) continued without interruption until the outbreak of the French and Indian War in 1754, which preceded by two years its European counterpart, the Seven Years' War (1756-63). Most of these incidents were in the Ohio Valley, including George Washington's expedition which surrendered at Fort Necessity, so that the first British army under General Braddock was dispatched to that area through Pennsylvania in 1755. In the meantime the French had built a large stone fortress at Ticonderoga, in the style established by Louis XIV's famous military engineer Vauban. From this fort in 1755 advanced an army under Baron Dieskau which was defeated at the southeast end of Lake George by a combined force of New York troops and Indians under William Johnson, who thereby earned the title of baronet.

The challenging presence of Ticonderoga made the Hudson Valley once again the cockpit of America, for it was obvious that nothing but a formal siege by a large professional army would capture this bristling fortress — one of four which the French had built, the others being at Louisbourg and Frontenac, the front and back gateways of Canada, and at Quebec. Therefore, where Leisler's expedition had been a fur-traders' raid, and those of 1709 and 1711 little more, those to come were by British armies experienced in European wars, and almost as much invasions of the Hudson Valley as they were of enemy territory. In 1755 one last intercolonial expedition, commanded by Governor William Shirley of Massachusetts and largely manned from New England, set off for an unsuccessful attack on Niagara. The following year British redcoats began massing at Albany, accompanied by large levies of provincial troops, creating an army far larger than had ever assembled before in America.

New York contributed some soldiers to this provincial army, and Dutch merchants were active among its suppliers. Some of the merchants of New York and Albany held important contracts, as did the Cuyler family of both cities, which provided some supplies for the Niagara expedition and then lost heavily when the French captured Oswego and destroyed the stores. Most of the big British army contracts went to merchants in London and their New York correspondents, but subcontracts for procuring such commodities as flour, forage, and beef on the hoof had to be let to local merchants with contacts in the countryside. The need for these food-stuffs brought unprecedented prosperity to the Dutch farmers, who found other sources of profit in selling horses and wagons to the army. Artisans found employment building temporary winter shelters for the soldiers and bateaux for river and lake transportation, and many bateauxmen and teamsters were needed to move men and goods to their destination.

For Albany, the experience was overwhelming. The population of the city was perhaps 3,000; that of the county — the entire settled area north of Kingston, including the Mohawk Valley — about 17,500. By comparison, there were 13,000 people in New York City (half as many as in Boston or Philadelphia), and about 96,750 in the whole colony. The British army assembled in 1758 numbered 6,000 redcoats and 9,000 provincial auxiliaries; when the inevitable camp followers are added, it is probable that this force exceeded the population of the entire county. The British officers and some of their men, at one time to the total of 1,400, were quartered in the burghers' homes; the remainder lodged in tents and barracks in the fields around the city. The provincial troops camped on the east side of the river, around the Van Rensselaer manor house of Fort Crailo, on the curb of whose well tradition relates that Dr. Richard Shuckburgh sat to write "Yankee Doodle." This tradition has been disproved, but the well is still there in the yard of Fort Crailo (now a museum illustrating the eighteenth-century Dutch way of life) and it is perhaps not necessary to detect the actual imprint of the satiric British surgeon's breeches to appreciate it as a symbol of an important step in the emergence of American identity.

The Albany Dutch hardly knew what to make of this friendly

invasion. Some of them, especially the young people, welcomed the soldiers and fraternized with them socially, attending
the plays put on by the officers — and in the case of at least one
patrician young lady, trusting not wisely but too well in a colonel's
promise of marriage. Others, particularly the older burghers, were
shocked by such goings-on, both in their own right and as evidence
of erosion of Dutch identity. Domine Frelinghuysen added fuel
to the fire by his thunderous denunciations of immoral behavior,
in particular one play, a sexy farce in which the representation of
women's parts by men, in the absence of actresses, did not strike
the Dutch as funny. He also fulminated against the Anglican
Church, which for the first time in the city's history (because of
the presence of British officers) boasted a congregation socially
equal or even superior to the domine's own. All this was observed
by a precocious little girl named Anne McVicar, the daughter of a
Scottish officer who was treated with great kindness by the
Albany Dutch women, particularly the childless Madam Margaretta
Schuyler. Fifty years later — when she had become the mother of
twelve children, the mistress of a school for girls in Scotland, and
a student of Scottish folklore — the then Mrs. Grant wrote a book
about her childhood experiences in Albany, centered on the
sterling character of Madam Schuyler, which despite the defects
of memory and the limitations of a child's point of view, creates
an astonishingly vivid and accurate picture of the Albany Dutch
in this difficult period of transition.

While the British army was still organizing itself in 1757, the
French took the offensive, besieging Fort William Henry on the
site of Johnson's victory, and ambushing with great loss a relieving
force under Colonel Ephraim Williams (whose will provided the
founding bequest of Williams College). Much of the garrison was
massacred after it surrendered. The next year General James
Abercrombie attacked Ticonderoga with 15,000 men. After the
death in a skirmish of his able and popular second-in-command,
Lord Howe, Abercrombie made the mistake of ordering his
infantry to charge before the artillery was ready to blast a path
for them. With incredible bravery the Highlanders rushed into the
trap of entangled trees the French had felled before their en-
trenchments and pressed forward in the face of withering fire;
two-thirds of the Black Watch regiment were killed or wounded
before they were permitted to withdraw and return to Albany.
Then, for anticlimax, General James Wolfe took Quebec, the

French called in their frontier garrisons, and in 1759 — the "Annus Mirabilis" when it seemed that nearly every day brought a new British victory in some part of the world — General Jeffrey Amherst marched into Ticonderoga without a battle. The next year he captured Montreal, and the army transferred its base there, the 10,000 redcoats moving in triumph up the Mohawk and down the St. Lawrence to overawe the former French Indians with the massed spectacle of British power. For the Hudson Valley Dutch the war was over.

The Albany Dutch were left to pick up the pieces with a mixture of relief and regret. With the soldiers went the horde of sutlers and contractors whose competition had irritated the Albany merchants to the limits of their patience. They had defended themselves in the traditional manner of a Dutch commune, entrenching themselves behind their civic privileges and using them as weapons. Englishmen so unfortunate as to be haled into the Albany courts complained that it was impossible to get a favorable verdict from an Albany jury, and the city assessors deliberately tried to tax the newcomers out of existence. One of them described this incident:

> The good people of Albany has taxed our new merchants smartly, they have only made 4 of them pay a hundred pounds the 12th part of the taxes of this city — the merchants deneyed paying the tax, they distrained their goods, the merchants petitioned the Gen'l [Amherst] that as followers of the army they were oppressed by the Albanians, they have not yet rec'd an answer — the mayor said in the street, he thought to resign his mayorship, but he would keep it one year to pleague the Irish — well said, Mr. Mayor [Sybrant Van Schaick].[1]

But with the transients went all the army trade from which the Albanians had profited and enough of the Scots and Scotch-Irish merchants became permanent residents to organize a Presbyterian church in 1761 and two years later erect an imposing Georgian house of worship.

Furthermore, bitterness left over from incidents of the war was perpetuated and exacerbated by some long-drawn-out lawsuits, fought obstinately by tactless Englishmen who settled in the city and disregarded the ill opinion of their Dutch neighbors. General John Bradstreet, the hero of the capture of Fort

Frontenac in 1758 and British Quartermaster General, became involved in an acrimonious contest with the Dutch Reformed Church over damages for the use of the church pasture by the troops. As part of his case, Bradstreet proposed to attack the church's title to the land by challenging the legality of the city charter; his own counsel advised him this was going too far, but the Albanians of course heard of it — Bradstreet was choleric and anything but discreet — and were incensed. At the same time William Marsh, another English appointee, challenged Harme Gansevoort's claim to the office of city clerk. Marsh was irascible and supercilious, and on his first appearance before the Albany Mayor's Court he deliberately insulted it by taunting its members with their Dutch heritage and accusing them of inherent disloyalty to the King. Acquaintance with Bradstreet and Sir William Johnson only reinforced his arrogance, which provoked the Albanians to fight back with every possible legal maneuver and delaying tactic until after four years he finally won a decision awarding him the office on a technicality. The Albanians, however, refused to allow him to exercise it, insisting that he appoint a respected Albany lawyer of Johnson's faction as his deputy.

In the midst of these irritating incidents, local factional alignments were shifting. The new patricians, who had been in power for nearly a decade when the army came to Albany, had begun to divide among themselves. Some of them, including Mayor Sybrant Van Schaick, found it to their advantage to do business and cooperate politically with Sir William Johnson. Others, led by Volkert P. Douw and Harme Gansevoort, wanted nothing to do with him. The fur-trading old patricians, being out of power, were quietly throwing their support to whichever of these factions appeared to forward their advantage at the moment. This appeared to create openings for ambitious plebeians like Abraham Yates, a shoemaker turned lawyer who sought election to the Assembly in 1761 when the two new patrician incumbents fell out with each other. Yates believed he had considerable support as a dark horse, but a few days before the election the incumbents made up their quarrel and the intrusive plebeian was frozen out.

Yates' campaign introduced into Albany a new feature in New York politics, the organized party in which professional politicians rely for their power on the votes of a body of independent electors held together by issues. Previously, provincial politics had been conducted by gentlemen who based their political power on their wealth and social position, and regarded as a formality the often uncontested elections by a limited electorate over which they had many means of control. But as settlers came into the province from New England, where voters expected to think for themselves and vote their own minds, the Assembly opposition, led by the Livingston family, saw an opportunity to build an additional base of power. Working out its technique primarily among non-Dutch voters in the southern part of the colony, it won control of the Assembly in 1761, when Abraham Yates sought to be its candidate to win Albany County away from the influence of Johnson and the faction organized by his uncle's brother-in-law, Lieutenant Governor James DeLancey.

Of course the Livingston party did not rely entirely on the personality and appeal to humbler voters of the plebeian Yates to win support among the Albany Dutch with their cherished patrician tradition — in fact, the reelected Assemblymen were also Livingston supporters. Some Albany patricians were related to the Livingston family. Some old patricians hated Johnson as a competitor in the fur trade, and a number of new patricians hated him because they owned land in the Mohawk Valley where his influence was all but supreme. Furthermore, before the war the Livingston faction had won the adherence of zealous Dutch Calvinists, including Domine Frelinghuysen, by its fight against permitting the Anglican Church to dominate King's College (now Columbia), the colony's first institution of higher learning. The party eventually lost this battle, but remained opposed to any extension of the Anglican establishment, thus securing the support of many Dutch Reformed. As a result of this controversy, the Dutch Reformed Church refused the offer of a theological chair in the new college and founded an institution of its own in New Jersey, Queen's College (now Rutgers) at New Brunswick.

In the meantime, the Dutch-descended merchants of New York City were becoming increasingly dissatisfied with imperial trade policies, although they had long since learned the English language and considered themselves completely assimilated and loyal subjects of the British empire. The war had brought them unprecedented prosperity, which gave way to depression when the military forces stationed in the city were transferred to the West Indies in 1761. It also brought to the attention of British officials some aspects of New York commerce which the merchants would have preferred to keep to themselves, particularly their extensive smuggling trade with Holland. Tea, gunpowder, guns for the Indians, sailcloth, and linen were still much cheaper in Amsterdam than in London, and ships sent to the West Indies loaded as much of their return cargo at Curacao as at the British islands — and the irregular coast line around New York offered many inlets where such cargoes could be unloaded before the ships came to the attention of customs officials. But Governor Charles Hardy began to suppress this trade in 1757, and after the war the general's tightening of imperial trade regulations made it clear that such irregularities would no longer be so easily tolerated.

The Sugar and Stamp Acts then struck the colonies a double blow. The Sugar Act bore especially hard on New York, for the colony imported quantities of sugar and molasses from the West Indies as raw materials for its refining and distilling industries — and four out of five of the principal sugar refiners were Dutch families. The merchants not hit by the Sugar Act were hit by the Stamp Act, which taxed the principal documents used in commercial transactions. It is therefore not surprising that the Stamp Act Congress was called by and held in New York, or that three out of five of the colony's delegates — all leading New York merchants — were descended from prominent Dutch families. The city also quickly organized a formidable body of Sons of Liberty, which resisted the landing of the stamps and mobbed some British officials.

The Huguenot DeLancey family, which had previously encouraged mob violence in New York City as a political weapon, actively promoted the activities of the Sons of Liberty at this time. Some of the members of the Sons were certainly Dutch artisans, and its activities were certainly compatible with the Dutch custom of plebeian unrest, often prompted by dissident patricians. Its leadership, however, and probably much of its membership was not Dutch, and its tactics cannot be ascribed primarily to Dutch tradition. One of these leaders, Isaac Sears, explained the silent connection with the DeLanceys, and doubtless with later patrician Patriots, in this way:

> His not associating at our Meetings, I excused on the following Account, — That as his Family and Connections were superior to any of those that assembled on those Occasions: Every Thing that should have been there transacted would have been principally imputed to his Influence; and if

we had failed in our Attempt, he would have been the first Victim: which, I thought was a Burthen that we could not reasonably impose upon him.[2]

The reaction of the Dutch in Albany offers an interesting comparison with that of those in New York. Although 48 Albany merchants promptly signed a protest against the Stamp Act, at first they seem to have paid little further attention to it, perhaps regarding it as one more trade regulation to evade. Then in January 1766, after their Livingston-faction delegates returned from the Assembly with news of the events downriver, it apparently occurred to Albanians to use this issue as a weapon in their local disputes. The Albany Sons of Liberty, who at this time included many young men from new patrician families, demanded that several merchants of the pro-Johnson faction (some Dutch and some English) disclaim publicly all intention of becoming stamp collectors. All did so at once except postmaster Henry Van Schaack, who hesitated; his hesitation was interpreted as a refusal and the Sons of Liberty mobbed his suburban house one winter night. He was not at home, but they seized his sleigh, set it on fire, and drove it in flaming triumph to and through the city; it seems surprising that this did not start a general conflagration, but perhaps the snow on the roofs protected the houses. Both in its participants and its nature, this incident seems far more consonant with an Albany tradition of pranks by young patricians and the Dutch tradition of blunt practical jokes as weapons of political controversy than with the grim mob violence of the Sons of Liberty in New York, which included an incident similar in nature but apparently very different in tone, of the burning of the coach of a hated British official.

The Stamp Act and subsequent acts in restraint of trade incensed primarily the merchants; when nonimportation was developed as a weapon against these acts, the artisans soon found that it led to unemployment and insisted that it be relaxed. But the Quartering Act controversy of 1767 provoked general resistance in New York as in no other colony. One reason, of course, was that New York City had been designated the British army headquarters for North America, so that there were more troops in this colony than any other. But another was certainly that New York, above all the other colonies, had experienced occupation by the British army during the war and knew what it meant. So long as the troops purchased supplies from and spent their pay in the colony they were not unwelcome, but when it was asked to raise revenues for their support, the Assembly balked. Parliament thereupon passed an act restraining it from doing business if it did not comply, and the Assembly backed down. The following year, after an election in which the Livingston faction lost their majority, the Assembly again passed some anti-imperial measures, and the governor dissolved it. It is to be noted that in these years when they were struggling for power in the colony, both the Livingston and DeLancey factions supported anti-imperial measures whenever they thought it would gain them support among the people — indeed, there were times, as during the Stamp Act protest, when the DeLancey leaders favored more radical action than the Livingstons. The election of 1769 was hard fought as the Livingston party sought to regain its majority and the DeLancey faction to exclude it altogether. The latter were overwhelmingly successful; three members of the Livingston family were defeated at the polls and the fourth prevented from taking his seat on a technicality.

Leadership of what was left of the opposition, therefore, devolved upon Philip Schuyler of Albany, first elected in 1768. Schuyler was a grandson of Johannes Schuyler, whose career as a fur-trading patrician had been marked by his leadership of the raid on LaPrairie and the Schenectady massacre and his marriage to the widow of a prominent Leislerian; Philip Schuyler's career showed similar military and maverick characteristics. He early combined his military and mercantile interests by serving as a supply officer for the New York troops during the French and Indian War, and in that capacity became good friends with the irascible Bradstreet, who otherwise detested the Albany Dutch. This friendship went so far that in 1761 Schuyler went to England to settle Bradstreet's official accounts, and while he was gone Bradstreet advised Mrs. Schuyler to hire unemployed army laborers to build the beautiful Georgian Schuyler Mansion which still stands in downtown Albany. Schuyler was also a large owner of frontier lands at Saratoga (now Schuylerville), a personal friend of Governor Sir Henry Moore, and more acceptable to Sir William Johnson than any other Albany Dutchman. At the same time he was counted as a friend by the Sons of Liberty, although with Dutch prudence neither they nor he kept any written record of the extent of his knowledge of or involvement in their doings.

But for the time being there was not much this opposition

Major General Philip Schuyler, by John Trumbull.
Courtesy of The New-York Historical Society, New York City

could do; the victory of the De Lancey faction was complete. It was at this point that the De Lanceys began that movement toward supporting the Crown which eventually made them New York's Loyalists. In 1770 the new patricians were swept from the Albany administration, Mayor Volkert P. Douw being replaced by Abraham C. Cuyler, the 28-year-old son of the last fur-trading mayor. This extremely youthful age for this exalted position may indicate the overwhelming influence of the Cuyler family, but it may also suggest that the De Lancey faction had some difficulty in inducing any Albany Dutchman to accept the office from their hands. The other appointed officials included City Clerk Stephen De Lancey, imported from the downriver leadership, and a number of recently arrived British merchants; new patrician representation on the Common Council was also cut back to a minority. The new patricians thereupon laid low, attended to their business, and waited upon events, while into the vacuum rushed such ambitious plebeians as the Yates family.

The Yates family inherited from a seventeenth-century British soldier their name and some English characteristics, such as Abraham Yates' penchant for writing histories of events in which he participated, but all of them married Dutch wives and by this period they were fully adjusted to the Dutch tradition. Some of them, like Abraham Yates, began as Albany artisans, others had prospered in Schenectady; all of them were ambitious to become patricians, but they sought some other route than making a fortune in commerce. Abraham Yates' success as a professional politician helping to create the electorate of the common man — though rudely interrupted by his defeat in 1761 — showed them how. In 1763 Abraham Yates was elected to the Albany Common Council from the Third Ward, in 1771 his cousin Robert Yates won election from the First Ward, and in 1772 another cousin, Peter W. Yates, joined them from the Second Ward. But apparently three Yates upstarts occupying those venerable seats at once was too much for the new patricians, who challenged the validity of Abraham Yates' reelection in 1773. After hearing considerable evidence of improper influence on voters by both sides, the Common Council decided for Yates' new patrician opponent, and soon thereafter passed the city's first election code.

Such local conflicts, and the tensions arising from them, certainly had more impact on the Albany Dutch than the Boston Tea Party of 1773 and the Intolerable Acts of 1774, which inflamed

New England to the brink of revolt. The merchants of New York, however, recognizing the threat to their trade, refused to permit any tea to be landed. At the same time they recognized the challenge to their control of civic affairs presented by the increasingly well-organized — and secret — Sons of Liberty and Committees of Correspondence. When these radicals called for the election of delegates to the First Continental Congress, therefore, Dutch and English merchants joined to urge formation of a Committee of Fifty-One to organize resistance within the bounds of moderation. Chosen as chairman was Isaac Low, a brother-in-law of Abraham C. Cuyler, and among its members was a brilliant young Dutch lawyer named Peter Van Schaack, a brother of Henry Van Schaack and a cousin by marriage of Henry Cruger, the American-born and Dutch-descended mayor of Bristol, England.

This prudent moderation remained characteristic of New York City's response to the growing pressure for revolution until news arrived of the outbreak of fighting at Lexington. Immediately the Sons of Liberty plunged the city into a week of rioting — again entirely consistent with the inherited expectations of Dutch plebeians, although it is improbable that they were responsible for it. The British governor could not, and the city officials would not, restore order by military force, so the leading merchants called for the election of a new Committee of One Hundred on which the radicals had more representation. This unwieldy body sent delegates to the Second Continental Congress and more or less directed revolutionary activities in the city, but the various factions within the city for the most part effectively neutralized each other. The First Provincial Congress, replacing the Assembly, met in the city in the fall of 1775, thereby providing zealous Patriots with an outlet for their activity. For the most part, however, New York City Dutch merchants were willing to wait and see what the Revolution would bring.

Albany's response to the Battle of Lexington was rather different. No one rioted, but a Committee of Correspondence led by Abraham Yates flung off its veil of secrecy and called a general public meeting for May 1, 1775. The people gathered at the Third Ward market house, in the middle of what is now Broadway opposite the United States Post Office, and elected a Committee of Safety representing all shades of opinion from City Clerk Stephen De Lancey to Yates himself. A few days later this com-

mittee asked the 18 rural districts of the county to elect representatives to it, and selected delegates to the Provincial Congress.
When news arrived of the seizure of Ticonderoga by Ethan Allen
and his Green Mountain Boys, with the support of some
Connecticut troops under Benedict Arnold, a group of new
patricians demonstrated their revolutionary zeal independently by
canvassing the city for contributions toward their support.

In the meantime, the Continental Congress had selected
George Washington as commander in chief and appointed four
major generals, one of whom was Philip Schuyler. He was
directed to raise a "Northern Army" distinct from the forces
besieging the British in Boston, and to follow the route of 1759
and conquer Canada. This expedition, of course, had roots in New
York Dutch tradition much farther back than 1759, not the least
of which was that a Schuyler was in command of it. Schuyler
invited many of his friends among the younger Albany patricians
— both old and new — to serve as officers, and exerted his great
personal influence to resolve their disputes over rank and to
overcome their Dutch caution against committing themselves too
far too soon. He also drew on his credit and that of the Albany
merchants to assemble supplies, and only three months after
Lexington and six weeks after Schuyler's appointment, this last
Albany Dutch expedition against Canada marched out of the city
with the solemn blessing of Domine Westerlo and his congregation.
As Leonard Gansevoort, a member of the Committee of Safety,
described the scene to his brother Peter, who was already in the
field:

> General Schuyler has Yesterday been in the Dutch Church and desired
> the Prayers of the Congregation for himself and the Army under his
> Command which he received, and I sincerely lament that you were not
> present that you might have heard it. Mr. Westerlo's prayer was so very
> pathetic and so well adapted that he drew Tears from the Eyes of al-
> most all there present. May God grant that a happy Reconciliation take
> place upon Constitutional Principles and prevent the further Effusion
> of Blood.[3]

The Dutch, therefore, progressed to revolution by a different
route than the English colonists, but they arrived at the same
place. They entirely agreed with the English that their liberty was

in danger, but they defined liberty more in a sense of freedom from foreign tyranny than in the context of a struggle against the King and Parliament. Before the outbreak of the Revolutionary War, this feeling was strongest in the cities of Albany and New York. The burghers of Albany, who still controlled the city government, demonstrated Dutch resistance to invasions of civic privilege. The Dutch merchants of New York resented imperial policies which interfered with their illegal trade with the West Indies and the Netherlands. Artisans in both cities expressed their dissatisfaction in the tradition of strategically timed riots. Though the Dutch throughout the province welcomed the protection and profit offered by the British army, they feared its domination — and resented taxation for its support. Zealous Dutch Reformed pastors and laymen feared encroachment by the Anglican Establishment to the detriment of their tradition of toleration. For all these traditionally Dutch motives, Dutch colonists in America gave their support and their active assistance to the various revolutionary bodies, from the Sons of Liberty to the Continental Congress, which the English colonists created to carry their revolt into action.

8

The Siege of the Hudson Valley

THROUGHOUT the colonial period the Hudson Valley Dutch colonists' experience of warfare resembled that of their seafaring countrymen. They were attacked by small raiding parties of French and Indians, not so different from enemy privateers harassing trade, and they retaliated in kind, but never had any occasion to draw upon the long Netherlands tradition of extended siege warfare, developed to a fine art by Prince Maurice and William III. They had built palisades around their villages and drilled as a burgher guard, but they had never stood shoulder to shoulder on those walls, men and women side by side, and thrown any missile they could lay hands on at assaulting troops, as had the burghers of Leyden. They had suffered occasional interruptions of trade, but they had never eaten the last scrap of food and surrendered to avoid starvation only to be massacred, as had the burghers of Haarlem and Zutphen. They had been conquered by the English but they had never endured the revocation of their cherished privileges, as had the burghers of Ghent. They sometimes felt themselves threatened by English innovations, but they had never learned to encourage those whose strength was failing while guarding against subversion by those who did not want to fight at all, as had the burghers of Antwerp. They had seen the destruction of Indian war, but they had never been driven to cut the dikes and destroy their own homes to save their lives, as had the people of Holland and Zeeland. But when the Revolutionary War came to New York they had to do all of these things in one way or another, for the war amounted to a seven-

year siege of the Hudson Valley, to which the Dutch responded
with the stubborn steadfastness their ancestors had shown throughout their long history of sieges.

The war did not begin as a siege but with a raid into Canada
in the colonial fashion. By this time the logistics of such expeditions had been perfected, and Schuyler transported his army without difficulty to the head of Lake Champlain. There it began to
be plagued by disease, more fatal than fighting to most armies in
an age which understood neither the principles of contagion nor
the methods of mass sanitation. Nevertheless, it captured the
gateway fort at Saint John's on the Richelieu River in November
1775, and marched into Montreal soon afterward. A detachment
went on to Quebec to cooperate with the force led by Benedict
Arnold which had marched, with incredible hardship, through the
wilderness from Maine, but the combined assault on New Year's
Eve failed, and General Richard Montgomery, one of the ablest of
Schuyler's young officers, was killed. Still the little army im-
pudently besieged the stone walls of Quebec, fighting smallpox
and winter weather as gallantly as they did the enemy, until the
ice went out and Colonel Guy Carleton relieved the city with a
British fleet.

In the face of amphibious attack there was nothing for the
Americans to do but retreat, first to Montreal, then to the head of
Lake Champlain, then down the lake to Ticonderoga, where, eyes
glazed with fever, they looked back to Canada and defied the
British to come on. Schuyler, ill himself, had returned to Albany
to forward supplies — for the army needed everything — and Congress appointed General Horatio Gates to command the troops "in
Canada." Since these troops were for the foreseeable future in
Ticonderoga, however, and since both Gates and Schuyler were
jealous of their individual authority, this divided command was a
fertile breeding ground for jurisdictional disputes. The British,
meanwhile, advanced to the head of Lake Champlain, but they
could go no farther without vessels, which they set about building
with characteristic thoroughness. At the foot of the lake Benedict
Arnold, who had been·a sea captain before the war, imported ship-
wrights from New England and the race was on to build a navy
that could control the lake.

In the meantime the cannon from Ticonderoga, which Colonel
Henry Knox had sledded down the frozen Hudson and over the
Berkshires to Boston, had enabled Washington to drive the British

out of that city in March. An immigrant English artisan named Thomas Paine had written a pamphlet called *Common Sense* which convinced many ordinary people throughout the colonies that the time for peaceful reconciliation with the mother country had passed. In the long, hot June days the Continental Congress in Philadelphia debated the question of formal separation from England, and on July 2, 1776, it voted to approve the Declaration of Independence. The Declaration was read to the people of Philadelphia on July 4, and five days later, on July 9, it was adopted by the New York Provincial Congress.

The British fleet soon appeared off Sandy Hook, under the command of Admiral Lord Richard Howe and General Sir William Howe, younger brothers of the Lord George Howe who had been killed in Abercrombie's assault on Ticonderoga in 1758. Washington stationed his army on Long Island, where General Howe attacked and easily defeated his inexperienced soldiers. But a foggy night and a contingent of New England fishermen expert with boats enabled Washington to extricate his army by a retreat across the East River. When the British followed him to Manhattan, Washington abandoned New York City — then confined to the area below the present City Hall — and withdrew to Harlem Heights. There, on the site of the present Columbia University campus, his rear guard checked the British advance long enough to permit the rest of the army to retreat over King's Bridge at the north end of the island. Behind them, as the British marched into the city, someone started a fire, by accident or design, and most of Dutch New York went up in flames. The siege of the Hudson Valley had begun. Its consequences were foreseen at once by William Smith, an early Patriot leader who became a Loyalist partly because he feared the siege would destroy the liberty he cherished: "Poor N. York! To the general Foresight of the total Loss of Trade and her becoming by the Means of Hudson's River and her scanty Sea Coast, the Theater of this unnatural War, is in a great Measure to be imputed the Backwardness of Multitudes in adopting the common Principles of the Continent."[1]

For the moment, the British were intent upon capturing Washington and his army — "the fox," they called him after a bugler at Harlem Heights taunted the Continentals by playing a hunting "Tally Ho" instead of the signal for a charge. And the campaign of the fall of 1776 was in some respects not unlike a fox hunt. Washington's army retreated into Westchester, turned at

• Montreal

Valcour Island ✵
Oct. 11, 1776

Fort Ticonderoga •

• Skenesborough

• Oswego

• Fort Stanwix

Oriskany ✵
(Aug. 6, 1777)

Saratoga ✵
(Sept. 19 — Oct. 17, 1777)

Schenectady •

• Bennington

Schoharie •   • Albany
**MANOR OF
RENSSELAERSWYCK**

Fort Stanwix Treaty Line, 1768

• Kinderhook

Catskill •   • Claverack

**LIVINGSTON
MANOR**

• Kingston

**HARDENBERGH
PATENT**

• New Paltz

**BEEKMAN
PATENT**
• Poughkeepsie
• Fishkill

• Newburg
West Point •

**PHILIPSE'S
HIGHLAND PATENT**

**CORTLANDT
MANOR**

**PHILIPSE
MANOR**
• Tarrytown
• White Plains
• Yonkers
New York •
Long Island ✵
(Aug. 27, 1776)

New Brunswick •

New York at the
Time of the Revolution

- - - - - Present-day state lines

.... Boundaries of manors
and patents

✵ Battles

• Towns

bay, and checked the British advance at White Plains, then slipped across the Hudson and disappeared into New Jersey. The British fleet sailed up the river to reduce Fort Washington, on the Manhattan heights above the site of the present George Washington Bridge; the garrison of Fort Lee, across the river on the Jersey side, narrowly escaped. Then a force under Lord Cornwallis landed in New Jersey and pursued the "fox" from the Hudson to the Delaware in crisp December hunting weather. But the wily Washington dodged across the Delaware, taking the boats with him, and Cornwallis' advance guard of Hessian mercenaries settled down in Trenton to enjoy a German Christmas. It was their last revel, for that night Washington doubled back across the Delaware, surrounded the town, and awakened the merrymakers to a grim morning-after with the fire of his guns. A week later he defeated Cornwallis' main force at Princeton, and the hunter, suddenly finding himself the fox, turned tail and ran back across New Jersey to the protection of the British fleet. Washington followed deliberately and set up winter quarters at Morristown, and the Dutch farmers of New Jersey discovered what it meant to be caught with full barns between two hungry armies.

Overrun by first one army and then the other and finally left as a no man's land between them, Dutch New Jersey thus became the theater of a vicious guerilla war. When foragers swept through the countryside, seizing all the food and fodder they could find, making distinctions only in that they sometimes paid farmers whom they believed to be on their side and usually plundered those they believed to be on the other, it is hardly surprising that many Dutch farmers, especially those nearest to New York City, declared themselves to be Loyalists. Those nearer Morristown had the same inducement to declare themselves Patriots. But the situation was much more complex than this. The Jersey Dutch had been bitterly divided for two generations over religion, and, as has been pointed out, it is probable that this conflict was underlain by clashes of folk traditions from different regions of the Netherlands. There was in Bergen County a strong element from the southern Netherlands and another numerous group from the north, including a considerable contingent of fiercely independent Frisians, and as farmers it seems likely that rural parochialism was more familiar to them than the commercially motivated tolerance of the cities, but this requires further study.

At this point it can only be proven that in communities

whose Dutch Reformed churches had split into Coetus and Conferentie factions, or even into two congregations, members of the
Coetus group were very apt to become Patriots and supporters of
the Conferentie, Tories. It seems likely that loyalty to such abstrac-
tions as the Continental Congress or the Crown weighed much less
with them than the fact that, in the Dutch tradition, they were
fighting mad at their neighbors over religious doctrines, differences
in inherited ethnic traditions and local customs. Numbers of
Bergen County Dutchmen enlisted in Loyalist regiments, and
proved to be among the most valuable of the Royal American
troops. The corresponding bitterness against these men among
their former friends and neighbors was experienced by one of their
wives, Catherine Van Cortlandt of Morris County, who was driven
by ill treatment to join her husband, a Loyalist officer in New
York and eventually to settle with him in England. The Van
Cortlandts, in New Jersey as in New York, were members of the
landed gentry and therefore not typical Dutch Tories, but even if
the feeling against them included as much social and economic as
political resentment, it illustrates the extent to which bitterness
could go in Revolutionary New Jersey:

> Our dear children are again taken from school in consequence of the
> cruel insults they daily receive for the principles of their parents. . . .Many
> of our female neighbours have been here, but I find their visits are only
> to gratify curiosity and to add insult to our unremitted distress. One of
> them who lives across the river, whose family we took so much pleasure
> in relieving when friendless, made a return of gratitude yesterday by a
> humane speech. She said that formerly she always respected you and
> loved the ground over which you walked, but now could with pleasure
> see your blood run down the road. . . .The farmers are forbid to sell me
> provisions, and the millers to grind our grain. Our woods are cut down
> for the use of their army, and that which you bought and left corded
> near the river my servants are forbid to touch, though we are in the
> greatest distress for the want of it, as you may suppose when I assure you
> that our dear children have been six weeks without any other covering to
> their tender feet but woollen rags sewed round them to keep them from
> freezing.[2]

The military movements of 1776 effectually sealed off the
mouth of the Hudson, so that the people of the Hudson Valley
could neither export their produce nor import goods from all over
the world as they had been accustomed to do. Perhaps half the

population of the colony of New York lived in the part now occupied by the British army — and since eighteenth-century soldiers
were not the citizen-draftees or volunteers of today but dropouts
from society who could find no better employment or were
pressed into service by methods similar to the "crimping" of
sailors, such occupation was likely to be rough indeed. As if this
were not enough, the upper Hudson Valley — including a large
proportion of its Dutch inhabitants — had at the same time to
meet General Sir Guy Carleton's force poised to strike from the
north and an even deadlier threat from within. For the diverse
peoples of the upper valley were by no means all in favor of the
Revolution. The Scots and Irish tenants imported to the Mohawk
Valley by Sir William Johnson (who had died in 1774) remained
loyal to his heirs and to the Crown until Schuyler sent a body of
troops to seize their arms and Sir John Johnson and many of his
followers escaped to Canada. Schuyler, following in the footsteps
of his great-uncle Peter Schuyler, beseeched the Iroquois to stay
out of this white man's quarrel, but with Sir John urging them to
take up the hatchet once more for the British King, there was no
knowing how long they would remain neutral.

There were also tenants at odds with their Patriot landlords on
the Van Rensselaer and Livingston manors. In the tense first two
weeks of October 1776, when Carleton's little fleet on Lake
Champlain was reported to be ready to sail, the Livingston Manor
militia was constantly marching in search of Tories who "skulked"
in the woods, its effectiveness materially diminished by members
"more or less disaffected which renders our plans Commonly
Exposed before Executed."[3] When word arrived that Arnold's
tiny fleet had engaged Carleton's squadron at Valcour Island and
had gone down to gallant defeat, the Albany County committee
called out the militia to resist invasion. But many of the men from
Rensselaerswyck refused to march, gathering instead in the woods
in large armed parties. They were not eager to fight either with the
militia or with the Loyalist volunteers. One who was captured
explained their attitude thus: "that the people he met are friends
to the country but that they won't fight if they can help it, and
so agreed at said meeting; that the reason for not fighting for the
country is, that they will not be against the King."[4] The situation
remained tense until it became obvious that Arnold's defeat had
been a victory after all, for it was now too late in the season for
Carleton's army to advance.

This threat of subversion from within proved to contain an even greater danger the next spring, as rumors of another British invasion flew up and down the river. Early in May 1777, highly placed Patriots heard a report that the British fleet was approaching Peekskill. Perhaps in response to this report — or perhaps by spontaneous combustion after a rescue, and recapture by Patriots, of a group of Tories who had been arrested — the tenants of Livingston Manor arose in counter-revolution. But the report was false, the British troops never appeared, and the Tory tenants, without equipment or military experience, were quickly put down by the local militia, assisted by that of Dutchess County and neighboring Massachusetts. Subsequent investigation by the provincial Committee for Detecting and Defeating Conspiracies revealed that nearly all the tenants on Livingston Manor — most of whom were English or German, but some of whom were Dutch — had been concerned in this plot, and at the same time disgruntled tenants on lands owned by other members of the Livingston family in the Hardenbergh Patent west of the Hudson were also marching off to join the enemy. The Livingstons themselves, who clearly had no idea how three generations of shrewd dealings and out-and-out sharp practice had antagonized their tenants, were astonished to discover what a powder keg they had been sitting on, and, in fear for their lives, blamed the tenants for ingratitude. William Smith, Jr., the former Patriot leader who had been unable to accept independence and was under polite house arrest at the home of his Livingston in-laws, described the reaction of Lord of the Manor Robert Livingston III:

He did not utter a Sentiment which he did not contradict and frequently in express Terms, except his Execrations upon his Tenants — His Fears have driven him to Temerity. He exclaims agt. setting up any Governt. at this Juncture — Poor Gent — He says his Tenants owe him 10,000 pounds sterling — He can't bear the Thought that his Indulgences show that he has no Influence upon them — Much less that they are in such a Temper as to prevent him from riding about in his own Manor — and seeing no Safety but in their Expulsion hints his wishes that they may all be hanged and their children starved.[5]

Meanwhile in London, a British general named John Burgoyne turned his fertile imagination from writing plays to devising strategy, and convinced the ministry that a simultaneous invasion of the Hudson, Champlain, and Mohawk Valleys could not fail to bring the colonies to submission. He accordingly arrived in Canada in the spring of 1777 with 8,000 English and Hessian troops, ready to start where Carleton had left off. This time there was no spunky little navy to dispute the passage of Lake Champlain, and Burgoyne, his 8,000 men, and all their baggage cruised serenely to Ticonderoga, arriving at the beginning of July. American General Arthur St. Clair, who had only 2,000 inexperienced men to defend the sprawling white elephant of a fortress, designed for the intricate defensive tactics of the French professional army and stripped of its own armament for the siege of Boston, decided that he could not hold it, and on July 5 retreated. This move, however militarily advisable, shocked those who remembered how a comparably outnumbered French garrison had held the fort against Abercrombie in 1758. But the French victory had been very largely the result of Abercrombie's incompetence in the assault, and when Burgoyne's men succeeded in placing cannon on a nearby mountain which commanded the fort, St. Clair hastily extricated his army from the great stone walls which had suddenly become a trap, marching them off to join Schuyler and fight another day.

The loss of Ticonderoga discouraged the Continental Congress and many others, but it did not discourage the Hudson Valley Dutch, in whose hands, with the support of some Continental troops, the defense lay for the crucial next six weeks. As the invaders approached the settled areas, Schuyler on the upper Hudson and 28-year-old Colonel Peter Gansevoort on the upper Mohawk prepared a stubborn Dutch defense whose principal feature was an ingenious use of the forces of Nature to fight for them. They had no dikes to cut, so they set militiamen to cut down trees instead, obstructing with a fantastic tangle the few roads and the waterways. Where these ran through the marshy ground between the Hudson-Champlain and the Mohawk-Oneida watersheds, such obstructions created artificial swamps too wet for marching and wagons and not wet enough for boats. The invading armies, trying to build roads for their heavy cannon and baggage trains, churned the ground into soupy mud until Burgoyne's army literally bogged down in the 22-mile portage between Lake Champlain and Fort Edward on the Hudson River.

In the meantime a smaller force of British soldiers, Tories, and

Fort Stanwix; photograph of a model made in 1897. *Courtesy of the Gansevoort-Lansing Collection, the New York Public Library, Astor, Lenox and Tilden Foundations*

Indians commanded by Colonel Barry St. Leger besieged Gansevoort's post at Fort Stanwix, now Rome. When they demanded its surrender, Gansevoort invited his second-in-command, New York Son of Liberty Marinus Willett, to respond with a fluent oration, reserving for himself a silence which conveyed louder than words his determination to "defend this fort to the last extremity."[6] The Mohawk Valley militia, Dutch, English, and German settlers under General Nicholas Herkimer, marching to his aid, was ambushed by the Tories and Indians at Oriskany on August 6. The militia gave as good as it got in vicious hand-to-hand fighting between former neighbors and friends, but it was unable to reach the fort and General Herkimer received his death wound; the men returned to defend their homes.

The next night Willett sneaked through the enemy lines to seek help. When he reached Schuyler's camp, the main army was anxiously awaiting Burgoyne's advance, but Schuyler detached Benedict Arnold with 1,300 men to relieve Fort Stanwix. Arnold marched up the Mohawk with cautious haste, calling out the militia as he went and keeping careful watch against another ambush. When he approached the fort he tried psychological warfare. On the way he had captured a half-wit named Hon Yost Schuyler, whom the Indians regarded with the awe they accorded to anyone in his condition. Hon Yost was sent to St. Leger's Indians with a story about the size of Arnold's force designed to play on their superstitions. The ruse worked; the Indians fled and St. Leger, his soldiers, and the Tories had no choice but to abandon their siege and follow.

Because Colonel Gansevoort did not write his memoirs as did Willett, or become enshrined in local folklore by a heroic death as did Herkimer, it was not realized until recently how tight the siege was, and how much the success of the defense depended upon sheer Dutch stubbornness. As in Schuyler's army, the men came from several colonies, and most of them were not Dutch; their Dutch commanders designed Dutch strategies, however, and inspired them with Dutch determination not to give in. St. Leger and his troops, having dispersed the militia at Oriskany, brought up their cannon and settled down to a regular siege. The garrison had plenty of food, but was short of gunpowder. They therefore simply sat in silence as St. Leger's trenches closed in and British smiths converted four little mortars into howitzers to blast a hole through the earthen wall of the fort. The final assault was to have been delivered on the very day that Gansevoort and his garrison woke up to find that the British army had decamped. St. Leger's force never stopped until it got back to Canada; Arnold's made made sure it was gone for good and then returned to the main army, and the garrison of Fort Stanwix settled down to wait for the outcome of the rest of the campaign. In the Continental Congress, the news snapped John Adams out of his depression over the loss of Ticonderoga, so that he wrote to his wife, "Gansevoort has proven that it is possible to hold a fort."[7]

In the meantime, Albany Dutchmen and women tightened their belts and prepared for the worst. The tradition that Mrs. Schuyler set them the example by firing the grainfields at their Saratoga estate with her own hands is entirely in character for the people who cut their dikes. Back in Albany, refugees from the outlying districts poured into the city. The Committee met every

Drum captured from the British after the siege of Fort Stanwix, August 22, 1777. *Courtesy of the New York State Military Museum, State Capitol, Albany*

day, providing food and shelter for them, rounding up Tories, and sending them to secure places outside of the county. Domine Westerlo held daily services in the church to pray for deliverance from the hand of the invader. The burghers sent all the supplies they had to the army, including the lead weights from their window sashes. The Committee stood ready to sink the fleet of river sloops, owned in Albany for generations, as soon as the commanding general should give the word. Some patricians thought it wiser to send their womenfolk into the country, but Colonel Gansevoort's intrepid fiancée Catherine Van Schaick did not want to go.

Her letter as she left sums up both the mood in Albany and the spirit of the Dutch women:

> Now there semes to be no place for us to flee, but O I hope the Omnipotent God has left a Zoar for us to flee unto, out of the burning fire of War, as he did for Lot out of Sodom. I can [not] overcome a Reluctance of your leving me on so great a Hazard, as never to see me more. I have had hopes of seing you here, but now I must give up all. O when shall that hapy Period arive that we again shall meet, I hope in short, if not or never, may he that has laid the yoke on me help me to bear [the] burthen, then will the yoke be easy and the burthen Light, but now in my distress it is all dark and glomy before me. these are Mountains wich I cannot as yet ovelook, might I once see you if not, may I as often hear of you as posible, then I will have somewat to Comfort my distressed mind.[8]

The successful defense of Fort Stanwix was the one bright spot in a dark summer for the colonies. In the meantime, Sir William Howe drew off Washington's army from the Hudson Valley by attacking Philadelphia, where he won the battles of Brandywine and Germantown, forced the Continental Congress to withdraw to York, and occupied the city. Sir Henry Clinton delayed in New York, however, waiting to advance up the river until Burgoyne should emerge from the wilderness. It was no encouragement for the Dutch that in these tense days Congress superseded Schuyler by Gates. The importance of Gates' popularity among the New England militia, who flooded in after the sensational murder of Jane McCrea and the victory at Bennington of John Stark and the Green Mountain Boys, would have been hard for them to understand. Nor was the ensuing battle of Saratoga their battle, although New York troops fought bravely in it. Burgoyne was eventually overwhelmed, as was appropriate, by the united strength of the northern colonies. But Schuyler and the Dutch had done their part, and more than their part, considering their numbers, in stopping St. Leger and stalling Burgoyne for that crucial six weeks that gave New England time to realize the danger and get to the battle.

But Burgoyne himself pointed to the essential accomplishment of the Dutch when, explaining his failure to Parliament, he said: "Would the Tories have risen? Why did they not rise? . . . A critical insurrection from any one point to create division would probably have secured the success of the campaign."[9] After the events of

166 STUBBORN FOR LIBERTY

1776 it was entirely reasonable to assume that the thinly populated upper Hudson Valley would submit to a show of force as readily as had the much more densely settled area around New York, where the people not only acquiesced in military occupation and sold their harvests for British gold, but turned out in considerable numbers to form Loyalist regiments. And in fact, as the events on Livingston Manor proved, the mid-Hudson region was riddled with Loyalists ready to rise. Had British communications been better, holding the tenants in check for six months, the outcome would have been very different. Howe's not unintelligent maneuver to draw Washington's army into another theater of war succeeded. Clinton's puzzling foray into New Jersey (when hindsight insists he should have been sailing up the Hudson to assist the beleaguered Burgoyne) might have accomplished its presumable purpose of collecting an overwhelming force of Loyalists and setting in motion a domino process of counterrevolution, to conquer the rugged mid-Hudson region for him while his warships forced the crucial Highland forts.

But the Tories had shown their colors too soon, and the Dutch Patriots had them well under control; and Clinton finally started up the river too late to assist Burgoyne, who, contrary to all probability, was on the verge of surrender to a determined, half-disciplined army of militia. Clinton burned Kingston and the Livingston home at Clermont, but even with this encouragement the tenants were disarmed and powerless, and the shoals in the river made it dangerous for his warships to approach Albany, where the stubborn Dutchmen, not for a moment overawed, had the situation firmly under control. The nutcracker approach had seemed unbeatable, but the Hudson Valley Dutch were a hard nut to crack, and in the end it was their traditional resources for resistance that dealt with each problem as it came along and so — all unconsciously — took the greatest possible advantage of British lapses in timing and communication, which against a less determined people might not have proven fatal to their plan of invasion.

The Battle of Saratoga was the last major engagement in New York State, for the British shifted their theater of operations to the southern colonies. But the siege of the Hudson Valley was far from over; indeed it was just entering its most grueling stage. The British still held New York City, closing the river to commerce and forcing the Dutch to subsist as best they could on what they could grow, make, or bring in by wagon at great trouble and expense from other colonies almost as hard-pressed as their own. Dutch farmers continued to cultivate their fertile fields when the enemy let them, and although many farms in the Mohawk Valley were devastated by Tories and Indians and many in New Jersey were repeatedly ravaged by foragers from both armies, those in between still produced enough food so that no one in the Valley went hungry, and there was even some left over to send to Washington's army. Manufactured goods were another story, for the valley had relied on trade for these and had even fewer industries of its own than its neighbors. The Dutch mended their tools as best they could and wore out their clothes — and since one wag in New Jersey suggested that the Dutch women's ample petticoats be confiscated to clothe the ragged troops it seems they had a supply sufficient to last for several years. Their greatest need was for guns and ammunition, which they tried to make for themselves with little success, but these could fortunately be teamed in from the iron works and powder mills of Pennsylvania.

Thus sustained, the Dutch fought back against the enemies within. The Jersey Dutch spent all seven years of the war in a savage guerilla war of raids and reprisals against each other. Some of these raids included movements by one of the armies, but most of them were conducted by Patriot militia and Tory partisans defending their friends in their stone farmhouses or attacking their enemies in theirs. This was siege warfare on the individual level, and the militia on both sides developed it to a point that would have been worthy the attention of Prince Maurice. The highly individual character of this conflict is one of the possible indicators of a strong continuing Frisian tradition in this area, where personal animosities were clearly more important than community loyalty, in contrast to the attitude of the Dutch in Albany, Schenectady, and the rest of the upper Hudson Valley. They also made a fine art of spying and counterspying, aided materially by the fact that they spoke among themselves a language which neither British nor Continental officers understood; it is a measure of Major John Andre's imagination and effectiveness as Clinton's chief of intelligence that he made it his business to learn it. When they were captured, the Patriots unquestionably suffered more than the Tories, for the Continentals only had facilities to imprison a few of the most dangerous and usually released the rest on parole, but the British had no compunction about throwing anyone they suspected into the filthy, disease-ridden prison ships in New York harbor, where the unascertainable death toll is known to have been appalling. Such prisoners whose patriotism was determined by their religious beliefs must have felt themselves indeed martyrs in the tradition of their ancestors imprisoned by the Spanish Inquisition.

This guerilla war was most bitter in New Jersey and the adjoining corner of New York on the west bank of the Hudson below the Highlands, because it was territory not permanently occupied by either army, but was a source of supply for both. The Dutch of occupied Manhattan, Staten Island, and Long Island of course had no opportunity to fight in this way, even if they were not among those who made these counties strongholds of Loyalism long before the invasion. Those of Westchester were often involved in spying — it was from local traditions of this area that James Fenimore Cooper derived the materials for his first historical novel, *The Spy* — but since there was no Continental army near them, they were subject only to British foraging and had no support for extensive Patriot guerilla activities. It is also probable that preexisting religious disputes were less divisive in this region than in New Jersey, where the memory of Frelinghuysen and his contentious disciples was very much alive. Furthermore, in Westchester the great landlords, such as the Philipse family, were Loyalists, so tenants ambitious to own their own farms had good reason to lean toward the Patriot cause but not to lean too far within the observation of British foragers. After the war, when the Philipse estate was confiscated and sold, many of the purchasers were these tenants who had prudently preserved their farms by neutrality.

In the Mohawk Valley civil war was started by those Tories who had fled to Canada under pressure from their Patriot neighbors and returned in arms to retaliate in company with bands of Indian raiders. The moving spirit behind this campaign was the family of Sir William Johnson, to whom the majority of their Scots and Irish tenants remained loyal even to the sacrifice of their homes and lands. The Mohawks also, under the leadership of Molly Brant's brother, Joseph Brant, left their ancestral lands for Canada and then returned to ravage them. The Dutch settlers stayed on their farms and fought back, all of them as determined as 80-year-old Douw Fonda, who was finally scalped on his own doorstep. Fighting back was difficult because no one could tell where or when the raiders might strike next. Colonel Gansevoort's regiment, still stationed at Fort Stanwix, could therefore be of little help — to the intense frustration of its fire-eating young commander — and the militia had to depend upon themselves.

The opening engagement of this civil war was the Battle of Oriskany. After the siege of Fort Stanwix, the Tories and Indians did not return until the next year. Then they made up for lost time, burning Cherry Valley and ranging as far as the Wyoming Valley on the Susquehanna in Pennsylvania, where they committed the Wyoming Massacre on the site of Scranton. The following year the Patriots counterattacked, sending the Sullivan-Clinton expedition to destroy the Indians' base in the fertile Genesee Valley. Nevertheless, the Indians regrouped in Canada and retaliated in 1780 by destroying the settlements along Schoharie Creek. Another party penetrated to the Hudson at Catskill and kidnapped a number of Patriot leaders. Still another descended upon Albany, intending to abduct General Schuyler from his suburban mansion, but the attempt was frustrated by the General's ruse of shouting orders to a nonexistent troop of defenders while help came from the city. Tradition — again probably without foundation in fact — relates that a deep cut still to be seen in the stair rail of the mansion was made by a tomahawk flung at Schuyler's daughter Margaret as she fled up the stairs with her baby sister in her arms. There were also raids on frontier settlements in Ulster County and the Minisink Valley. These raids continued sporadically until the end of the war.

In the meantime Washington's army, having endured the winter at Valley Forge and driven the British out of Philadelphia, returned to the Hudson Valley to keep watch on the enemy in New York. First it made its headquarters at Morristown, as before, but after the discovery of Benedict Arnold's treasonous attempt to give West Point to the British, Washington moved his headquarters to a Dutch farmhouse in Newburgh. (This farmhouse became a museum in the nineteenth century.) It was from this camp that his army marched off to help the French fleet trap Cornwallis at Yorktown. The boers of Orange County, whose Patriotism was so staunch that they had been entrusted with the custody at Goshen of those Tories deemed most dangerous, particularly welcomed those of their defenders who spoke their own language. As Colonel

Regimental flag of Colonel Peter Gansevoort's 3rd New York Continentals.
Courtesy of the Albany Institute of History and Art

Gansevoort wrote to his wife from Orangetown (now Nyack): "the inhabitants are all Dutch people from whom I can git every think [*sic*] by speaking Dutch to them."[10]

But the river remained closed for another two years after Yorktown, until peace was finally concluded at Paris in 1783. Simeon Baldwin, a young man from Connecticut who had come to Albany in the summer of 1782 to teach in the city's first academy, made many penetrating observations about the Dutch, described in his diary the effect of the news upon the city:

> March 26th. Heard the glorious news of a general peace among the belligerent powers of Europe and America. It was brought by express

into Albany. The people by the crier were desired to meet at the City Hall immediately. The letters were read and 3 cheers universally given. Other demonstrations of joy were suspended till official accounts should come to hand. No place on the continent which is so far from the enemy is so immediately affected as this; shut out from any sea port; trade, their dependence entirely stagnated and the most affluent families reduced to poverty. It does one good to see the general joy, which sparkles in the eye, enlivens the countenance, animates the feelings of all, especially the unhappy who could say, Nos patriam fugimus.[11]

The burghers' immediate response was in the form of private parties at which their abandonment of all restraint in circulating the flowing bowl offended this Yankee, who preferred not to overindulge. Three weeks later, he described the official celebrations as follows:

April 22d. Met with the citizens about 10 o'clock at the City Hall. Had a long procession from that to the hill preceded by the common council cannon and bells constantly contributing their aid to enliven the position. A long table was provided the liquor ready, and 13 toasts were given with a huzza and 13 cannon to each. This took up most of the forenoon. Went to dinner, returned in the afternoon, repeated one toast over a cup of wine; satisfied my appetite with seeing instead of eating the roasted ox. In the beginning of the evening fire was set to a large pile of piece wood prepared for the purpose, round a pole with a large barrel of tar on the top. It made a beautiful appearance. We had no proper fireworks of powder. Some were drunk; many were merry; all all [sic] were happy. The city was illuminated till 11 o'clock and appeared very beautiful, during which the streets were crowded with people of every kind and sex. The gentlemen of the city spent the night and following day in debauchery and carouse so that 'twas almost thought a duty inseparable from a true whig and patriot to make himself a convert to the depravity of their table and practice. I was strongly solicited to join in this peculiar method of demonstrating joy but found means to evade it.[12]

Thus the Hudson Valley Dutch endured what was in some respects the longest and most severe ordeal of the entire Revolutionary War. They were too practical to think of their everyday endurance as heroic, though they were quick enough to acclaim Peter Gansevoort as "the Hero of Fort Stanwix," and since it was not their custom to write memoirs or histories of their experiences, they have not received the credit due to them. Of course, they were only a minority in New York's war effort, as they were by this time a minority in the population. But the Dutch contribution was significant because so many of them were in positions of military or civilian leadership, because the geographical area in which they were most numerous was so strategically located, and because their tradition of local autonomy and defense was exactly what was needed to organize the most effective resistance against the type of forces which attacked them. It would seem exceedingly significant in explaining the failure of Burgoyne's invasion, that at his objective he encountered the dogged, unexpected resistance of the Hudson Valley Dutch, defending their community with the determination and ingenuity of their ancestors in the Netherlands.

9

E Pluribus Unum

THE Union of Utrecht of 1579 had created the United Netherlands as a war measure. In 1581 the Seven Provinces declared their independence of Spain, and in 1588 they organized the Dutch Republic. Seven jealous provinces composed of numerous competing cities and parochial rural districts agreed to stick together for the purpose of fighting the common enemy. The States-General raised funds for the war and handled foreign relations while the Stadholder conducted military operations. Gradually, as the fighting became less desperate and commerce increased, the States-General assumed the added function of presenting competition from degenerating into unprofitable anarchy by creating such monopolistic organizations as the East and West India Companies. When religious strife threatened to tear the country apart, it reluctantly abandoned its principles of toleration and local privilege to accept the Calvinist establishment of the Synod of Dort. But these were the only respects in which the Dutch Republic was formally unified. The foundation of this unity was an unspoken agreement shared by the Dutch people to respect in each other the same loyalty to communal privileges and local customs that they claimed for themselves. Thus the Dutch were able to form a single nation, in peace as well as in war, despite their ethnic, linguistic, religious, socioeconomic, and political diversity.

This traditional attitude was of great importance in New York's transition from colony to state because there was so much diversity within the province. The colonists came from a variety of nations — not only Dutch and English, but Highland and Lowland

Scots, Protestant and Catholic Irish, and French Huguenots and German Palatines, all very much aware of their independent ethnic traditions. There were differences of economic interest, social aspirations, and adjustment to English rule between merchants and artisans; landlords, tenants, and yeomen farmers; and between burghers and boers. Religions included Anglicanism, established in England and the southern colonies; Presbyterianism, established in Scotland; Congregationalism, established in New England; and the Dutch Reformed, established in the Netherlands — as well as a variety of evangelistic sects established nowhere. In New York they all had to cease relying on the support of the government and stand on their own, retain the loyalty of their members, and sustain their ministers by voluntary contributions.

Important political diversity grew out of the Revolution itself, often colored by preexisting loyalties and grudges. There were many Loyalists in New York — some observers estimated more than in any other colony — many of them concentrated in the downriver area. Dedicated Patriots were as conspicuous a minority in most communities when they heard of the battle at Lexington and Concord as Calvinists had been in the cities of Holland and Zeeland when the "Sea Beggars" came ashore and called upon the people to resist Spanish tyranny. The rest of the people were of all shades of opinion between these extremes, but hardly any of them dreamed in the first year of the war that it would lead to a lengthy conflict or to independence from Great Britain. Many, indeed, supported the Second Continental Congress in the hope that it would lead to peaceful reconciliation. This diversity prompted the election of no less than four Provincial Congresses within that year, the first of which restored order in New York City after the Battle of Lexington in 1775 and the last of which ratified the Declaration of Independence in 1776. The task before the Patriot leaders in this momentous year was first to define their cause and then to persuade this diverse people to unite behind it. They started by urging people to sign the "Association," an agreement not to purchase British goods which, after the fighting started, was often expanded by local committees to include a pledge to bear arms if called upon or at least not to fight for the King. "Non-Associators" were subjected to all sorts of informal penalties from social pressure and economic harassment to confiscation of arms and even tar and feathers, depending on the strength of local feeling.

The Dutch were certainly not the prime movers in the drive to independence, although there were Dutch leaders all across the spectrum of opinion and many Dutch were members of the various Provincial Congresses and active on their committees. To see the Dutch tradition in action, it is necessary to look at the localities which were its fundamental units. The local records of Albany, the largest and most important town still run in the Dutch tradition, are fortunately among the most complete, and illustrate many of the problems with which local Dutch leaders had to cope. The first, of course, since the revolutionary committees were entirely extralegal and had for long been secret, was winning the support of the people. Abraham Yates, the chairman of the Albany Committee, was adept at appealing to the common man, but the patricians who held the key to power in the city had expressed their opinion of him by overturning the Third Ward election of 1773. Yates immediately called upon the people to elect a Committee of their own choosing, whose members included all shades of opinion from extreme Tories to extreme Patriots, and trusted to time and events to shape it more to his liking. The first step in this shaping was to expand this committee to include the county as well as the city. Although the members were still of all shades of opinion, this gave the Patriots the machinery to exert pressure from the city upon rural districts or vice versa — a pressure which they used to great advantage.

The patricians, in the meantime, were becoming involved in a number of Patriotic activities, many of which took them out of the city. It was they, partly from custom and partly because they could afford to serve, who were elected to the Provincial Congresses; Volkert P. Douw, for example, was Vice-President of the First Provincial Congress. Others enlisted in Schuyler's army and marched off to Canada. This left Yates exactly where he wanted to be, in control of Patriot activities in Albany, although an incident in July 1775 touched off a traditional Dutch reaction which warned him that he could go too far. When there appeared upon a public bulletin board an anonymous letter libeling General Schuyler, the patricians stirred up a mob which surrounded the building where the Committee was sitting, and demanded that the writer be identified and punished. The committee accordingly investigated, and found him among its own members — Peter W. Yates, a cousin of Abraham, who in the next twenty years was to get in trouble several times for lack of political tact. He was forthwith expelled from the committee and the mob subsided, having reminded Abraham Yates that he was not the only one with influence over the people.

For the next year the Committee walked the tightrope of public opinion, administering the Association, warning and sometimes disarming non-Associators, and gradually taking over the functions of the city government as the city officials discredited themselves by their own actions. Mayor Cuyler, for example, whose family was still active in the Canada trade, started for Montreal in the summer of 1775 on a so-called business trip, but was stopped on the way by a Patriot detachment and ignominiously returned to the city. When the Provincial Congress passed an act for confiscation of the arms of Loyalists in the spring of 1776, the mayor, the other city officials, and the leading English merchants were accordingly disarmed. The last straw came on June 5, 1776, when Cuyler and the city's other Loyalists held a public party at Cartwright's Tavern in honor of the King's birthday. The next day the Committee placed him and most of the other revelers under arrest and, a month before the Declaration of Independence, the English colonial civil government of Albany ceased to exist.

Assuming another traditional function of the Albany magistrates, the Committee participated with General Schuyler in requesting the Iroquois to remain neutral. It also cooperated with the committee of Tryon County (which had been set off in the Mohawk Valley in 1771) in circumscribing the activities of the Johnsons, confining members of the family who were arrested, and eventually forcing Sir John Johnson and his followers to flee to Canada. Closer to home, the Committee had a special problem in its own delegation from Kinderhook, the home town of Henry and Peter Van Schaack, to which they had retired to wait out the conflict as "neutrals." In the first semiannual elections, Henry Van Schaack was elected to represent his neighbors, whom he described as so reluctant to sign the Association that he hesitated to circulate it among them.

But there were also more ardent Patriots in Kinderhook — many of them Yankee settlers — and many small Dutch farmers who detested the Van Schaack family for having engrossed some of the town's common lands by a bit of sharp practice some years before. In May 1776, therefore, when the town's electors duly returned a delegation headed by Van Schaack, another election

Peter Van Schaack. From Henry C. Van Schaack, *Life of Peter Van Schaack* (New York, 1842)

held a few doors away by the officers of the militia had quite different results. The Albany Committee, called upon to settle this dispute, decided for the militia group, and the Van Schaacks were promptly arrested as Tories. Kinderhook then had a little revolution of its own, to facilitate which the Albany Committee exiled both Henry and Peter Van Schaack to New England, despite their anguished protests that they were not Loyalists at all but neutrals.

In July 1776, when the Albany Committee was well organized and serving as the only functioning government in the city and county, Abraham Yates became a member of the Fourth Provincial Congress, where he was promptly chosen chairman of a committee to draft a constitution for the new state. This process is so commonplace today that we tend to forget that it was something new in 1776. Most nations vested their concept of sovereign power in the persons of their kings, and even the cherished British "constitution" was a body of unwritten tradition focused upon a few basic documents drawn up for quite different purposes. But the Continental Congress, having hit upon the idea of vesting sovereignty in the people rather than the king, and of telling the world so in a written document, went on to advise the newly independent states to provide themselves with written documents defining the powers and duties of the people's government.

New York was in the midst of the military crisis created by Howe's seizure of New York City and Carleton's threatened invasion from Canada. There was also a serious disagreement between Yates and his plebeian supporters, who wanted a government giving wide powers to the people and their elected representatives, and the province's patricians and landed gentry, led on the committee by Robert Livingston and John Jay, who wanted a form of government like that of the colony, with a limited electorate and powerful appointed administrative officials. The stalemate between these two groups continued for several months until leaders outside the Provincial Congress, particularly General Schuyler, aware of how badly a settled local government was needed for the war effort, pressed for the completion of the constitution. Finally on April 20, 1777, the Committee reported a compromise draft, which was accepted. The State of New York was born.

The first elections under the new constitution were held in June 1777, as Burgoyne prepared to advance over Lake Champlain; the candidates for governor were Philip Schuyler and George Clinton (second of that name and a distant relative of the first), both of whom were serving in the army. With the occupied downstate areas out of the picture, Schuyler, with his patrician background and firm support among the Albany Dutch, appeared to be a shoo-in, but Clinton rallied his own mid-Hudson region and attracted unexpected backing from soldier voters, to win by a narrow margin. Schuyler, whose wife's mother was a Livingston, believed that one reason for his defeat was the resentment of the Livingston tenants against their landlord (the tenant rebellion of 1777 took place during the campaign and many resentful tenants refused to vote at all).

County and local governments, which extralegal Patriot committees had taken out of the hands of Loyalist officials, were also restored to normal, including the charter government of Albany. Clinton appointed Albany's second mayor of English descent, John Barclay, son of one of the city's colonial Anglican rectors, and Patriot English residents were elected to the Common Council frequently, although Dutch patricians — and some plebeians — continued to be elected also. The colonial tradition which almost amounted to cooptation among the patricians was broken, but not violently, and the Dutch patricians adjusted to a new pattern in which they could keep their power if they could learn to rely primarily upon their appeal to the voters rather than upon their wealth and social position.

One of the most pressing problems facing the new state government was dealing with the disunity created by the Tories. Those who threatened armed rebellion or open subversion had already been arrested and sometimes exiled by the local committees or forced to flee by their Patriot neighbors. The Albany Committee, for example, had shipped Mayor Cuyler and his wily brother Henry off to Connecticut soon after their arrest in 1776, and kept them in confinement in various locations until it was possible to send them under guard through the British lines. There was also a jail for Tories in Albany, which was usually overflowing throughout 1776 and 1777, and especially dangerous characters were sent to the prison camp at Goshen or to prison ships at Kingston — where conditions were probably little better than in the British prison ships at New York. The Fourth Provincial Congress established a "Committee for Detecting and Defeating Conspiracies" which was deluged with complaints against individuals alleged to be Tories and rumors of Tory plots, especially in the downstate area before it was occupied and in the Neutral Ground thereafter. It was this committee, which had its own intelligence network and post riders, and could even draw on troops to break up these plots if necessary, that helped local authorities to put down the Livingston Manor tenant rising and restore order afterward.

The new legislature established a full-time state Commission for Detecting and Defeating Conspiracies and similar commissions in each county. Only the most dangerous Tories had been imprisoned; the rest had been released, with a warning, on bail, or "on their own recognizance" and left to the surveillance of their Patriot neighbors. This was the most efficient way of dealing with them in a state which had no organized police force other than the militia, whose most onerous and time-consuming duty was maintaining local order — an almost impossible task in communities with a high proportion of Tory sympathizers and few reliable Patriots. Some of these Tories on bail made no more trouble, but others took advantage of the generally unsettled conditions to commit all sorts of crimes which were not necessarily prompted entirely by political antagonism. "Tory crimes" included murders and assaults upon local Patriots, and such "robberies" as that of the house of Hendrick Van Rensselaer at Claverack in 1777, for which 16 persons were arrested, including accessories before and after the fact. The Commissioners for Conspiracies punished some of these offenders themselves, but turned others over to the civil courts as soon as they reopened under the new constitution.

At least as important in the Commissioners' work was dealing with those individuals who obstinately refused allegiance to the new state. The county committees had been penalizing "non-Associators" from the beginning, but the pledge of Association had no legal force, resting entirely upon the power of public opinion. Then in 1778 the Legislature passed "An Act more effectively to prevent the mischiefs arising from the Influence and Example of Persons of equivocal and suspicious Characters, in this State" which provided for the administration of a loyalty oath, and for expulsion from the state of all who refused to take it. The Albany Commissioners immediately presented this oath to a body of "equivocal and suspicious characters" the Patriots had been watching for years, including the Van Schaacks and their friends from Kinderhook and two brothers-in-law of Mayor Cuyler. The latter waited until the last moment and then took the oath and settled down to be good citizens; the former refused. Thirty-one persons were accordingly exiled in the summer of 1778, 14 of them from Kinderhook, including Peter and Henry Van Schaack, despite their protests to such highly placed Patriot friends as John Jay.

Peter Van Schaack, in particular, who had supported the revolutionaries of New York City in their early measures of resistance, was certain that his exile was unfair. He was the first upper Hudson Valley Dutchman to graduate from King's College, and had been regarded as one of the most promising young lawyers in pre-Revolutionary New York City. But like his brother Henry, he had risen by the favor of the De Lancey faction and was suspect by Patriot Dutchmen for that reason even before the brothers retired to Kinderhook (only to find their family's local position undermined by the resentment of their irate neighbors). Nevertheless, Peter Van Schaack, despite failing eyesight, the extended fatal illness of his wife, and the deaths within five years of six of their nine children, improved his retirement and later his exile by writing fine-spun defenses of his neutral position. It is extremely interesting that these writings, though framed within the context of English revolutionary debate, are founded upon the Dutch tradition of moral liberty rather than the English tradition of political liberty. Jay and his other Patriot friends agreed they were acutely reasoned, but unfortunately divorced from the brutal reality of the situation in Kinderhook. They did, however, grant Peter Van Schaack permission to go voluntarily to England for medical treatment for his eyes; his brother Henry was exiled but remained in occupied New York City.

The Van Schaacks, who have become the most famous Dutch Loyalists because they were perhaps the most articulate, were atypical for that very reason. However, a statistical analysis of the Albany records reveals a great deal about humbler Dutch Tories in that county. In the sic years covered by the published minutes (1775-81), about 1,200 persons were arrested for Toryism in Albany County, of whom about 400, or one-third, had Dutch surnames. This percentage was approximately that of the Dutch in the general population as indicated by the militia lists. These proportions were likewise consonant in all of the county's 18 rural districts except Kinderhook, where the local circumstances already described produced a large percentage of Dutch Tories, and Schenectady, adjoining the Johnson country, where nearly all the Dutch were Patriots. Incomplete records make it impossible to compile statistics for the city of Albany, but many of the city's British merchants were arrested as Tories, while the only Dutch patricians even suspected were Mayor Cuyler and his immediate relatives. Apparently the Albany Dutch closed ranks in favor of the Patriot cause and used it as a weapon to expel unwanted intruders upon their civic privileges.

In the two-thirds of these cases in which the offense is known, the misdeeds of these predominantly rural Dutch Tories were about evenly divided between active and passive. The most frequent active offense was robbery (42), followed by going to the enemy (35), attending Tory meetings (31), and sheltering or rescuing Tories (24). These accounted for over ninety percent of the total (140), a scattering being arrested for murder (1), kidnapping (1), disorderly conduct (1), counterfeiting (3), and high treason (2). Nearly two-thirds of the passive offenders refused a pledge of allegiance, either the Association (19) or the loyalty oath (56). Another significant group were wives of Tories who had fled to the enemy (20), who were sent to the British lest they become public charges. The rest were charged with depreciating Continental currency (12), refusing to testify (9), careless talk (7), toasting the king (4), possessing Tory literature (2), and simply "disaffection" (2), for a total of 131. There were 199 whose specific offenses were not recorded.

After the war was over, the people of the state divided sharply about what to do with the Tories, especially those in the southern half of the state. This was now recovered, but the property of Patriots had been freely used and destroyed by the invaders, and many Patriots had fled to become a burden on the rest of the state. Some Tories had been exiled; many had fled on the departing British fleet, which took them to Canada where some, including Abraham C. Cuyler, found new homes. Some, like Peter Van Schaack, had gone to England, where they sought and eventually obtained compensation for their losses from the British government. The state confiscated and sold a great deal of Loyalist property, especially great landed estates like that of the Philipse family. These estates were broken up among small holders, either by direct sale to the former tenants or by sale to speculators who then resold the land to farmers. The treaty of peace provided that confiscations and other legal proceedings against Loyalists should cease, but none of the states paid any attention to this clause.

Nevertheless, most of the Loyalists were not cut off forever from their homeland, although those who had fought in the Loyalist regiments or made themselves obnoxious, like Mayor Cuyler, were usually forbidden by their neighbors to return. Most of the ordinary Tories, especially in the rural districts, simply faded into obscurity, working their farms and gradually overcoming the ostracism of the community, although memories of bitterness continued to be handed down within families for generations, especially in New Jersey. In 1784 the legal decision in *Rutgers* v. *Waddington* opened the way for former Loyalists to recover their legal and civil rights and some, at least, of their property, and in 1786 the Legislature passed an act permitting the return of those whose only offense against the Act of 1778 had been neutrality. Peter Van Schaack, who was specifically named in the Act, thereupon returned to Kinderhook where he married again, sired a second family, and, though blind, became a beloved and respected lawyer and teacher. His sharp-tongued brother Henry preferred to make his new life in Pittsfield, Massachusetts, where he soon fell back into the habit of taking the unpopular side of controversial issues.

The Van Schaacks and others like them profited from the turn of events; as political differences developed between conservative and radical Patriots, the former found it to their advantage to take up the cause of the former Tories in return for their support when their political privileges were at length restored. As one of these conservative leaders later explained:

> Soon after we regained possession of New York, we permitted the Tories to enlist under our banners; and they have since manfully fought by our side in every important battle we have had with the democracy; some of them in the character of officers, and others in those of common soldiers. And when monies have been necessary to support our cause, many amongst them never scrupled to pay their quota of the general tax. Moreover we ought not to forget their zealous and useful service in our great contest for the constitution.[1]

As soon as the Hudson River was reopened, Dutch merchants hastened to revive their shattered commerce, although the severance of imperial connections deprived them of their traditional market in the West Indies, and the entire nation was in the throes of a postwar depression made worse by the depreciation of Continental currency and by deliberate British dumping of manufactured goods at cut-rate prices. Some New York merchants tried to take advantage of their liberty of trading directly with the Netherlands to recreate a market for Dutch goods, but after 100 years of trading with the English this market was not as large as the merchants hoped. Other Dutch entrepreneurs were building sawmills to tap New York's wealth of lumber, and purchasing increasing quantities of potash from frontiersmen who prepared it as a by-product of clearing their lands. The development of the New York frontier had begun, and Hudson Valley Dutch capital, invested in land, in trade, in local industries, and in improvements for transportation, was in the forefront of it.

In the meantime, the Hudson Valley Dutch continued to participate in politics on all sides of important issues. During and immediately after the Revolution, the citizens united behind Governor Clinton, who ran without opposition in 1780 and in 1783 easily defeated Philip Schuyler. Schuyler, after his electoral defeat and removal from command in 1777, had retired to private life but by no means from public affairs. He continued to correspond with George Washington and state leaders and maintained an extensive intelligence network based on his traditional family trading connections with Canada; awareness of the latter probably contributed to the British desire to kidnap him in 1780. He also retained the position of leadership in the Livingston faction, into which he had been thrust in 1768, as the Livingston family found their unpopularity increasing as a result of their relations with their tenants, their all-too-obvious ambition to engross every office they could reach, and family feuds among themselves. But after the recovery of the southern part of the state Schuyler ceased to run for governor, pointing out that he was not personally known there, and confined himself to the task for which he had proven himself best suited during the war, behind-the-scenes organization and management of the party which was publicly headed by his son-in-law Alexander Hamilton, and included another of his sons-in-law, Stephen Van Rensselaer (the "Last Patroon"), and most of the Dutch patricians.

Most of the Dutch plebeians, on the other hand, aligned themselves behind Clinton, under the leadership of Abraham Yates and local leaders like him from the middle and lower Hudson Valley. It was at this time that the middle Hudson region, which had received most of its settlers in the preceding two generations, began to come into its own. Its Dutch leaders were from substantial boer families, such as Peter Van Gaasbeek of Ulster County, Egbert Benson of Dutchess County, and William Van Ness — and in the coming generation, Martin Van Buren — of Kinderhook. The longer-settled present-day Rockland County (then part of Orange), forced by the British occupation of New York City to

live without its traditional market, learned to stand on its own
feet; one of its prominent Dutch leaders who served in the Second
Continental Congress and the state government was John Haring.
The followers of these men included Dutch and Yankee farmers,
some of whom had purchased forfeited Loyalist estates on which
they had previously been tenants, as in southern Dutchess County
(now Putnam County). Others were still tenants of Patriot landlords, but as before the most discontented tenants were of New
England extraction; Dutch tenants were apparently more willing
to follow the political leadership of their landlords well into the
nineteenth century.

   Schuyler and Alexander Hamilton — trying to put together a
party to oppose Clinton in the state — advocated revision of the
Articles of Confederation to strengthen the national government,
initiating the call for the Annapolis Convention, which led to the
Constitutional Convention. New York's delegates to the latter were
Hamilton and Albany Dutchmen Robert Yates and John Lansing,
Jr. Yates's and Lansing's preference for a more workable confederation rather than a strong national bovernment reflected the
conception of union which had worked in the Netherlands for
two centuries. The whole delegation left the Convention when it
became obvious that neither such opinions nor Hamilton's desire
for a quasi-monarchy would prevail, and only Hamilton returned
to sign the final Constitution as the best compromise that could
be secured.

   New York deliberated long over this document, being the last
state to ratify before it went into effect. It now appears that the
two factions made it an issue in their growing power struggle with
each other, but that they were not really very far apart in their
views. The Federalists — Schuyler and Hamilton's faction —
wanted unconditional ratification; the Anti-Federalists, led by
Clinton and including the Yates organization, wanted various
modifications to insure the rights of the common man. When
ratification by New Hampshire and Virginia insured that the new
form of government would become operative in any case, the two
sides quickly resolved their differences and some of the Anti-
Federalist majority agreed to vote for ratification. The contest has
been depicted as much more dramatic than it actually was, since
neither side really wished to remain out of the new nation.

   The role of the Dutch in achieving this national unity was not
on the floor of the Poughkeepsie Convention, for many of those

who ran as Federalists — including the Albany slate — were defeated in the election. But Schuyler, Leonard Gansevoort, and their friends went to Poughkeepsie as observers, and cooperated with such distinguished downstate delegates as Robert Livingston and John Jay in lobbying for the national interest. For this purpose they undoubtedly brought into play all of the informal, extrapolitical pressures customary in colonial politics, to reverse the result of the election — but it must be remembered that elections in colonial New York were not sacrosanct as they were in New England, or ideally are in America today. The electorate was limited, voting was public, and it was normal practice for voters to sell their support to the highest bidder. Many country elections were uncontested ratifications of a gentlemen's agreement among the principal local landowners. In the cities, bidding for votes was openly mercenary, as in Albany in 1773, and often marked by riots, reflecting the Dutch tradition of popular expression through civic disorder. Thus, Schuyler and his party looked back to an eighteenth-century view of the electoral process, while Yates and his party looked forward to that of the nineteenth century.

This difference in point of view, when coupled, as it often was, with patrician disdain for his plebeian origins, helps to explain the embittered attitude of Abraham Yates' "History of the Movement for the United States Constitution." He interpreted ratification as a conspiracy by a few self-seeking politicians, an interpretation for which he had ample ground both in 30 years of his own experience and in the Dutch tradition. For Yates was after all an ambitious plebeian striving to become a patrician by the influence of a fortune, not in gold, but in the golden opinions of the voters. Time after time he had amassed such a fortune, by winning or appearing certain to win an election, only to have the enjoyment of its profits snatched from him by the connivance of patricians who dismissed him as though he did not exist. The silent cooperation of men who had known each other from childhood and worked together for many years could appear very like conspiracy to an outsider, particularly since conspiracy was quite customary in the highly personal local government of the Netherlands. It worked both ways, since it was the only means plebeians had to force their needs on the attention of patricians who chose to ignore them. But Yates never published this bitter history, perhaps partly because in the end he got something he had always wanted after all, when in 1790 the Clintonians appointed him Mayor of Albany, and Abraham Yates, plebeian, had attained the highest local summit of patrician ambition. It may well be that this triumph meant more to him than any other, for Abraham Yates' outlook was always incurably local, and the parochialism which embarrassed him in the legislature and the Confederation Congress was a last expression of the Dutch particularism which had made Albany almost an independent city-state a century before.

In many ways Yates' administration was the last golden sunset of Dutch Albany, for Yankee settlers were flooding into the Mohawk Valley and farther west and Yankee traders were settling in Albany to supply their needs. Schuyler and the patricians, perpetuating the Dutch tradition of thinking largely in the promotion of commerce, pooled their resources for this purpose. They chartered Albany's first bank, a company to bridge the Mohawk at Cohoes, and companies to build canals between the Mohawk and Lake Oneida and the Hudson and Lake Champlain, thus linking a familiar Dutch form of engineering to the eventual development of New York's uniquely successful canal system. After the depression of the 1780s, trade was booming; the patricians oversubscribed the stock of these companies almost before the books were opened. But then sunset gave way to fiery twilight in 1793 as three disgruntled slaves set a blaze in their master's stable that burned down a third of the city, including many of its old Dutch houses. This was only one of seven disastrous fires in the 1790s in which Dutch Albany, like Dutch New York, ended its history in flames. Then in 1797, a year after Yates' death, the Legislature selected Albany as the permanent capital of the state, and its destiny took a decisive turn toward the American future rather than the Dutch past.

Another last recapitulation of a Dutch tradition was investment from the Netherlands in the development of the new state and nation. The Dutch Republic had observed the American Revolution with great interest, and was the first nation to salute the American flag at sea; prominent Dutch liberals such as Baron Van der Capellen advocated the American cause, and, perhaps most helpful of all, Amsterdam bankers — still the leaders of European finance — floated loans to help the new nation meet the cost of war. But perhaps the most important of these Dutch investments came in the 1790s, when a syndicate of Amsterdam capitalists called the Holland Land Company engaged in several development programs in western New York. One of these, a scheme for the mechanized production of great quantities of maple sugar on a tract north of Oneida Lake, failed because of various technological and labor problems and left only such Dutch names on the map as Boonville and Barneveld, New York.

The Holland Land Company's most extensive project was the development of 6,000,000 acres in Pennsylvania and western New York on which they founded towns at Batavia and another New Amsterdam, now Buffalo. Their New York State agent, Joseph Ellicott, successfully surveyed the New York portion of this tract and eventually sold most of it to Yankee farmers, whose interests he represented in Albany, playing an important part in the routing of the Erie Canal across that part of the state. But the investors' plans were upset by events in the Netherlands, where Napoleon's armies briefly snuffed out Dutch independence and prompted the permanent transfer of the center of world finance to London. The investors of the Holland Land Company were eventually content to sell their lands for little more than the return of their original investment.

The Dutch contribution to the creation of unity within New York, and to making New York a part of the Federal union, was only partly the work of Dutch leaders. The Dutch were perhaps more significant as shrewd and intelligent followers who shaped the principles of unity enunciated by such men as Hamilton into practical action on the local level, which was as yet the only concrete political reality for most people. Schuyler, like Hamilton, was capable of a national vision, which, as might be expected of a Dutchman, he focused upon the development of strong commercial ties. His Anglo-Dutch conception of government by landed gentry and patricians did not, however, fully comprehend the reality of the ambitions of the plebeians, the independence of the boers who were learning to transfer their loyalty from religious to political principles, or the importance of the opinions of individual voters fostered by New England town meetings. Abraham Yates and other plebeian leaders understood these factors better, and their success in using them to win election eventually forced the Schuyler group to meet them on their own ground and thus to expand their own conception of American unity. The participation of such former Loyalists as the Van Schaacks as leaders in Schuyler's organization emphasizes that the unity being formed out of diversity in the State of New York was broad enough to include everyone, even those who in the heat of controversy had been proscribed. Thus the Dutch, who were such an important element of the unique problem of the diversity of New York, also made from their inherited tradition a significant contribution toward its solution.

10

Folklore, Fiction, and Fact

AS THE Dutch tradition ceased to be embodied in a cohesive ethnic group, it attracted the attention of some of America's early men of letters. Most of them were not of Dutch descent, although the few who were included one of the greatest American authors, Herman Melville. They therefore observed Dutch culture from the outside, having little or no knowledge of the Dutch language, literature, or standards of values, and used their observations within the context of their own inherited literary traditions, which were very different from those of the Dutch. Writers of Scots descent often used the distinct characteristics of the Dutch way of life as reference points for moral criticism of the dominant American standards taken for granted by their contemporaries. Those working in the English romantic tradition used Dutch folkways as picturesque items of local color in sentimental novels. And later in the nineteenth century the story of the Dutch Revolt of 1565 inspired John Lothrop Motley, one of the great historians who were making the epic of the achievement of popular liberty one of the major themes in American historical writing. Many of these works were widely read and have become classics in American literature, and so have created an image of the Dutch in America which is only partly an accurate reflection of the actual Dutch tradition.

The first and by far the most famous of these writers was Washington Irving. Irving was born in New York City in 1783, of Scots and English parentage, and grew up there when Dutch was still spoken in the market where the boers of New Jersey, Man-

191

hattan, Staten and Long Islands sold their produce. The young Irving thus picked up some knowledge of the Dutch language with which, on country rambles and the leisurely sloop voyages which were then the only means of river transportation, he collected a wealth of folklore from garrulous old wives and old salts. The first product of this curiosity was *Diedrich Knickerbocker's History of New York* (1809), whose content of Dutch folklore has only recently been recognized by folklore specialists, one of whom wrote that this book "is probably Irving's only work in which the form and style as well as the content were near the folk level."[1]

But *Knickerbocker's History* is far more famous as the first work to inform Americans in general of the broad outlines of the history of New Netherland. Irving had very little information to go on — only the first pages of William Smith's *History of New York*, which named the Dutch governors and related a few events. It has also been suggested that he was familiar with a few contemporary Dutch accounts of New Netherland; that by Johannes De Laet was available in Latin and French translations, and Domine Megapolensis' description of the Mohawks had recently been reprinted in an English version, but the works of Adriaen Van der Donck — which he specifically mentioned in the Introduction — and David P. de Vries he would have had to read in the original. The results of these investigations appeared in a community just beginning to be aware of its past, for in the first years of the nineteenth century, members of the newly founded New-York Historical Society were starting to inquire into the subject. When it came time to commemorate the bicentennial of Hudson's voyage in 1809, their celebration took the form of a banquet followed by an oration by a local minister with antiquarian interests. Such a celebration was quite appropriate in the Dutch tradition, but Irving, anticipating a later American custom, thought it also ought to be marked by the publication of a history. His own work, published on December 6 (the Dutch feast of Saint Nicholas), served this purpose, with a satiric jab at the Dutch for not having done it themselves.

The historical context of *Knickerbocker's History* was not inaccurate as far as it went, but in the absence of translations of the records of the Dutch colony it could not go very far beyond the names of the Dutch governors, de Vries' and Van der Donck's opinions of them, and such general facts as the conflict with New England, the conquest of New Sweden, and of course the final

surrender to the English in 1664. Beyond this Irving was left to
rely entirely on his imagination and such scraps of folklore as were
still attached to the names of the first settlers by their descendants.
He, therefore, created the unforgettable characters of "Wouter
the Doubter," "William the Testy," and "Peter the Headstrong"
(*hardkoppig Piet* — could this have been a surviving folk sobriquet?). These chief executives originally possessed traits satirizing
the Presidents of the United States after Washington, particularly
William the Testy, who represented Jefferson, but it is important
to note that Irving edited out these topical allusions in the 1848
edition, which is the one most likely to be enjoyed by modern
readers. Irving also parodied a number of conventions common in
histories popular among his readers, such as beginning with the
creation of the world and drawing extended parallels with classical
antiquity. The account of the bloodless capture of Fort Christina
in the manner of a Homeric conflict, complete with individual
encounters of heroes and intervention of deities, but finally
brought down to earth by the ignominious tumble of the heroic
Stuyvesant into a cow-pat, is a comic tour de force.

To provide a context for these mock-heroic events, Irving
imagined exploits for ancestors of the Dutch families then prominent in the city, such as Olof Van Cortlandt's hapless voyage to
Communipaw (New Jersey), which was later illustrated in a
painting by John Quidor that effectively captured Irving's delicate
atmosphere of fantasy. The descendants, however, were not
amused. Among themselves they enjoyed broad postprandial
narratives and the dialect tales of the sloop captains, but to be
ridiculed with their own tradition of humor by this young English
upstart was something else again. Furthermore, the difference was
becoming marked between the cosmopolitan burghers, who adjusted to the dominant culture of the new nation in the interests of
commerce, and the boers, who clung to the dialect and folkways
of their ancestors, and Irving's knowledge of folklore was clearly of
boer origin. In turning it against the patricians he was observing
an existing diversity, but also meddling in an internal conflict he
did not fully understand. The New York patricians' insistence
that Irving's picture of the Dutch was false was therefore partly,
but only partly, justified.

The use in *Knickerbocker* of authentic folklore as a basis for
moral criticism of the social standards and political practices of
Irving's New York reflected that eighteenth-century Scottish

"Voyage from Hell Gate to Communipaw," by John Quidor. *Courtesy of Wichita Art Museum, Wichita, Kansas, the Roland P. Murdock Collection M115.54*

literary tradition which had produced a galaxy of moral philosophers and the ballad collections of Walter Scott. Scott himself, when later presented with a copy of *Knickerbocker* by one of Irving's traveling friends, spoke highly of its humor in the tradition of Swift and Sterne, but confessed that the New York political allusions were lost on him, and apparently did not recognize the Dutch folklore as folklore at all. When Irving moved to England after the War of 1812 he visited Scott, who entertained him most hospitably and later assisted him in finding a publisher for *The Sketch Book* — a circumstance which provoked a rumor that the

"Great Unknown" might have written this work by "Geoffrey Crayon."

The Sketch Book, representing the English rather than the Scots side of Irving's heritage in its picturesque descriptions and its romantic nostalgia for "Merrie England," contains Irving's best-known "Dutch" stories, "Rip Van Winkle" and "The Legend of Sleepy Hollow." The framework of the story of "Rip Van Winkle" has been shown to be a German folk tale, though it is not unlikely that if more were known about Hudson Valley Dutch folklore, a similar story about a lazy hunter meeting the "spooks" of a captain and crew playing ninepins on the Donderberg (Thunder Mountain) might be discovered. The moral conflict between the easygoing Dutch and the bustling Yankees, by no means to the advantage of the latter, recalls the Scots moral criticism of *Knickerbocker*. The picturesque arrangement of details, the nostalgia for a lost world remembered from childhood, and the lure of the supernatural, all recall the romanticism of Wordsworth and Coleridge, the latter a close associate of Irving's long-time friend, the painter Washington Allston, who, like Irving, was living in England after the War of 1812.

"The Legend of Sleepy Hollow" likewise embodies a German folk tale, a moral conflict between Dutch and Yankees, and picturesque descriptions of the boer way of life. Because the story turns upon a contest between human characters rather than a conflict of abstract values, it illustrates the Dutch way of life even more vividly than does "Rip Van Winkle," whose lazy, hen-pecked hero is a figure in the folklore of many peoples. The abundance of the Van Tassel farm, the plump charms of the kittenish Katrina, and the rough practical jokes of Brom Bones all reflect keenly observed characteristics of boer culture. (The Van Tassel homestead has been identified as the Van Alen house at Kinderhook, now a museum, which Irving saw while visiting a friend at the time he was completing *Knickerbocker*. Since Sleepy Hollow itself, the grim scene of British Major André's capture, is near the real Van Tassel farm in Tarrytown where Irving later made his home, both towns claim — with equal justice — to be the scene of the story.)

It is important to note that the German and English character-istics of these stories, though to a certain extent adulterating their depiction of the Dutch way of life, helped them to communicate its existence to a very wide audience. When Irving had tried to use materials from Dutch folklore in *Knickerbocker* they had been misunderstood even in New York and overlooked by Scott, an experienced collector of folklore. But German folklore, as collected by the Brothers Grimm and others and translated by Scott, was both intellectually respectable and widely popular in Europe. Romantic nostalgia also struck a responsive chord in England, as Irving proved with the beloved "Christmas at Bracebridge Hall" sequence in *The Sketch Book*, which initiated the revival of the holiday customs of "Merrie England" by the English themselves. Therefore, when Irving presented Dutch materials within this familiar framework, they could be identified and appreciated by readers to whom the structure of Dutch folk tradition was unintelligible. These readers were numerous indeed, for not only was *The Sketch Book* a best seller in its own right in both England and America, but its Dutch stories were later brought to an even wider audience in America by Joseph Jefferson's play "Rip Van Winkle," and in the British Empire by the English acceptance of *The Sketch Book* as a masterpiece of prose style suitable as a text for teaching English to colonials and foreigners.

Two later Dutch stories by Irving should also be mentioned, although neither became as famous as those in *The Sketch Book*. "Dolph Heyliger," interpolated in *Bracebridge Hall*, tells of a poor boy from New York who follows a ghostly hint of good fortune to Albany. There in the "Vanderheyden Palace" (an actual Albany Dutch house once owned by the Loyalist patrician Vanderheydens who moved to England early in the Revolution) he falls in love with an heiress whom he marries after he returns home and finds a buried treasure where the ghost had indicated he should look. "Wolfert Webber," also written in the 1820s, likewise describes a Dutchman's attainment of wealth by the virtues of perseverance and making the most of available resources. Webber, a boer unable to make ends meet by cabbage farming on Manhattan Island, engages in an unseccessful search for pirate gold but then makes an unexpected fortune by leasing his farm for building lots for the expanding New York City.

When Irving returned to America after 15 years in Europe, he bought and rebuilt a Dutch farmhouse near Tarrytown which he named "Sunnyside," and became America's first literary institution and an object of pilgrimage in his lifetime. The publication of his collected works in the mid-nineteenth century, a venture probably suggested by the success of a similar edition of Scott's works, brought a revised *Knickerbocker* before the public as a

"The Return of Rip Van Winkle," by John Quidor. *Courtesy of the National Gallery of Art, Andrew W. Mellon Collection*

"classic" rather than a topical work, and placed the Dutch stories on the bookshelves of Americans who aspired to be "cultured" and also among readings widely used in the expanding common schools. Thus Irving's prestige as America's first internationally acclaimed author helped to fix his interpretation of the Dutch at the very heart of the emerging American national literature.

The popularity of *The Sketch Book* doubtless prompted some of Irving's friends who had Dutch ancestors to try their hand with American Dutch materials. James Kirke Paulding, a first cousin of one of the captors of Major Andre, had been one of Irving's collaborators in his first work, *Salmagundi*, and his brother married Irving's sister. Paulding was very much aware of his Dutch heritage, which he later depicted:

> I am by the Fathers side *pure* Dutch — both my Grandfather & Grandmother, whom I remember, were Dutch — spoke Dutch — and read Dutch out of an old Dutch Bible with Silver Corners & Silver clasps. By my mother, I am adulterated with some French & English Blood — but I am so far a Dutchman yet, that, I hate all interlopers, and reverence Old customs.[2]

Paulding also recalled that it was his essay on Dutch New Year's customs in *Salmagundi* which gave Irving part of the idea for *Knickerbocker*, and Irving's correspondence reveals that he showed that manuscript to Paulding before it was published. Here perhaps is part of the explanation of the mystery of where Irving acquired his Dutch materials, for the Pauldings were a substantial Westchester boer family, except for James K. Paulding's father, who became a New York merchant and made an advantageous marriage with a daughter of the Ogden family, which also intermarried with Livingstons and Van Cortlandts. James K. Paulding, therefore, inherited the boer rather than the patrician Dutch tradition, but as a member of a burgher family with more education than most boers found it necessary to pursue, and was therefore in a position to view both burgher and boer traditions with understanding, affection, and detachment. Washington Irving's intimate association with his brother-in-law and his friend placed him in a particularly favorable position to absorb this attitude, which is essentially that of *Knickerbocker*, and may have offered him an opportunity to learn both the spoken and written Dutch language. It would also account for that almost uncanny awareness of sensitive points for satirization unlikely to be obvious to an outsider, which so incensed Irving's Dutch patrician contemporaries.

The popularity of *Knickerbocker*, with all its satirical allusions to contemporary politics, did little immediately to encourage an interest in their heritage among the Dutch; the international success of *The Sketch Book* had a very different effect. The name of "Knickerbocker" — originally that of a substantial boer family from northern Dutchess County, one of whose scions, Harmen

Knickerbocker, settled near Schagticoke and was a well-known member of Congress at the time the book appeared — came to be adopted as a sobriquet for the Dutch tradition of New York City, upon which was founded that romantic nostalgia which Irving claimed was a part of the sense of locality which American communities needed to develop. This happened so fast that patrician Gulian C. Verplanck, who in 1818 publicly excoriated Irving for ridiculing the heritage of Verplanck's ancestors, became in 1822 the editor of the *Knickerbocker Magazine*, devoted to exploiting the literary primacy of Gotham.

The same spirit prompted Paulding, who had become a novelist as well as an essayist, to write *The Dutchman's Fireside* (1831), in which he drew heavily on Anne Grant's *Memoir of an American Lady* to recreate the way of life of a colonial Dutch family of the patroon class. The story described the initiation of a young Dutchman to adulthood by participating in the Indian trade, serving in the French and Indian War, and winning his sweetheart from a British rival. But Paulding's own knowledge of the Hudson Valley Dutch enabled him to bring out the darker side of a tradition which Mrs. Grant had depicted as a model of wise innocence for the instruction of young ladies. The young trader was nearly murdered by drunken Indians who wanted to steal his goods, the heroine was attacked by an Indian seeking revenge for a wrong done him by her father, and the British rival for her hand was killed in the ghastly heroism of Abercrombie's assault on Ticonderoga.

Another writer of Dutch descent, Charles Fenno Hoffman, was also closely connected to Irving by ties of family and friendship. One of his works was a pioneering history of Leisler's Rebellion (1845), which the next year became the subject of an unsuccessful play by still another Dutch-descended author, Cornelius Mathews. Like Paulding, however, Hoffman's most widely read work on the Dutch tradition was a novel, *Greyslaer* (1840), which related the tribulations of a young couple of the patroon class who were separated by the events of the Revolution in the Mohawk Valley. Much of this sensational tale has been traced to other sources, such as a celebrated crime of Hoffman's own day, which suggested the villain's attempt on the heroine's virtue, and was also made the subject of a grimly realistic novel by William Gilmore Simms. The use of a fair and a dark heroine (the former murdered by Indians in the first chapter) and a thrilling sequence in which the dark heroine is abducted by Tories and confined in their cave hideout (now Howe Caverns, Schoharie County) were probably suggested by James Fenimore Cooper's *Last of the Mohicans.* The hero, meanwhile, also following Cooper, joined the Patriot forces until military movements in the aftermath of Saratoga gave him an opportunity to rescue the heroine. In the climax of this blood-curdling tale, the heroine with deep and characteristically Dutch piety persuades the hero to forego his plans of violent vengeance for her wrongs because he would thereby stain his own immortal soul.

Cooper, developing the American historical novel in imitation of a different side of Scott from that which attracted Irving, also contributed about this time to fictional interpretation of the colonial Dutch. His novel *Satanstoe* (1845), like Paulding's, drew heavily upon the work of Anne Grant, emphasizing particularly the Dutch way of life at Albany, where Cooper had attended school about 1800. He depicted the city vividly, dramatizing the high spirits and pranks of the young patricians, and made the most of a thrilling opportunity for the hero to rescue the heroine during the spectacular spring breakup of the ice in the river. This volume was the first of a trilogy; in the second, *The Chainbearer* (1846), he created the character of the surveyor Andries Coeje-mans, a wise folk hero intended as a Dutch Natty Bumppo. The third volume, *The Redskins* (1846), moved away from depiction of the Dutch to direct participation in the Anti-Rent controversy of his own day, in which, although Dutch-descended landlords were involved, Cooper detected no Dutch characteristics.

Still another figure from Dutch folklore introduced into American mythology at this period was Santa Claus. The annual visits of the good saint, who on December 6 showered children with goodies — or switches — were one of the most durable and beloved Dutch traditions of New York. Even Dutch patricians who were in every other respect fully assimilated to English culture took pride in their association with this worthy, and when a Dutch ethnic society was formed in imitation of those honoring Saint George, Saint Andrew, and Saint Patrick, it took the name of Saint Nicholas and held its annual banquet on his feast day. The other ethnic societies acted in these years as political pressure groups, but the Saint Nicholas Society, founded in Albany in the 1820s and moved to New York in the 1840s, seems to have been primarily a social organization. Dutch descendants, like Paulding, who wished to call attention to their ethnic identity, often did so by referring to Saint Nicholas as a cultural landmark.

Saint Nicholas was contributed to the cultural heritage of all American children by Clement C. Moore, an Episcopalian professor who wrote "A Visit from Saint Nicholas" for his own children in 1822. Moore's wife was a Van Cortlandt, and the elaborate Saint Nicholas festivities customary in her family are suggested by a wooden cookie mold in the form of the Saint now on display at Van Cortlandt Manor, Sleepy Hollow Restorations. The mold makes a cookie about two feet high, which when elaborately frosted, made a memento of the Saint much too large to be found in a child's stocking — or wooden shoe. The poem was published in a Troy newspaper in the 1840s and rapidly reprinted; one early edition showed the Saint arriving in his sleigh in a little town of step-gabled Dutch houses. It became widely popular as a recitation for children, and was caught up in the essentially German wave of Victorian sentimentality over Christmas, and later in twentieth-century commercialization, until the master of Santa's Workshop at North Pole, New York, is hardly recognizable as his Dutch original.

The following characterization, from an oration delivered by Albany Dutchman Abraham Lansing to the Saint Nicholas Society of New York in 1892, will illustrate the nature of the Dutch folk figure:

Santa Claus is an embodiment of human attributes and their exponent . . . He is presented to us as a pattern, not as a preceptor. He does not simply teach the lesson of benevolence and kindness, he illustrates them by his deeds. He is the model of an active, discriminating, practical generosity, imparting wholesome truths by means of his own excellent and wholesome example . . . His realm is that of childhood and his mission is to mold its plastic mind and direct the formative processes of its character and, if I accurately recall the traditions of my childhood, he is the friend of all children, but he is the discriminating benefactor of those who are reasonably deserving . . . He stirs the expectant world of childhood with the pleasures of anticipation and hope; coming, as other substantial blessings and really great events are apt to come, silently, he arrives on tip-toes in the night-time; locks cannot exclude nor doors withhold him from his purposes . . . He is the joyous energetic emissary of Christmas and filled with its spirit, and his own heartiness and happiness are an illustration of the pleasures of unselfishness . . . Now, it has been a fashion to make merry over the Dutchman's peculiarities, but it occurs to me that they are peculiarities which are capable of realizing both in fancy and fact just such complete and excellent characters as that of this delightful old friend of our childhood. We judge a mechanic by his works. You cannot, as a rule, judge a Dutchman by his professions, for he seldom makes them; you must judge him as he asks always to be judged, by the result of his labors. And it seems to me very plain that no intelligence but that of a very high order, and no manhood but a very sound manhood, could have conceived and realized this salutary and beautiful illusion of Santa Claus. And the point which I wish particularly to make to-night is that Santa Claus is a Dutch creation. He comes straight from that elder Amsterdam, his headquarters during his earthly sojourn, and if you take away from him his thoroughly Dutch characteristics you ruin him.[3]

In view of the well-known close relationship between the "Knickerbocker" authors and the painters of the Hudson River School, and the great tradition of pictorial art in the Netherlands, it is rather surprising that hardly any of the Hudson River artists were of Dutch descent. The one who was, John Vanderlyn (grandson of Pieter Vanderlyn of Kingston, the only one of the Hudson Valley limners who has been identified), went to Europe to study about the turn of the nineteenth century, under the patronage of Aaron Burr. There Vanderlyn became a specialist in the depiction of scenes from classical history, in accordance with the prevailing fashion. On his return to the United States was less successful than he expected because he insisted on investing his time and resources in "panoramas" — representations of European cities in which Americans were less interested than he hoped. The other artistic cynasty among the colonial Dutch, the Duyckinck family (glass-makers, portrait painters, and dealers in paint), had made a fortune by various means and deserted the practice of the arts. There was also one important nineteenth-century architect of Dutch and Huguenot ancestry, Minard La Fever, whose elaborate edifice for the Washington Square Dutch Reformed Church (1837-41) was an early example of the American Gothic Revival. This building, though its immediate models were English churches, recalled the Dutch patrician tradition in which churches were splendid civic monuments at a time when most American congregations were still building very simple meeting houses.

The next generation of the cosmopolitan Dutch patricians in New York was led by Evert Duyckinck, a descendant of the Duyckinck artistic dynasty, who employed his leisure as editor, encyclopedist, bibliophile, and patron of young authors. A number of his proteges were of Dutch descent, including Cornelius Mathews, Herman Melville, and Walt Whitman, and it is interesting to speculate that the obscurity which frustrated readers of their own time in the works of all three may have been caused by elements derived from their Dutch heritage. Melville's novel *Mardi* is a case in point. This puzzling book — in which a group of characters, seeking the kidnapped heroine through a South Seas archipelago, enliven, interrupt, and sometimes seem to forget their quest in philosophical and literary discussion — was the fruit of Melville's introduction to Duyckinck's library, table, and salon. Its partly digested literary allusions alone made it difficult reading for Americans whose principal reading matter was newspapers and current novels. On top of this, Melville offered them a severe moral criticism of the Manifest Destiny democracy of 1848, reflecting both his Scots paternal heritage and his mother's Dutch point of view, a combination recalling that of *Knickerbocker's* political satire. As if this were not confusing enough, it seems likely that the basic structure of the work — the story of the hero's irresistible attraction to an ambiguous enchantress who finally compels him to fling himself into a deadly pool — may be derived from one of the few Hudson Valley Dutch dialect folk tales which have been collected. With all these unfamiliar elements, it is hardly surprising that readers expecting a yarn of nautical adventure did not know what to make of *Mardi*, which was a dismal failure.

Later in his career, as Melville sought to regain the popularity he lost when his genius outran his audience's expectations of an author, he tried to make use of a Hudson Valley setting for *Pierre*, a Gothic tale of love and death in which the scion of a patroon family is torn between the attractions of fair and dark heroines. Melville used the patroon tradition, which he demonstrated to be older than that of post-Restoration English aristocracy, to establish the atmosphere of decaying antique ruin customary in this kind of romance, but once again the Dutch tradition was too unfamiliar for most readers to understand what he was trying to do. Most of his other works show less obvious evidence of his Dutch inheritance. His first sea story, *Typee* — significantly the favorite of his Dutch uncle, Peter Gansevoort — contained vivid descriptions of a South Sea island observed with the accuracy and fidelity of detail of the Dutch painters. His major work, *Moby Dick*, denounced the deadly sins of pride and avarice with a fervor reminiscent of Frelinghuysen's sermons, and his late long poem,

Clarel, explored the soul's pilgrimage in quest of truth which pious Hudson Valley Dutch men and women made the pursuit of their retirement years.

Some of Melville's shorter poems, published only after his works were rediscovered by twentieth-century scholars, illustrate other aspects of his interest in the Dutch tradition. The longest, "At the Hostelry," probably written soon after a visit to Europe in 1857 during which he toured art galleries, imagines a colloquy on the nature of art among a group of Dutch and Italian Old Masters. "On the Housetop," depicting the New York draft riots of 1863, compares this disturbance with civic unrest in the medieval Netherlands as described by the Burgundian chronicler Froissart, to evoke a remarkably powerful condemnation of man's inhumanity to man. "A Dutch Christmas in the Time of the Patroons" describes homely customs probably observed at Melville's mother's family home at Gansevoort, New York. And perhaps most interesting as a commentary on the Knickerbocker tradition is "Rip Van Winkle's Lilac," a prose-poem putting Irving's folk hero into another dimension as a lover of beauty and a public benefactor. Melville envisions Rip, having carelessly thrust a switch into the ground before his home, returning from his long sleep to find the ruined house overgrown with a lilac bush so lovely that all his neighbors come to it for slips to beautify their own yards — a Dutch custom which an oral informant says was widespread in the rural Hudson Valley well into the twentieth century.

Rural Dutch folkways also formed the substance of an almost forgotten novel by the Rev. David Murdoch, *Dutch Dominie of the Catskills* (1861). The Dutch domine, fiery Patriot leader Johannes Schuneman, had been one of Murdoch's predecessors in the Catskill Reformed Church, and there is clearly a great deal of local oral tradition within the conventional framework of love between the daughter of a Dutch Patriot and the son of a Dutch Tory. The author fuses the two principal events of the Revolution in Catskill, Schuneman's leadership of defense during the Burgoyne campaign and the Tory and Indian raid of 1780, and adds a romantic subplot concerning a supposititious daughter of the British commander kidnapped by the Indians. The most unusual — and most Dutch — feature of the story is the character of the heroine, who combines a fervent piety, frequently quoting the Bible in Dutch, with an intrepid skill in woodcraft that enables her to help her father rescue the kidnapped English girl and then hide in the woods with her during the raid without the slightest infringement upon her own femininity. In the meantime, her lover is converted to the Patriot cause by the brutality of the other Tories and the energetic example of Domine Schuneman, and the pair are reunited in the ruins of her burned home after he helps the Patriots rescue the raiders' captives.

Another novel involving Dutch characters in a romance of love and Patriotism was Amelia E. Barr's *The Bow of Orange Ribbon* (1886). This story began in Stamp Act New York with the seduction of a burgher's daughter by a British officer, the scapegrace younger son of an earl. After a secret marriage, an elopement, and 10 years in England, where she ran a model Dutch household while he ran a course of fashionable profligacy, he was reformed by her faithfulness and returned with her to New York to join the Continental Army. The heroine's family were all characteristically Dutch — her testy, upright, conservative father; her socially ambitious mother; her exemplary but unimaginative older sister and commercially successful but self-righteous brother-in-law; and her sympathetic brother, who was disappointed in his love across ethnic lines because the Jewish girl he cared for refused to put love ahead of her duty to obey her elders. The heroine herself was a devoted and competent Dutch housewife — unshakably honest, forthright, and firm in principle.

Still another author of this period who depicted Mohawk Valley Dutch characters was Harold Frederic, who was born in Utica and was of Dutch and German descent. Frederic became a journalist in Albany, and at the age of 27 received an assignment as the *New York Times* correspondent in London, where he spent the rest of his life. A minor but pivotal character in his first novel, *Seth's Brother's Wife,* was a Dutch political boss of the Van Buren type, Abram K. Beekman, who reappeared briefly in the bestselling *Damnation of Theron Ware.* Much more fully developed was Douw Mauverenson, the protagonist of *In the Valley,* a traditional romance of the Revolution in which a plebeian Patriot hero and an aristocratic Loyalist villain competed for the hand of a beautiful heroine of a Loyalist family.

But Frederic, whose insight into human nature went far deeper than this conventional conflict, depicted Douw dismissed as a vulgar Dutch "outsider" by the English gentry among whom he was ambitious to be accepted, and then discovering that the Patriot patricians of Albany were not only Dutch but as cultured as the English aristocracy. "Heretofore, I had suffered not a little from the notion . . . that gentility and good-breeding went hand in hand with loyalty to everything England did, and that disaffection was but another name for vulgarity and ignorance."[4] In the end, furthermore, like Hoffman's Max Greyslaer, Douw chose to rescue rather than kill his rival when he found him wounded after the Battle of Oriskany, but he made this choice in response to the prompting of his own conscience rather than the pleading of the pious heroine. The fundamental moral concern of all of Frederic's works, which was generally misunderstood despite their popularity, also recalls the emphases of the Dutch tradition in much the same way that Herman Melville's does.

Finally among nineteenth-century American authors, Boston historian John Lothrop Motley was inspired by the history of the Dutch Revolt as an epic of a people's achievement of liberty. Motley was interested only in the experience of the Dutch in Europe; his work ended before the founding of New Netherland, and he was apparently unconcerned with the contribution of the Dutch to American liberty. The wide popularity of his works, with their unforgettable characterizations, therefore created an image of the Dutch tradition among American readers which was far removed from the "Dutch-ness" of Rip Van Winkle. Motley's works contributed to misunderstanding of the nature of Dutch culture in America because, as will be seen, they were shaped as much by English literary conventions as by their historical content. In *The Rise of the Dutch Republic* (1856), Motley related the events from the accession of Philip II to the assassination of William the Silent, in an atmosphere recalling that of Shakespeare's history plays. He divided this drama into five "acts" consisting of the administrations of the five governors Philip sent to the Netherlands — the vacillating Margaret of Parma, the brutal Duke of Alva, the efficient Requesens, the romantic Don John of Austria, and the intriguing Alexander of Parma. Under the pressure of these various forces of tyranny, the Dutch suffered for the first two "acts," then roused themselves to heroic heights of resistance in the third and fourth, and achieved a victory of sheer endurance under the reverses of fortune in the fifth.

Motley's characterization was equally Shakespearean. Philip II resembled Richard III, the monstrous tyrant who filled the stage with his vicious and cruel wickedness, and gloried in his villainy for its own sake. Cardinal Granvelle, Margaret of Parma's scheming adviser, recalled Iago, as did a number of other Catholic clerics. The Duke of Alva, swimming in blood, went beyond Shakespeare to the extravagant melodrama of Marlowe's *Tamburlaine* and numerous Jacobean dramas. The unholy intrigues of the ecclesiastical figures and the gruesome horrors of the Inquisition were presented from the point of view of the entirely fictitious sensational "Gothic" romances popular since the end of the eighteenth century.

By contrast, William the Silent appeared as a national hero of "spotless marble," similar to Shakespeare's Henry V or, closer to home, George Washington as depicted by Irving, Jared Sparks, and Parson Weems. His greatest moment was marked not by action but by the silent force of his character as he quelled an angry mob simply by sitting on his horse in front of them. Motley expressed his opinion of William in one of his letters:

> I flatter myself that I have found one great, virtuous and heroic character, William the First of Orange, founder of the Dutch Republic. This man, who did the work of a thousand men every year of his life, who was never inspired by any personal ambition, but who performed good and lofty actions because he was born to do them, just as other men have been born to do nasty ones, deserves to be better understood than I believe him to have been by the world at large. He is one of the very few men who have a right to be mentioned in the same page with Washington.[5]

The principal theme of this epic interpretation of the origin of Dutch national identity was the victory of liberty over tyranny, considered as an instance of the cosmic struggle of good and evil. As David Levin explains it:

> His story of those thirty years of bloodshed proclaims two complementary "laws": that liberty and religious truth, always indestructible, are invincible when defended by a brave, energetic people; and that in such a conflict tyranny, however powerful, inevitably defeats itself, because its methods and its men are as unnatural as its ends. To this theme the rarity of patriot victories becomes a distinct advantage, for the power of the drama lies in the struggle against overwhelming adversity. The most terrible defeats do not destroy liberty, and tyranny's most crushing victories lead only to frustration.[6]

But it is important to emphasize that, although Motley's interpretation was based on literary models, it was solidly supported by facts. Like the other great Romantic historians of Boston, William H. Prescott and Francis Parkman, Motley based his story upon exhaustive research in the primary sources. The most grue-some of the Gothic horrors he so clearly relished — such as the siege and massacre of Haarlem and the tortures of the Inquisition — were amply supported by documentary evidence.

After *The Rise of the Dutch Republic*, Motley wrote *The History of the United Netherlands from the Death of William the Silent to the Twelve Years Truce* (1861-68), in which Philip II once again appeared as the villain, but there was no single hero to personify the virtues of the Dutch people. Then he completed the trilogy with *The Life and Death of John van Oldenbarneveld* (1874), in which that statesman was depicted as a martyr in the cause of liberty, and Prince Maurice as a military hero undone, like Othello, by the idleness of peacetime and the evil promptings of jealousy. Thus Motley completed his epic, in accordance with the literary preference of his times overestimating the roles of characters he depicted as almost more — or less — than human, and underestimating that of social and economic factors. He was also somewhat too willing to impose an essentially literary unity on a complex and diverse period of history. Nevertheless, Motley's interpretation of the Dutch tradition, like Irving's, became stand-ard in America, and has not yet been revised for general readers in the light of the work of more recent historians in the Netherlands.

The Dutch tradition, therefore, became enshrined in the American literary tradition as it was interpreted by a number of writers, most of whom were not of Dutch descent. To readers of Irving it appeared as an object of humor, whose most conspicuous characteristics were those that aroused laughter — whether satiric or loving — in others. To readers of Paulding and Hoffman it appeared as the foundation of a sturdy independence of character in colonists and Patriots. To countless children it appeared as the beloved figure of Santa Claus. To readers of Melville it did not appear at all as Dutch tradition, but as impenetrable obscurity. To readers of Murdock and a number of other novelists in whose works boers were minor characters, it appeared as a picturesque, piquantly different way of life on farms overflowing with abun-dance. To readers of Motley it appeared as the superhuman endurance which kept William the Silent and the Dutch people fighting for liberty in the face of years of inhuman Spanish oppression. All of these characteristics were without question present in the Dutch tradition, but authors of other backgrounds interpreted them in terms of their own standards, without realizing that they were distorting the proportions of that tradition.

11

The Americanization of the Dutch

HAVING contributed materially to the founding of the new American nation, the Dutch soon ceased to be a distinct ethnic group within it. They did not organize politically on ethnic lines, their church soon completed the process of becoming an American denomination, and their language survived only as a dialect spoken for a time in remote rural areas. But Americans of Dutch descent participated actively in the economic, political, and social developments of the nineteenth century, and the contributions of a number of them showed the continuing influence of elements of the Dutch heritage. And finally, new groups of Dutch immigrants came from the Netherlands, dissatisfied with religious and economic conditions they left behind and seeking to build a new life in the Midwest. The Dutch, therefore, continued to have an important impact upon American culture which often went unrecognized by people whose conception of "Dutchness" had been formed by the literary works of Irving and Motley.

Dutch patrician civic organization, still visible in Albany at the beginning of the nineteenth century, quickly fell into disuse. After the mayoralty of Abraham Yates, Yankee immigration became an invasion, and the bustling newcomers quickly lost patience with the traditional ways of the burghers, such as their long waterspouts which extended over the street to a single central gutter — in the Netherlands a canal. The Yankees, however, complaining in a newspaper campaign that the spouts interfered with vehicles, forced the city council to ordain that they be cut off, but did not provide for the rebuilding of the streets with side gutters, so that the water ran right back into the burghers' cellars.

But this change, earthshaking though it seemed at the time, was minor compared to the shift in neighborhoods created by the increasing population and expanding functions of the city. The patrician families continued to live in their ancestral homes until about 1800, when the district around the intersection of State Street and Broadway became commercial, and the remaining Dutch houses were turned into shops. Then in the next generation, with the building of the Erie Canal, the "canal basin" — the terminal harbor for canal boats — was located where the New York Central tracks and the Riverfront Arterial now run. The entire neighborhood turned almost overnight into a bustling port with warehouses, accommodations of all kinds for the rough "canallers," and slums where the immigrant Irish longshoremen lived. The patricians had to give up their new Federal mansions only a few years after they were built and move to the new streets on top of the hill where the State Capitol and state office buildings now stand.

The Dutch Reformed Church likewise adjusted quickly to changing circumstances. After the death of Domine Westerlo in 1790, the Albany church never called another minister from the Netherlands, and most of his successors were not of Dutch extraction. The congregation built a new church on North Pearl Street, completed in 1806 and still in use, but the schism reconciled by Domine Westerlo had broken out again and soon thereafter a portion of the members seceded, after which the church ceased to be a symbol of ethnic unity and became merely another American denomination. This process was accelerated by events within the entire communion, such as the Synod of 1790, which reconstituted the church as a body within the United States of America and provided that English should thenceforth be the language of worship. That this change represented a need felt by boers as well as burghers is suggested by the new English Psalter prepared by a committee headed by Domine John H. Livingston, which drew upon the version of Isaac Watts, beloved by Presbyterians, rather than the Anglican version of Tate and Brady, and abandoned the complex meters of the familiar Genevan melodies for the four-square English ballad meter of popular hymn tunes. But all these changes, and remaining bitterness from the Revolution, were too much for some New Jersey and New York churches of the former Coetus faction, who seceded in 1822 to form a new denomination, the "True Reformed Church."

The abandonment of the Dutch language by the churches indicates that, by and large, the parishioners were ceasing to speak it in their homes. Among the burghers, the Revolutionary generation in Albany spoke Dutch by preference to the end of their days, and looked upon English as a learned second language in which they could not express their deepest feelings; as one of them wrote her son: "I am not able to inform you all the particulars of her death. If it please the Lord that I may see you again I hope to tell you in my own language, but when shall that be?"[1] But the written language of this generation was English, even in their most personal letters. At first they wrote with the rather stiff artificiality of a language learned from books, taking allusive and metaphoric English literary devices quite literally. Gradually they learned to write more colloquially, but in the light of the remark just quoted it is interesting to observe that there were areas of experience, such as religious feeling and popular superstitions, which they did not commit to writing at all, and that the personal feelings they did express, though certainly genuine, fell into the formal conventions of sentimental rhetoric.

Children born in the early nineteenth century, therefore, of course knew Dutch and spoke it to their parents, but used English for all their everyday affairs and did not speak Dutch to their own children after they left the nursery. Those children, therefore, who came of age during the Civil War, recalled only a few nursery rhymes and endearments, and did not know the language as a medium of communication. Nevertheless, an interesting bit of oral tradition concerning the transmission of this language was passed on to the present writer in 1959 by Huybertje Pruyn Hamlin, who was born in 1872, a child of her elderly father's second marriage to a young wife. John V. L. Pruyn was born in 1811, and in the 1840s made a trip to the Netherlands where he addressed a meeting in the Dutch language he had learned as a boy in Albany. No one in the audience could understand him until a very old man stood up and said he remembered hearing it in *his* boyhood in church services conducted by a very old minister; he called it "Bible Dutch." It would be quite possible that the minister had been born before the end of the seventeenth century, which accords with the fact that Hudson Valley Dutch did not participate in any of the linguistic changes in the Netherlands after 1664 and therefore became an interesting "fossil" dialect.

Some boers continued to speak this dialect among themselves

throughout the nineteenth century, but, like the burghers, they used English as their written language, and study of the dialect was neglected until almost everyone who understood it had died. Nevertheless, as a spoken tongue it preserved its Dutch character, as a Dutch visitor who heard it in the rural Valley in the late nineteenth century observed: "it was more or less corrupted, of course, and often ungrammatical, but the accent was correct and had a native even though dialectical flavor, quite distinct from the pronunciation of a foreigner."[2] It resembled the German dialect of the "Pennsylvania Dutch," in that those who spoke the dialect to their families and friends usually spoke English to everyone else. Because the "Pennsylvania Dutch" were more numerous, and also because they made some efforts to use their dialect as a written language, it attracted more attention and survived longer than Hudson Valley Dutch, but both dropped out of use with the spread of compulsory central schooling and the invasion of rural homes by radio and television.

Perhaps the greatest change in the boers' way of life resulted from the abolition of slavery in New York. Dutch boers, who owned from one to three slaves apiece, had been since colonial times by far the largest users of slave labor in New York. Most of these slaves were owned in the southern counties around New York City, particularly Kings and Richmond (Staten Island), in which they comprised one-sixth of the total population, and above all Queens, where one-third of the people were black. Since these were the counties most inclined to Loyalism and occupied by the British during the Revolution, their structure of slavery was completely disrupted, first by the British invitation to slaves (of Patriot owners) to attain freedom by enlisting as laborers with the British army; and then by the flight of many Loyalists and the confiscation of the property of many others when the Patriots regained the territory.

The depression after the Revolution and increased immigration from New England and abroad provided a more adequate supply of free labor, so that slavery was neither as necessary nor as profitable as it had been in the colonial period. New England immigrants also included some highly vocal opponents of slavery on moral grounds, whose arguments for the most part went over the boers' heads. This was partly because, since the Dutch worked alongside their slaves and for the most part treated them as servants rather than chattels, strictures directed at the inhumanity of plantation slavery did not really fit their circumstances. Nevertheless, the Yankees persevered, and in 1799 forced through the New York legislature a gradual emancipation law under which all slaves in the state were to be freed by 1827. The colorful Colonel Erastus Root of Delaware County described boer resistance to this measure:

> The slaveholders at that time were chiefly Dutch. They raved and swore by *dunder* and *blitzen* that we were robbing them of their property. We told them they had none, and could hold none in human flesh while yet alive, and we passed the law.[3]

At the same time, the numerous children of Hudson Valley boers were participating in the westward movement. Descendants of New Jersey families crossed Pennsylvania, some settling there for a generation before they followed the well-worn route south through the Valley of Virginia and then west over the Appalachians to Kentucky and Tennessee. Others went straight west across Pennsylvania to the Ohio River, and floated down it on flatboats to many settlements in the Northwest Territory, such as New Jersey speculator John C. Symmes' Miami Purchase around Cincinnati. Families from the mid and upper Hudson Valley went west by the Mohawk River and the Great Lakes to northern Ohio, Indiana, Illinois, Michigan and Wisconsin. Since they did not settle in homogeneous communities like the Connecticut settlers of the Western Reserve or the Pennsylvania Germans in the Muskingum Valley, these settlers have for the most part merged into the anonymous masses of American frontiersmen.

Andrew Ten Brook, whose family trekked from New Jersey to Pennsylvania, and then to Ohio and Indiana, and who happened to write a memoir of his experiences in his old age, will therefore have to serve as an epitome of many. The Ten Brook family was evidently already in the habit of migrating, for Andrew's grandfather was born in Hunterdon County, New Jersey, on the extreme westward fringe of colonial Dutch settlement, and during the Revolution was a tavern-keeper near Trenton. After the war he and his family moved to Lycoming County, Pennsylvania, where they throve on a leased farm on the Susquehanna River near Williamsport. Andrew was born there in 1810, but when he was six years old, the call of the West became irresistible, and his father assembled his resources and packed the family into a

Conestoga wagon for the trip to Ohio. First they had to backtrack 100 miles southeast to Reading to pick up the great road that was the remote precursor of the Pennsylvania Turnpike. On reaching the Ohio River at Wheeling they bought a flatboat and floated down the river to Cincinnati, near which they bought a farm.

But times were hard in Ohio and Ten Brook's father lost most of his cash reserve to a sharper who took advantage of the monetary confusion created by the circulation at a distance of notes emitted by unsound banks. Though in comfortable circumstances when they left Pennsylvania, the family had little besides its wagon, tools, livestock — and a windfall in the form of an unexpectedly repaid old debt, carefully saved to buy more land — when they moved on to the Wabash Valley in 1823. Andrew, then 13, recalled this journey vividly, including such Dutch touches as the family custom of eating mush and milk (at Albany, *suppawn*) for supper, and their careful attention to their dairy cows, first for milk on which they depended during the journey and the first winter when other food was scarce, and then for the butter and cheese which were their first "cash crop." Indeed, while his father and older brother did the heavy work of clearing land, Andrew's particular tasks were pounding corn into meal and keeping track of the cattle, which grazed in the forest but were carefully brought home every night to be milked — a chore which gave him the delightful opportunity to scout the woods, rifle in hand. As soon as a little ground was cleared, the Ten Brooks planted turnips and potatoes, which in another Dutch tradition they fed to the livestock as well as themselves, thus maintaining through the winter their supply of milk — and their production of butter and cheese, which Andrew sold in a nearby town. The money thus earned the thirfty boers invested in more farmland while it was still cheap, and in a few years recovered the substantial scale of living they had enjoyed in New Jersey and Pennsylvania.

In the meantime, Dutch patricians back in the Hudson Valley were profiting by the opportunities to augment their fortunes that frontier development offered. In the tradition established during the colonial period, many invested in land — forfeited Loyalist estates, and also the vast tracts opened up in western New York and beyond by post-Revolutionary agreements with the Indians. Since most of the settlers available for these lands were Yankees who insisted on owning their own farms, these speculators quickly developed a variation of the existing system in which they sold the land rather than leasing it, but did not transfer title until the mortgage was paid off. Few settlers had the capital to buy land outright; many found the struggle to meet the payments too much and defaulted, leaving the land to be resold to someone else. Since with the arrival of some settlers or improvements in transportation the value of the remaining lands increased, the speculators could hope for snowballing profits — sometimes. The path of these Dutch landowners, most of them Federalists, who continued the colonial tradition of investment in land under the conditions of the new nation, may be traced on the map by the names of numerous communities — Cortland and De Ruyter in central New York, Gouverneur and Lowville in the Saint Lawrence Valley, and, farther west, Lansing, Michigan, and Rensselaer and Van Wert, Indiana.

Another traditional Dutch investment was banking, and Dutch fortunes stood quietly behind many of the banks which made New York an early center of finance and enabled Wall Street to attain primacy over Chestnut Street in Philadelphia after the destruction of the Second Bank of the United States during the second administration of Andrew Jackson (1832-36). The role of Wall Street in engineering that catastrophe has been overstressed, however, since many New York magnates were perfectly willing to profit by working with the Bank rather than against it. An even more profitable project which may be attributed at least partly to Dutch initiative and insight was New York's canal system. It was Philip Schuyler, with a Dutch awareness of canals, who perceived the potentialities of New York's "water level" routes to the west and north and organized the first companies to exploit these by means of canals, and DeWitt Clinton, Dutch on his mother's side, who coordinated the contributions of many Dutch and non-Dutch engineers and entrepreneurs to create the Erie Canal.

But the Dutch by no means stopped there in exploitation of waterways and development of transportation generally. They were quick to perceive the potentialities of the steamboat; only four years after the successful Hudson River voyage of the *Clermont*, Nicholas Roosevelt built the first steamboat on the Mississippi, and Dutch investors hastened to participate in the steamboat companies which competed with the Albany sloop fleet on the Hudson. The first steamboats were experimental, expensive, and unreliable — likely to blow up or get stuck on the treacherous sand bars of the upper river, particularly when captains insisted

"Commodore" Cornelius Vanderbilt.
Courtesy of Vanderbilt Mansion, Hyde Park

on racing each other recklessly. But since they did not have to
wait for the wind and could make headway against the tide, they
soon took the passenger trade away from the sloops. Bulky and
nonperishable freight, however, such as grain, lumber, and hay,
continued to go by sloop until late in the century. The greatest
of all the steamboat entrepreneurs was a New Jersey Dutch sloop
captain, Cornelius Van der Bilt, who saw the possibilities in
steamboats, and organized a monopoly to control the competition

of rival steamboat lines. Then, in a familiar Dutch tradition, he went on to check the threat of competition by railroads by gaining control of those connecting communities along the Hudson River, and finally to challenge the New York Central which ran from Albany to Buffalo, consolidating it with the Hudson River lines to create the great trunk system which channeled much of the commerce of the West to New York City — and in the process making for himself one of the first really great American fortunes.

While the Dutch were thus quietly playing a leading part in the organization of American finance and commerce on a continental scale comparable only with the worldwide mercantile empires of the Netherlands and Great Britain, another Hudson Valley Dutchman was performing a very similar service for the American political system. Martin Van Buren was of boer stock, a son of one of those Kinderhook Patriot families that had seized power from the Loyalist Van Schaack faction during the Revolution. As a young law student he was well acquainted with Peter Van Schaack, whom he respected and loved, but he regarded the other, less tactful members of the family as his political enemies. Van Buren began his political career by helping to consolidate the Dutch-Yankee Jeffersonian organization of the newly created Columbia County in opposition to the Federalist "Columbia Junto," a task which he handled much as Abraham Yates had a similar one in Revolutionary Albany. Then he moved to the level of state politics, where he accomplished the same task over again, forming the popular "Bucktail" faction which in 1820 overthrew the patrician regime of DeWitt Clinton and then in 1821 rewrote the state constitution to provide a much wider suffrage — extended to all white men in 1826 — and many elective offices. Thus the aims sought by Abraham Yates in 1777 were finally achieved nearly a half-century later.

Then Van Buren went on to create the political machinery necessary to turn the winning of elections into the practical, everyday power to govern. His Albany Regency, the most efficient political organization in the United States at that time, combined Dutch organization of patronage and insistence upon absolute loyalty to the doctrines and discipline of the "community" represented by the party with Yankee use of issues to appeal to large numbers of ordinary voters. When the Regency sent Van Buren to the United States Senate, he immediately set about welding together diverse factions to create a similar party on the national level, supporting the presidential aspirations of military hero Andrew Jackson. The Democratic Party thereupon swept into power in 1828 and set a pattern which has become the dominant American political tradition. But this victory was in some ways the high point of Van Buren's career, for the diverse groups he had brought together to win the election had ambitions which, once they were in power, diverged sharply from each other and from the Dutch tradition, so that although Van Buren himself served Jackson faithfully, the coalition he had formed soon broke up in opposition to some of Jackson's policies, such as his war on the Second Bank of the United States.

Van Buren's own election as President in 1836, therefore, came as an anticlimax as well as the fulfillment of an ambition, for it took place in the midst of a severe depression brought on by Jackson's monetary policies, in which crisis the boer tradition was perhaps less helpful to Van Buren than that of the burghers might have been. His dilemma has been described: ˙

> Since there was no need for a national platform, the party could adhere to a vague, negative program, satisfy local demands, and still win three successive presidential elections. The Jacksonians would continue to be successful so long as they avoided taking a stand on issues that could not be translated into local terms. Should the administration ever force its lieutenants to choose between allegiance to the states and to the national organization, the party might well destroy itself.[4]

Furthermore, sharing the Dutch plebeian ambition to become a patrician, his conception of the style of life appropriate for the chosen ruler of an ambitious nation — fine wines and golden dinner services — antagonized some voters who felt that their Chief Executive should share the hard times with the people. After his defeat by William Henry Harrison in the "Log cabin and hard cider" campaign of 1840, Van Buren retired to Kinderhook, making an unsuccessful bid in 1844 for the Democratic nomination and in 1848 for reelection on the Free Soil platform.

For the most part, however, he retired to the boer way of life, enjoying farming his estate, "Lindenwald," at Kinderhook with the careful attention which characterized all his political manipulations. As James K. Paulding, also retired, observed to elder statesman Andrew Jackson:

Martin Van Buren. *Courtesy of Albany Institute of History and Art*

The same practical good sense, the same sober, consistent, and judicious adaptation of means to ends, which has carried him successfully through every stage of his political life, is discoverable in his system of Farming. His calculations are all judicious, his anticipations always well founded, and his improvements never fail to quit cost, at least. He is always Sanguine of success, because he prepares the necessary means, and never sinks under disappointment because he feels it is not his fault that he did not succeed. Hence the good fortune which his enemies ascribe to cunning intrigue, and which has acquired him the appellation of the Magician, is nothing more than the natural and just result, of the joint qualities of his head and heart. He is what I would call a wise man, for he looks at his own interests without disregarding those of others, or placing his happiness on the attainment of any one single object; and is neither elevated by prosperity or depressed by disappointment.[5]

The retirement of Van Buren marked the beginning of a period during which the Dutch tradition and the mainstream of American development diverged decisively. The Panic of 1837 demonstrated that the basic pattern of American economic development was the type of "boom and bust" in which fortunes quickly made were quickly lost, and the successful businessman was he who could bounce back from a failure by going back to small beginnings and inventing a new gadget or promoting a new boom-town by advertising its golden future. This was by no means a game without rules, or without a basis of confidence of its own — the range and audacity of the American concept of "full faith and credit" in its broader sense are seldom realized — but it was not the basis of patient accumulation over generations by which Dutch fortunes had been made, and many of them were lost in the vicissitudes of nineteenth-century business cycles.

Furthermore, the increasing identification of American liberty with egalitarianism ran directly counter to the Dutch tradition in which political liberty was perfectly compatible with social inequality. This was finally brought home to the remaining Dutch landlords during the Anti-Rent Wars of the 1840s, which prompted the voters of New York to insist that tenure by perpetual leasehold be abolished by the Constitution of 1846. It seems somewhat paradoxical that in the 1840s Dutch voters in New York inclined toward the Democratic Party — until it is recalled that their idea of democracy was derived from that of Van Buren rather than Jackson, and that the alternative was the Whig party created by militant Yankees from the raw frontier in the western and northern parts of the state.

It was just about this time that the Dutch tradition in America took on new life and some new directions as a result of renewed immigration from the Netherlands. This immigration, most of which went to the Middle West, is not in itself part of the story of the Hudson Valley Dutch, but since they were aware of it and some of them assisted it — and since some aspects of the present-day American conception of "Dutch" are derived from it rather than from the Hudson Valley tradition — it must not go without mention. It was prompted by a number of conditions created by the troubled history of the Netherlands in the nineteenth century, after Napoleon conquered the Dutch Republic and incorporated it in his Empire. The Congress of Vienna restored the independence of the Netherlands, but designated the then Prince of Orange as King William I and joined the southern provinces to his kingdom. The latter arrangement, however, did not work, because the French-speaking Walloons and the Catholic Flemish, resenting subjection to the Dutch, rebelled in 1832, and in 1839 were finally recognized by the powers of Europe as the kingdom of Belgium.

Within the Netherlands, the influence of Enlightenment ideas in the Dutch Reformed Church produced a schism when conservative congregations, including many pious common people, chose to stick to traditional interpretations of Calvinist doctrine and found themselves subjected to many penalties by the established Church. In 1834 these conservatives succeeded in withdrawing from the state church, but the position of the Seceders as they were called, was still precarious, and in the 1840s many of them made the very difficult decision to leave their homes and emigrate to America; in the end, over half the Seceders in the Netherlands did so. The immediate cause of their departure was the economic distress all over northern Europe in the 1840s as a result of crop failures, of which the most disastrous was the potato blight which threatened parts of Germany and the Netherlands as well as Ireland with famine.

Their decision once made, the emigrants organized their venture very carefully, arranging for the wealthier among them to make loans to the poorer for their passage and the purchase of land, and sending out an advance party to locate a suitable site for a settlement. Accordingly, a group of families led by Domine

A. J. Van Raalte sailed to New York in 1846, went on to Albany where they were generously welcomed by the Rev. Isaac N. Wyckoff of the Second Reformed Church and his congregation, and left their womenfolk and children there while the men went on to explore the frontier. After considering several locations they finally bought a large tract of land in southwestern Michigan which seemed to them to possess the types of soil with which they were familiar, and had potential advantages as a center of transportation when railroads and waterways then under construction should be completed. This site they immediately named "Holland." Some of their plans went awry, because several thousand of their followers poured into the settlement before shelter or facilities for securing supplies were really adequate for their reception, and because the leaders underestimated the difficulty of clearing the thick forest and draining the swamps. But after a very few years of severe hardship the settlers of this new Holland created a thriving cluster of communities named for the seven provinces of the Netherlands and other locations in the old country. Here, as in the Hudson Valley, the Frisians formed a numerous and distinctive group who differed from their neighbors about many matters, and who never hesitated to speak out and take action about their convictions.

As most of the immigrants came by way of New York and passed through Albany, Wyckoff continued to take an active interest in their welfare. In 1849 he visited Holland, Michigan, as a representative from the Reformed Church in America, to find out if the settlers needed any help and invite them to affiliate with the denomination. Material assistance they proudly but politely declined, requesting only ministers and teachers for their children; affiliation they finally accepted after Wyckoff made clear to them that American denominational organization was intended to protect the liberties of individual congregations, not to oppress them as did the state church in the Netherlands. This relationship lasted only a few years, however, before some of the congregations exercised their option of withdrawing to form a denomination of their own, the Christian Reformed Church. The Christian Reformed Church maintained strictly conservative Calvinist doctrines, founding Calvin College in Grand Rapids to train its clergy, and many congregations worshipped in Dutch until after World War II. But many of the Michigan Dutch remained in the Reformed Church of America, and it was they who founded Hope

College and Western Theological Seminary in Holland.

The colony at Holland, which came to be regarded as the center of immigrant Dutch culture in the United States, throve and grew, despite a disastrous fire in 1871 which, driven by a violent wind storm, destroyed most of the town. Its sons and daughters spread out to other parts of Michigan including nearby Grand Rapids, Kalamazoo, and a settlement in the forest near the tip of the "mitten." Settlers who had been farmers in the Netherlands rapidly learned to make the most of the fertile American soil, particularly muck and swamplands which American farmers had passed by as worthless but with whose possibilities the Dutch were thoroughly familiar; it was on such lands that the Dutch of Kalamazoo made comfortable profits by cultivating quantities of celery. Other Dutch immigrants preferred to settle in cities, such as Grand Rapids — where the influence of the Dutch tradition of cabinetmaking upon the city's emergence as a leader in American furniture manufacturing needs to be explored. Immigrants to Sheboygan, Wisconsin, supported the most widely read Dutch language newspaper, and in the suburbs of Chicago, Dutch settlers first made fortunes by truck gardening and multiplied them by selling their fields for building lots as the city grew.

A lesser but independent focus of Dutch immigration formed in south central Iowa, where a group of Seceder settlers under Domine H. P. Scholte located a settlement at Pella in 1847. Two years later, as the settlers were still struggling with the initial hardships of the frontier, their fortunes were suddenly made by gold-seekers rushing to California in 1849, who passed through Pella and eagerly paid top prices for all the supplies the Dutch could raise or secure from neighboring localities less advantageously situated.

Where Van Raalte's temporal leadership of the Holland colony was always an outgrowth of his spiritual leadership, Scholte was much more like an American promoter.

His versatility was truly remarkable. He served as minister, as editor of the English-language Pella *Gazette*, as lawyer, real estate developer, justice of the peace, school inspector, and mayor *ex officio*. Scholte was also an energetic capitalist. Besides owning almost one-third of the land in and around the town of Pella, his investments in local industry were substantial. He owned a brick kiln, steam flour mill, and limestone quarry, founded the Pella National Bank, and was a benefactor and trustee of the local college. Although he failed in his bid for nomination as state senator in 1852, he served as delegate-at-large and vice-president of the 1860 Republican national convention at Chicago.[6]

Although he initially favored the Whig party, in 1854 Scholte urged his followers to support the Democratic party, in opposition to the prohibitionist and nativist policies of the Whigs. In 1860, however, he sought to lead them into the Republican ranks over the slavery issue, they deserted him to stick by their earlier allegiance to the Democratic party — and have continued to stick by it, with a very few exceptions, until the present day. Perhaps this stubbornness indicates the influence of another group of Frisians, who were aware of their separate identity as early as 1849, when one of them commented upon their differences with the other colonists in a long letter to his relatives in the homeland. Soon after the Civil War, Pella, like Holland, produced too many sons for its land, and spun off a daughter colony in Sioux County in northwestern Iowa. A third generation from the Iowa counties and from Michigan homesteaded in the Missouri Valley on the border between North and South Dakota in the 1880s, where they shared the experiences of locusts and drought, when some gave up but those who hung on eventually prospered.

While these Dutch immigrants were participating in the classic nineteenth-century process of rapid "Americanization," the Hudson Valley patricians were continuing their slow adjustment to American culture, to which they still brought identifiably Dutch behavior patterns and values. Some Dutch customs, particularly those associated with Christmas and New Year's celebrations, continued to be observed in Albany until after the Civil War, when they finally fell into disuse. But the close family relationships and exclusion of outsiders, characteristic of the Dutch patricians, was extended to the English and Yankee families with which they intermarried, creating the tight, inbred "Knickerbocker" social world depicted by Henry James and Edith Wharton and still clearly visible among — and keenly sensed by — their descendants today. After the Civil War, these families by and large withdrew from government below the level of diplomacy and statesmanship, leaving the everyday practice of local politics to the representatives of the people — at this time, very largely Irish bosses. It is exceedingly interesting to note, however, that the Irish power structure which grew up in Albany, in particular, developed in the pattern set by the Dutch power structure which preceded it, so that the system by which the city of Albany is governed to this day is essentially that by which it has been ruled for over 300 years.

As Hudson Valley patrician families retired from politics, and many of them from commerce, living on income from their invested fortunes as did established patricians in the Netherlands, they followed their example one step further by devoting their leisure to scholarship, voluntary public service, and patronage of the arts. One example which must stand for many is the Schuyler family, the first of whom to be discussed was not descended from General Philip Schuyler or even from Peter Schuyler, but from one of Peter's brothers, whose descendants' economic level was nearer that of the more substantial boers than the wealthy patricians. Eugene Schuyler, son of George Washington Schuyler (who is best known today as the author of the family genealogy), began as a pioneer American scholar, the recipient of one of the first three Ph.D. degrees awarded in America, by Yale in 1861. He then studied law and went on to a career as an author and translator of works in Russian, and as a diplomat specializing in East European affairs.

Louisa Lee Schuyler, by contrast, was descended from General Schuyler through both her father and her mother, a granddaughter of Alexander Hamilton, and represents the socially concerned patrician lady of the late nineteenth century. Beginning her career of service by organizing the women's branch of the United States Sanitary Commission (precursor of the Red Cross organization) during the Civil War, she went on to introduce into the United States Florence Nightingale's reforms in nursing education and to organize the State Charities Aid Association for overseeing conditions in the often neglected public institutions for the indigent and infirm. Twentieth-century members of this public-spirited dynasty have included scholars such as historian Robert L. Schuyler and his brother, diplomat, banker, and art historian Montgomery Schuyler, and trebly-Dutch civil servant General Cortland Van Rensselaer Schuyler.

But concern for reform among late nineteenth-century descendants of the Hudson Valley Dutch was by no means confined to the patrician class. One of the most colorful Abolitionist

Louisa Lee Schuyler, by Leon Bonnat, 1883.
Courtesy of The New-York Historical Society, New York City

agitators was Gerrit Smith, whose father, Peter Smith, was a Rockland County boer who had made a fortune by joining John Jacob Astor in the western fur trade and investing his profits in upstate lands. Gerrit kept an open house for anti-slavery agitators on his estate near Utica, and was equally open-handed with financial support for their projects, of which the most famous was John Brown's raid on Harper's Ferry. He was also interested in other types of reform, and encouraged his cousin, Elizabeth Cady Stanton, to become one of America's leading feminists. Another group of Dutch reformers which has been studied is the Vrooman family of Kansas. The father, Hiram P. Vrooman was a son of a Mohawk Valley boer who migrated to Ohio, from which Hiram moved on to Michigan and eventually to Kansas. Beginning as a Van Buren Democrat, Hiram moved on to abolitionism and then, after the Civil War, to the Greenback party, which sought to solve social problems by economic reforms. His five sons all became professional reformers, Frank and Hiram G. as ministers in quasi-Pietist splinter sects, Harry and Walter as Socialist publicists, editor and orator, respectively, and Carl as a promoter of agricultural improvements. All were strongly influenced by Christian Socialism, and Walter made special efforts to introduce in America the social work emphasized by the English reformers of Ruskin Hall. Thus the Vroomans carried to an extreme the Dutch plebeian values of Van Buren — liberty for the common man to be achieved by economic improvement and secured by political organization, all underlain by fervent religious concern.

Therefore, it is hardly surprising to find a number of Dutch Americans among the leaders of the Progressive movement. Beyond a doubt the most conspicuous was Theodore Roosevelt, who was born in a family whose elder members still recalled some of the Dutch language and grew up in a New York whose leading families still included many with Dutch roots. In his public career as Governor of New York, Secretary of the Navy, Vice-President, President, and ex-President, he demonstrated a number of Dutch characteristics, such as awareness of the proper role of military leadership in a democratic state and the importance of an efficient political organization, capable of a creative relationship with large economic concentrations. In the next generation, Franklin D. Roosevelt demonstrated some of the same characteristics in a very similar progression from the Navy Department to the governorship of New York to the Presidency during a dozen years of unprecedented world crisis. He was, however, much less conscious of his Dutch heritage than was his wife Eleanor, who came from Theodore Roosevelt's branch of the family.

Another aspect of patrician Progressivism was contributed by Theodore Roosevelt's friend, Edward Bok, whose family, though patricians in the Netherlands, had been forced by financial reverses to come to America and, for a time, to share the hardships of poor immigrants in New York City. Determined to free his family from poverty and restore them to their proper position, Edward from a precociously early age spent his after-school hours in all sorts of profit-making enterprises, eventually finding his opportunity in journalism, where after working as advertising manager for a publisher, he became at the age of 30 editor of the *Ladies Home Journal*. In efforts to increase its circulation he created the modern women's magazine, designed as an instrument of the adult education advocated by the Progressives, with many reader-service departments and firm editorial stands on moral issues of concern to women such as venereal disease. Bok finally accomplished his ambition of joining America's patricians by marrying his boss's daughter, and founding a dynasty of public servants. (One of them, his grandson, Derek Curtis Bok, is now president of Harvard University.) His autobiography, *The Americanization of Edward Bok*, became a best-seller in 1923, and with the proceeds he endowed a number of public benefactions including America's most famous civic carillon, the Bok Tower near his retirement home in Lakeland, Florida.

Dutch participation in Progressive educational reform is exemplified by the career of Charles Van Hise, a classmate of Robert LaFollette at the University of Wisconsin who in 1903 was the latter's candidate for president of that institution. Van Hise, descended from the Van Nuys family of New Jersey, was a geologist who had made significant advances in research techniques and had administered government geological surveys and mineralogical searches in Wisconsin. As president of the University, he participated creatively in that part of LaFollette's "Wisconsin Plan" which envisioned the state capitol and the state university (at opposite ends of the main street of Madison) as active partners in improving the condition of the people of the state. University experts in many fields were called upon to make recommendations concerning proposed legislation and, after it was passed, to take a leading part in putting it into effect. During the tense years of

World War I, Van Hise's administration of the university displayed the Dutch virtues of moderation, tolerance, and diplomacy in dealing with vociferous minorities who thought patriotism more important than academic freedom. The part played by some Dutch-descended intellectuals on the other side of the question is illustrated by the activities of historian Claude H. Van Tyne of the University of Michigan, who led a movement to curtail the teaching of the German language by his university. He took a leave from his academic position to make propaganda speeches for the National Security League's program of "Patriotism through Education" and to rewrite school history texts, eliminating favorable references to Germany and unfavorable references to England and France.

Also in the early twentieth century, the Dutch colony surrounding Holland, Michigan, brought forth two statesmen who cannot be overlooked. Both represented the conservative rather than the progressive wing of the Republican party, which had won the allegiance of the Holland Dutch during the Civil War and has retained it until the present day. Gerrit J. Diekema, the son of a Frisian immigrant, won election to the Legislature from Holland in 1884, and from there went on to leadership of the state Republican party, becoming the best-known Dutch-American in Michigan and eventually being honored by President Hoover with appointment as Ambassador to the Netherlands. His younger colleague from the same area, Arthur H. Vandenberg, was a descendant of a Hudson Valley family, his father having moved from Coxsackie to Grand Rapids to seek his fortune. Vandenberg began his career as a Grand Rapids journalist, but was elected to the United States Senate in 1928 and remained there until his death in 1953. A Republican outstanding for both his intelligent conservatism and his diplomacy in a period of Democratic ascendancy, he gradually developed from an isolationist to a leading proponent of the United Nations under the stress of world crisis.

In economic enterprise, the Dutch invested existing fortunes in banking and finance or created new ones by audacious ventures in transportation and communication. In politics, they perpetuated the tradition of finding common ground on which diverse factions could meet, and of exercising the powers of the community's government for all its people, extending the concept of community from the local to the national level. They retained the traditional concept of liberty as a privilege to be enjoyed rather than a right

Senator Arthur H. Vandenberg. *Courtesy of the Michigan Department of State, State Archives. From the collection of the Michigan History Division*

to be taken for granted, and concentrated upon the practical mechanisms of making liberty work, rather than upon spinning abstract theories about it. They maintained an emphasis upon the importance of moral and religious values which, instead of making political issues of religious doctrines, sought ways of applying moral standards in public affairs as well as in private behavior. In all of these ways, the example of the leaders was no more important than the practice of their followers, ordinary people who created that foundation of popular support without which no American public figure can survive.

12

Recovering the Dutch Tradition

ALTHOUGH the history of the Hudson Valley Dutch has been neglected, a considerable amount of information about them has been accumulated, partly by their own efforts, partly by those of others. The State of New York very early translated some of the records of the Dutch period and collected others from the Netherlands, and private individuals preserved and sometimes published large collections of family papers. Descendants of Dutch colonists formed a number of genealogical societies which promoted the study of the history of the Dutch as well as celebrating the Dutch heritage. A number of popular writers have written well-received books using Dutch materials. In the last generation, scholars have investigated a number of aspects of Dutch culture and museums have recreated the material side of the Dutch way of life for increasing audiences.

Colonial historians of New York paid little attention to the Dutch as an ethnic group. Even Cadwallader Colden, whose *History of the Five Indian Nations* was written as part of the campaign to unseat the Albany magistrates as Indian Commissioners, did not explore the significance of the fact that his antagonists were of Dutch descent. William Smith, whose *History of New York* was primarily concerned with the misdeeds of royal governors and the rise of the Assembly, dealt with the Dutch period summarily in his introduction. Probably Colden could not read the Dutch records; Smith knew the language well enough to consult and translate a few of them. But for them the history of the province began in 1664 and it did not seem worthwhile to investigate the "prehistoric" Dutch period in any detail.

These Dutch records were made inaccessible by another barrier besides language, for between the seventeenth and eighteenth centuries there was a revolution in the art of handwriting. The beautiful script of eighteenth-century documents is still readily legible today, but seventeenth-century Dutch penmen used a rather different alphabet which cannot be deciphered now without special study and probably presented difficulties for eighteenth-century readers as well. As a result, seventeenth-century Dutch documents presented — and present — a double barrier to American researchers. This may have been one reason why a 1767 proposal to translate the Dutch records of the City of Albany was never carried out.

The first translator of these records was a political exile from the Netherlands named Francis Adrian Van der Kemp, a Frisian university graduate and minister of the leading Mennonite congregation at Leyden, whose activism in the cause of liberty led him to military resistance and consequent banishment. Early in the 1790s he and his family settled on a farm near Kingston, but after a few years they moved to a tract of virgin land in Oneida County where Van der Kemp tried to practice experimental farming. Farm laborers, however, were as unavailable there as elsewhere in early America, and neither Van der Kemp nor his wife proved capable of transforming themselves from burghers into boers in middle life. They therefore rented the farm and settled in the Holland Land Company's nearby town of Oldenbarneveld (now Barneveld or Trenton, N.Y.), where Van der Kemp lived the life of a leisured scholar, corresponding with numerous New Yorkers about agricultural improvements and writing numerous essays on religious and political controversies which he found it difficult to publish because he was unaccustomed to writing for American readers.

In 1818 DeWitt Clinton persuaded the Legislature to appropriate funds to pay for a translation of the Dutch records; Van der Kemp accordingly translated some 70 volumes in the next four years. After Clinton's defeat in 1823 the Legislature cut off the funds, and the project was left almost complete, but with some loose ends hanging and without its index. Later translators have dismissed Van der Kemp's work as unscholarly by modern standards, for with no information about the period beyond what he derived from the records themselves and little knowledge of the history of his native tongue, Van der Kemp simply transcribed the literal meaning of one document after another as it appeared to him. His work, nevertheless, made available the content of these materials for further study, although it remained in the state archives in manuscript and no historian appeared immediately to use it.

Another Dutchman aware of the need for preserving and publishing the documentary basis of New York history was Harmanus Bleecker of Albany, for whom the central city library is now appropriately named. Bleecker went to the Netherlands as a tourist in 1838, writing to an Albany friend of his warm reception:

> I send the enclosed papers containing notices of myself, with some reluctance. But considering myself as the representative of the descendants of the Dutch in Albany & that it is on that account principally that so much attention has been shown me here, I hope it will not be considered that I am gratifying my own vanity in forwarding them to you. I hope they will go to New York free from postage. You can have no conception of the pleasure that is given here, by the St. Nicholas celebrations in Albany.[1]

While he was there, President Van Buren appointed him head of the United States diplomatic mission to the Netherlands, a post he held for the remaining two years of the administration. His young Albanian secretary, John Romeyn Brodhead, a great-great-grandson of Theodorus Jacobus Frelinghuysen, discovered quantities of materials concerning the history of New York in the Dutch archives. With Bleecker's support, Brodhead prevailed upon the New York Legislature to appropriate funds to transcribe not only these documents, but also those in comparable archives in London and Paris. On these archives Brodhead eventually based his *Colonial History of New York*.

Brodhead, however, did not translate these documents for the use of others. That task was left for Edmund B. O'Callaghan, a physician from Ireland who came to Albany after participating in the Canadian Rebellion of 1837. In Albany he promptly became involved with the anti-renters and learned Dutch to seek evidence supporting their cause in the colonial records. This led him to write the first *History of New Netherland* (1846-48), in which he depicted the Dutch West India Company and its governors as oppressors of the liberty of the people. As a result of this publication he was appointed by the State of New York to translate

Brodhead's collections, in which position he published first the four-volume *Documentary History of New York* (1848-52) and then 11 volumes of *Documents Related to the Colonial History of New York* (1855-61), which were Brodhead's materials from Holland, England, and France. Later, O'Callaghan published several other collections of Dutch records, and his successor as state translator, Polish immigrant Berthold Fernow, published several more, including three more volumes of *Documents Related to the Colonial History of New York*. Taken together, these works provided a resource for studying the history of the province in its international context not even approached by any other state at that time.

Probably it was the appearance of these volumes which prompted public-spirited Albany editor Joel Munsell to begin publishing his collection of materials on the history of that city. Munsell, a Yankee journalist who had come to Albany in the 1830s and began his career by editing a muckraking newspaper called the *Microscope*, was as curious as a magpie about everything relating to old Albany. In 1850 he began a series of yearly volumes called *Annals of Albany*, into which he put a little of everything for everybody — journals of Hudson's voyage, accounts of the Schenectady massacre, eyewitness descriptions of disastrous fires, articles describing the fur trade and picturesque Dutch customs, excerpts from the Common Council minutes, lists of members of the city's churches and of the persons buried in their graveyards, and notes from the newspapers of his own day. When, after 10 years, the demand for these volumes ceased to justify their publication, he put the rest of his materials into a four-volume set of *Collections on the History of Albany*, including Common Council minutes of the Revolutionary period from 1745 to 1790, more church records, and an invaluable genealogical compilation based upon the registers of the Dutch Reformed Church. For specialized work these materials need to be checked against the originals if possible, because Munsell did not indicate where he made omissions, but his accomplishment in gathering together in one place so many sources for the history of early Albany was monumental, and has shaped all the histories of the city written since — these tend to fall apart where Munsell leaves off. This amazing compendium of local history was rivaled only by I. N. P. Stokes's massive *Iconography of Manhattan Island*, published in the twentieth century.

The Centennial of 1876 awakened many Americans to an awareness of their national past and prompted the organization of many genealogical societies, including the Holland Society of New York, founded in 1886. Membership in the Society was limited to men descended in the male line from, and therefore bearing the names of, Dutch settlers and "those of other former nationalities who found in Holland a refuge or a home, and whose descendants . . . came to this country as Dutch settlers, speaking Dutch as their native tongue. This shall also include . . . persons who possessed the right of Dutch citizenship within Dutch settlements in America prior to the year 1675."[2] The principal activity of the Society was, and is, its annual banquet, which maintains the Dutch tradition of good food, good drink, good oratory, and good cheer.

The first years of the Holland Society were in many respects golden years, for most of the members were New York patricians, men of wealth and position, who included bankers, corporation executives, civic leaders, and President Theodore Roosevelt. The annual banquets were major social functions at leading restaurants, with *cordon bleu* menus and speeches by the Ambassador from the Netherlands and similar dignitaries. Other events included an extra banquet commemorating the anniversary of the siege of Leyden, for which millionaire member Samuel Coykendall invited the entire membership to journey by a special train to the Kaaterskill Hotel on September 14, 1886. This was the first occasion on which the traditional *hutspot*, a stew of potatoes, carrots, and onion traditionally eaten by the burghers of Leyden on October 3, 1574, after they found it simmering in the cooking pots abandoned by the hastily retreating Spanish army, was featured on the menu; it later became part of the ritual of the annual banquet. In 1888 a large delegation of members made their first trip to the Netherlands, during which they were loaded with honors and feted by the officials of every city they visited. This trip and its successors were conceived not only as junkets but as efforts to promote amity between the Netherlands and the United States, which were carried on by correspondence and personal friendship between members of the Society and Dutch leaders who were sometimes highly placed in the affairs of their respective countries.

The Holland Society has also been active from the beginning in publishing materials about the Dutch in America, although the history projected in the original constitution has never been brought before the public. First came the *Yearbooks*, which quickly expanded from a record of proceedings at the annual banquet and accounts of special occasions like the trip to the Netherlands. They came to include historical essays by members and friends and, perhaps of greatest permanent value, primary sources, particularly church registers from Albany, Ulster, and Bergen Counties, fundamental to genealogists but also invaluable to historians. Similar materials published separately included the records kept by Domine Selyns (1916), works on Dutch houses by Helen Reynolds and Rosalie F. Bailey, records of the colonial New York Chancery Court (dealing with the settlement of estates) (1971), and four volumes of documents of the Dutch government of New Netherlands translated by A. J. F. Van Laer but left unpublished at his death (1974).

In addition to these books, the Society also publishes a magazine, *de Halve Maen*, which began in the 1920s as a newsletter for members and still retains that format. In 1943 it was expanded to include articles about the Dutch, some drawing upon the genealogical and historical research of members and others contributed by scholars in the Netherlands and America. This periodical, directed to an audience which, though not composed of scholars, is probably the most knowledgeable about the Dutch that could be assembled, contains much information about the New Netherlanders and their descendants which is not available elsewhere, and deserves to be more widely known. In the 1970s the Society has also sponsored two seminars on Dutch culture at Rensselaerville, New York, to bring together its members and interested scholars; the papers given at the second have been published in "Cultural Mosaic of New Netherland." Further seminars, including one on the Dutch in the Revolution, are planned as part of the Society's Bicentennial observance. The Society also maintains a library including many rare historical and genealogical resources for the use of members and scholars.

In its early years the Holland Society had a branch in Albany, but more recently this has been inactive. Instead, the Dutch Settlers Society of Albany was founded in 1924, extending membership to anyone descended by either male or female lines from the early colonists of the upper Hudson Valley. This Society devotes monthly meetings to study of the Dutch heritage, and publishes a *Yearbook* containing valuable articles, source materials, and genealogical compilations. Both of these organizations now believe that they honor their ancestors most effectively by collecting and publishing as much accurate information about them as they can.

Despite the Holland Society's exclusion of female members (who soon formed a society of their own, the Holland Dames), women have made a disproportionate contribution to what is known about the history of the Dutch. Feminine descendants of Dutch families collected and in some cases published quantities of family papers, oral traditions, and information about relics they had inherited. The first of these publications, in the centennial year of 1876, was Catherine Van Rensselaer Bonney's *Legacy of Historical Gleanings*, which consisted of two volumes of letters, illustrating the careers of her father, General Solomon Van Rensselaer, in the army before and during the War of 1812 and in New York politics subsequently; the adventures of her brother Rensselaer Van Rensselaer, who became involved in a revolution in Colombia in 1828 and then in the Canadian uprising of 1837; and her own experiences as a missionary in China. Another descendant of Albany Patriots, Katherine Schuyler Baxter, published *Godchild of Washington* (1896), assembling descendant's reminiscences of the Revolutionary members of Hudson Valley Dutch families.

Another fluent Dutch-descended authoress, Mary L. D. Ferris, descended from the Douw family of Albany but resident for most of her life in the suburbs of New York, wrote newspaper and magazine articles. Mrs. Ferris began to publish articles about old families in the Munsell tradition in the *Albany Argus* in the 1880s. She also contributed to such magazines as *Harpers*, urging the restoration of Fort Crailo in 1890 and about the same time writing a study of Dutch "monkey spoons" which is still authoritative. Later, as an officer of the Colonial Dames, she helped restore the Van Cortlandt Mansion in Van Cortlandt Park, New York City, and wrote the guidebook made available to visitors when in 1897 the Colonial Dames opened the house as a museum, which is unfortunately no longer in operation. Her vivid imagination also led her to focus her entertainments for the Colonial Dames on Dutch themes, using her inherited Dutch antiques and ancestral recipes for cakes, cookies, and punches, and to write numerous poems narrating incidents from family tradition for circulation — often as Christmas cards — to relatives and friends.

Silver mug with Douw family coat of arms; made by Jacob C. Ten Eyck of Albany, ca. 1735. *Courtesy of the Metropolitan Museum of Art, gift of Mrs. Abraham Lansing, 1901*

Other women of this group cherished Dutch relics and documents, although they did not write for publication. Catherine Gansevoort Lansing, the last of a patrician family, spent the last 20 years of her life preparing her ancestors' relics and papers for presentation to various museums. Many fine pieces of Gansevoort family silver are therefore available for study at the Metropolitan Museum of Art, and furniture in the Albany Institute of History and Art. But the center of her work is the massive Gansevoort-Lansing Collection at the New York Public Library. Its 400 boxes and 295 volumes of papers cover six generations of the Gansevoort family, including quantities of intimate letters between parents and children, brothers and sisters, husbands and wives, and aunts, uncles, and cousins, as well as the military papers of General Peter Gansevoort and his Civil War grandson, and legal documents and merchants' accounts, school compositions, and even a lock of Mrs. Lansing's father's hair. It is, therefore, a unique resource for the study of the gradual adjustment of Dutch patricians to American culture, as well as for the study of nineteenth-century family relationships.

At the same time, professional women authors began the study of the social history of the colonial Dutch, particularly the wealthy families whose way of life could be associated with that depicted in the paintings of the Golden Age. Alice Morse Earle included the Dutch in her works on colonial childhood and costume, and Esther Singleton wrote a series of books on life in colonial New York of which the first was *Dutch New York*. This work, which is still the most accessible treatment of many aspects of everyday life, gives the impression that the Dutch settlers were wealthy, cultured people such as some of them became in the generation after the English conquest. Two volumes on Dutch houses by Helen Reynolds and Rosalie Fellows Bailey, first published by the Holland Society and recently reprinted in paperback, include descriptions and pictures of many such homes in the Hudson Valley, invaluable because some of them are no longer standing, but these books attempt no analytical study of Dutch architecture.

Also centered on a woman, interestingly enough, was a *cause célèbre* which made a wide public aware of the Dutch. Anneke Janse, her husband Roelof, their two small daughters, and Anneke's sister and their mother, a midwife, all apparently from Norway, were among the first settlers of Rensselaerswyck in 1630. But Roelof, a seaman, did not prosper as a farmer, and his women folk disposed of quantities of household goods — quite possibly in the Indian trade — so the family left the Patroon's service in 1634 before the completion of their contract. But Roelof died in 1636, soon after they settled on a farm on Manhattan, and in 1638 Anneke married Domine Everardus Bogardus. Soon after this marriage she became involved in a colorful incident in which some of her husband's political opponents caused her to be arrested for indecent exposure in the streets of New Amsterdam. Anneke's defense was that while passing the blacksmith shop — the seventeenth-century equivalent of a gas station as a male gathering place — she had merely tidily lifted her skirts to keep them out of the filth which had accumulated in the street. This defense was ac-

cepted, and the incident illustrates one use to which sensation-
starved frontier colonists put their courts and also the earthy
humor and broad practical joking which was often a feature of
Dutch civic controversy. Thereafter Anneke became the mother of
four Bogardus children, in addition to her five by Roelof Janse.
After her second husband's death at sea, she went to Fort Orange
to live with her married daughter and "make a living" — presuma-
bly at the fur trade, since this was the principal occupation of the
town. At her death in 1663 she left a modest estate, of which part,
which descended to her four surviving children by Roelof Janse,
was the 62-acre farm on Manhattan Island which she had inherited
from him.

It was this farm which, over two centuries later, made Anneke
famous. After a number of transfers, the land became the
property of Trinity Church, and, with the rise in property values
on lower Manhattan, immensely valuable. But in one of these
transfers, one of Anneke's minor grandchildren had inadvertently
been omitted from the deed. His descendants discovered this fact
about 1750, and between then and 1847 sued repeatedly and
unsuccessfully to break the church's title to the land. In spite of
these legal defeats, the myth would not die; another suit was
instituted in 1909, and in the next quarter-century the cause
attracted much publicity. Lawyers, genealogists, and promoters
who scented an opportunity to make a fast buck thereupon
started searching for all the living descendants of Anneke Janse,
who turned out to be more numerous even than descendants of
passengers on the *Mayflower*. Finally, the Legislature passed a
special act quieting the title and forbidding any further suits, on
the grounds that similar irregularities would have called most titles
dating from the seventeenth century into question. It also became
clear that if the heirs had won, there were so many of them that
the share of each, even in the vast wealth in dispute, would have
been less than the contributions many of them were induced to
make toward the expenses of litigation.

In the course of this litigation, there grew up an even more
astonishing legend about Anneke's origins. All the evidence
now available indicates that she and her husband were both
ordinary people, born in Norway (though perhaps descended
from Dutchmen in the Baltic trade). The legend, however, made
Anneke out to be a granddaughter of William the Silent who had
displeased that prince by her insistence on marrying a commoner;

nevertheless, he had placed her share of his fortune in trust for her descendants in the seventh generation. This fortune was reputed to have accumulated to the sum of 100 million dollars in the early twentieth century. It is difficult to see how this story gained credence in the face of its glaring inconsistencies, but this mythic fortune was as glittering as the other, and only very recently has a patient genealogist finally dispelled the last shreds of it. According to this myth, Anneke's father, a son of William the Silent by a secret marriage, was named Wolfert Webber, and a New Netherlander of this name (from whom Irving doubtless derived that of his character) was her brother. It has now been proven, however, that this Wolfert Webber and his father of the same name, a respectable Amsterdam wine merchant, had no connection with either William the Silent or Anneke Janse.

In the meantime, much more documentary information about the Dutch had become available. In the 1890s the State of New York began to publish Revolutionary records, including militia lists and the proceedings of various governing bodies, such as the minutes of the Albany Committees of Safety and Conspiracies, and later the 13-volume Sir William Johnson Papers, completed in the 1960s. In the same years a Dutch emigrant to New York, A. J. F. Van Laer, served as State Archivist, making a life work of translating the Dutch records. Much more than a mere translator, Van Laer was also an imaginative editor and painstaking historian whose works not only rendered the text of the documents into clear and readable English, but provided authoritative footnotes identifying individuals whose names were subject to much confusion, and introductions making clear the significance of these documents within the context of seventeenth-century Dutch culture. He also called attention to many errors in the work of Van der Kemp, O'Callaghan, and Fernow, the first of whose work was marred by lack of fluency in English and the latter two by the fact that Dutch was for both an acquired language.

In 1911, Van Laer's work was interrupted by a disastrous fire in the State Library which raged for three days, destroying many documents and Van der Kemp's translation. Van Laer's son recalls:

> I can still see my father struggling with these papers. They had to be handled very carefully. He had envelopes in his desk drawer filled with small pieces of corners etc that had been broken off. These were sorted by sizes so he could select the apparent proper size and then try to fit it

in the proper corner according to the wording. A very tedious procedure but the only way to complete the wording except by guess, which he would never resort to.

I can also see him coming home from the fire, soaking wet. He went in with two firemen, who kept hoses on him, while he tried to rescue as much as he could over the three day period that the fire burned. As children we were more concerned about the change that fell out of his pockets as he undressed in the hall to keep from dripping water all through the house.[3]

Despite this setback, Van Laer published numerous volumes, including the Van Rensselaer family papers, the Albany court records, and some church records.

These records appeared just in time for the folk culture movement of the 1930s, during which "debunking" authors often selected vivid stories from the court minutes, focusing upon colorful characters and sensational incidents which gave the impression that the Dutch colonists — like the Pilgrims and the followers of Captain John Smith — were a rather unsavory lot after all. To a certain extent this demonstration that the first settlers were fallible human beings rather than faultless plaster saints was necessary and justified, but it was often carried further than the facts warranted. Popular works written at this time included Kenneth Roberts' best-selling novel of the Burgoyne campaign, *Rabble in Arms*, which rehabilitated the character of Philip Schuyler. Even more popular was the Maxwell Anderson — Kurt Weill musical comedy *Knickerbocker Holiday*, although the vast majority of those who still enjoy "September Song" do not realize that the drama characterizes a Peter Stuyvesant who was then believed by historians to be 20 years older than has since been proven to be the case. A children's book, *Seven Beaver Skins* by Erick Berry, also happens to be a superb regional novel about the adjustment of the Van Rensselaers' young colonists to life in the wilderness. Finally, another work by a woman descended from Hudson Valley Dutch families, Mary Hun Sears's *Hudson Crossroads*, relates in fictional form but with substantial accuracy the roles in colonial history of four generations of her ancestors as revealed by the documents published by the state.

Another expression of the Dutch tradition in terms of folk culture was the initiation of tulip festivals as civic celebrations featuring Dutch aspects of the community, the first of which began in Holland, Michigan. In 1935 a similar festival was initiated in Pella, Iowa, and another the following year in Pella's daughter community of Orange City, Iowa. These festivals, held in May, were timed to display the blooming of a great variety of tulips in public parks and private gardens, and also included parades, pageants, and the crowning of a Tulip Queen. Residents turned out in the provincial costumes of their ancestors and demonstrated Dutch folk songs and dances, costumed dignitaries enacted such ceremonies as scrubbing the main street with large brooms and wooden pails, and tourists flocked in to enjoy the flowers, the fun, and authentic Dutch food.

During and after World War II the spirit behind such enterprises was channeled into relief for the Netherlanders, who often responded with the gift of more tulip bulbs. Such a gift to the city of Albany from its "adopted" sister-city of Nijmegen prompted the establishment in 1948 of a Hudson Valley Tulip Festival; this included the traditional ceremonies of scrubbing State Street below the State Capitol, the coronation of a Tulip Queen, flower shows, and a gala ball. In 1959 Albany celebrated the 350th anniversary of Hudson's voyage with similar civic festivities climaxed by the visit of Crown Princess Beatrix of the Netherlands. Another very recent example of civic recognition of the Dutch tradition is a resolution of the New York City Council, promoted by Council President Paul O'Dwyer, supported by the Holland Society, many scholars, and others interested in the Dutch, and signed by Mayor Abraham Beame on January 8, 1975, to recognize 1625 rather than 1664 as the date of the city's founding.

Scholarship concerning the Hudson Valley Dutch in this period produced a single book, Ellis M. Raesly's *Portrait of New Netherland*, depicting the culture and literature of the Dutch colony. Then in the late 1950s and early 1960s a group of young scholars began working in the field, independently of each other. Their books began to appear in the late 1960s — five fundamental studies were published between 1967 and 1969 alone, and several others completed in the same years circulate among scholars as dissertations available on microfilm of Xerox copies. The published books include studies of the origins of New Netherland and of the West India Company, a life of Theodorus Jacobus Frelinghuysen, a history of the Albany patricians, and an analysis of the construction of Dutch barns. Still unpublished are dissertations on the Loyalists in New Jersey and the merchants of Albany. Works on religion in New Netherland and religious assimilation on the frontier have recently found their way into print. Some of them based on manuscript sources in the Netherlands as well as in America, these books offer for the first time an authoritative basis for interpreting the full range of the history of the Dutch colonists.

But these histories are only the beginning. Since the post-conquest Dutch left so few written records, the legacy of objects preserved by their descendants and in museums is of even greater importance than usual in reconstructing their way of life. Museums began to study their holdings of such objects about the time that the generation of young historians just described began their work, and a few catalogs have been published. The importance of Dutch silversmiths was demonstrated by a completely illustrated and very informative exhibition catalog, *Albany Silver* by Norman S. Rice. The paintings of the Hudson Valley limners were brought together in a fruitful conference at the New York Historical Society in 1967; the catalog of this exhibition unfortunately remains unpublished, and a work setting down what scholars know about these paintings is badly needed. Classification of Dutch furniture owned by museums is just beginning. Students of Dutch architecture are turning from assembling pictures of Dutch houses to analyzing Dutch techniques of construction, an approach which appears likely to produce very interesting results.

In the meantime, museum visitors have acquired a vivid picture of the Dutch way of life from exhibits of these artifacts. The "Dutch Room" at the Museum of the City of New York shows a typical patrician parlor of the late seventeenth century, and a "please touch" room for schoolchildren offers them an opportunity to handle cooking utensils and pat the fur of a real beaver-skin. Two rooms from the Jan Martense Schenck House at the Brooklyn Museum recreate the home of a substantial late seventeenth-century Long Island boer, and another room from the home of Nicholas Schenck offers a valuable comparison with the mid-eighteenth century. The Verplanck and Van Rensselaer Rooms in the American Wing of the Metropolitan Museum of Art show the highly assimilated style of life of pre-Revolutionary patricians and the leading manor family. Typical furnishings from an eighteenth-century family from Ulster County are displayed in the Hardenbergh parlor and bedroom at the Henry F. du Pont Winterthur Museum, Winterthur, Delaware. Numerous other mu-

Hall of Van Rensselaer manor house, Albany, built 1765-69.
Courtesy of the Metropolitan Museum of Art

seums, notably the New-York Historical Society and the Albany Institute of History and Art, display many fascinating individual items from their Dutch collections; the latter also has a large diorama based upon a series of paintings showing one of the streets of Dutch Albany as it appeared in 1805.

The Hudson Valley is also studded with historic house museums illustrating various aspects of Dutch culture, only a few of which can be mentioned here. Fort Crailo in Rensselaer depicts the early eighteenth-century comfort of manor lords. The Van Alen House in Kinderhook and the Bronck House across the river in West Coxsackie, both maintained by county historical societies, show the way of life of boers like those depicted in the Van Bergen Overmantel, which can be seen at the New York State Historical Association in Cooperstown. New Paltz presents an entire village of houses built by French Huguenots, whose style of life in some ways resembled but in some other important respects differed from that of the Dutch. This museum village is of special interest because it is the only one in the country maintained by an organization of descendants of an ethnic group of original settlers. Hurley contains a whole street of Dutch houses still in use as residences, and is open to the public on the annual "Stone House Day." Kingston has the Senate House and Newburgh Washington's Headquarters, both Dutch buildings made notable by their connection with events of the Revolution. And in the Dutch area of New Jersey there are numerous recently founded local museums whose Dutch holdings have not yet become widely known.

But perhaps the single most important museum of Hudson Valley Dutch culture is Sleepy Hollow Restorations at Tarrytown. This "Williamsburg of New York," supported by the same organization and using the same research techniques and interpretive approach made famous by Colonial Williamsburg, contains not one but three museums illustrating the development of the Hudson Valley Dutch way of life. Philipsburg Manor, reconstructed on its original site on the basis of painstaking archaeological, pictorial, and documentary research, depicts the seventeenth-century mercantile and landowning activities of the Philipse family, particularly their grist mill. Van Cortlandt Manor, in the original house, shows the possessions of an eighteenth-century Dutch family partly but not completely assimilated to English fashions; the kitchen, containing every imaginable utensil for the cookery for which Dutch housewives were famous, is particularly worthy of note. And finally, Washington Irving's "little Dutch snuggery" at Sunnyside, restored as nearly as possible to its state in Irving's lifetime when it was already a literary shrine, evokes the creative use which the nineteenth century made of the Dutch tradition.

Americans have been accustomed to think of archaeology as a means of exploring the ruins and discovering the remains of the ancient world, but scholars in Europe — especially England — have for some time been using its techniques to learn more about the Middle Ages. Fairly recently Americans have applied the same method to American history, rapidly surpassing even the English in post-medieval archaeology. Within the past decade, considerable attention has been focused on numerous "digs" performed at sites not suitable for the extensive reconstruction that have characterized such national landmarks as Williamsburg, Jamestown, and Plymouth. Such excavations, often undertaken when artifacts are discovered in the process of construction, or when sites are threatened by the progress of urban renewal, have been particularly valuable in uncovering information about the Dutch, whose principal sites of settlement are for the most part in repeatedly rebuilt center city areas. Most of this work has been done so recently and some of it under such urgent pressure of time, that the field reports have not yet been published, nor the significance of the discoveries been assessed.

Nevertheless, mention should be made of several digs at Albany, Kingston, and New York City, most of them conducted by the New York State Archaeologist in the Division for Historic Preservation of the Office of Parks and Recreation. That on the site of Fort Orange, in the path of Albany's Riverfront Arterial, has already been mentioned. Some discoveries there included the moat and the stone foundations on which the log fort was rebuilt in 1648. Inside the fort, excavation uncovered remains of traders' houses built against the fort's walls, their cellars dug out of the earth and lined with boards. Another excavation in downtown Albany, in 1972 and 1973, when some streets had to be dug up for construction of underground power lines, passed through a number of well-known sites including that of the colonial Dutch and English churches, and uncovered some of the city's earliest water pipes — hollowed-out logs — which may have been part of a water supply system observed in operation in 1678. Near Albany, the same office has excavated the sites of several farm houses, of

Portion of the floor and cellar wall of a trader's house built against the south wall of Fort Orange, ca. 1650. *Courtesy of the New York Office of Parks and Recreation, Division for Historic Preservation*

which the most substantial was the country home of the Douw family at "Wolvenhoeck," in Rensselaer, now part of the Port of Albany. Another significant project investigated the Schuyler house at "The Flatts," near Cohoes, on which the first house was built by Arent Van Curler in 1643; an interesting aspect of this dig is that some of the work was done by workshop programs for high school students and teachers.

The New York State Historic Trust, presently the Division for Historic Preservation, has also done considerable work at Kingston, particularly in surveying the fabric of the Senate House, which has long been a museum because it was used in 1777 as the "Capitol" of the State of New York; it was built in the late seventeenth century as a dwelling and was the home of several Kingston Dutch families. Other digs in Kingston have explored the ruins of the Louw-Bogardus house and near the Senate House have discovered some remains of the original stockade hastily built in 1658, as the Esopus Indians threatened their first attack. Interesting excavations in New York City include that of the Stadt Huys, the first City Hall, originally built as the City Tavern in 1641. Archaeologists exploring the site — 71 Pearl Street — in advance of construction of a new office building, discovered part of the original seventeenth-century foundations, a staircase probably from an eighteenth-century building on the site, and a wealth of artifacts including pieces of Dutch roofing tile. Another fascinating dig at the old Slip in the colonial port area yielded quantities of artifacts illustrative of New York's seventeenth- and eighteenth-century trade and shipping, many of them in an unusual state of preservation because the soil was permeated with quantities of tar, which sealed it from the air.

Perhaps the most unusual reconstruction of Hudson Valley Dutch culture is the sloop *Clearwater*, built in 1970 by a group of environmentalists in an effort to publicize their efforts to clean up pollution in the river. Since its first voyage under folk singer Pete Seeger — himself descended from a Hudson Valley boer family — it has toured the river, enabling visitors to became familiar with the construction and operation of these vessels that provided all transportation on the river for nearly two centuries. The Hudson River Sloop Restoration organization is also collecting information on the history of the sloops, and has published a remarkable portfolio of nineteenth-century engravings illustrating not only the boats themselves but also many aspects of life along the river — fishing, skating, iceboating. One of the most dramatic — and timely — shows sloops almost capsizing under immense loads of hay during a storm in New York Bay, reminding us that environmental and energy crises began long before the era of oil spills and embargoes.

There are also several trail-breaking studies of the Dutch in process. Those classifying furniture and investigating architectural construction have already been mentioned. Another is a survey of Dutch objects in local and major Hudson Valley museums. A dictionary of the Hudson Valley Dutch dialect will assemble some

7,500 words — every one that has ever been collected by a folk-lorist or found its way into writing. And an analysis of the registers of eight colonial Dutch churches in Albany County by the techniques of historical demography should open up a whole new dimension of understanding of the rhythm of life and the expansion of population in the families of both burghers and boers.

The study of Dutch culture has therefore been as diverse as that culture itself; each of these methods of preserving and recovering it has added something indispensible to the whole. Scholars and public-spirited civic leaders were early convinced of the necessity of translating and publishing as many as possible of the records of the Dutch and English periods. The efforts of descendants and other private individuals to collect and preserve family and local materials were equally important. So was the genealogical research of the Holland Society, and its simultaneous maintenance of the unwritten tradition of good fellowship and promotion of amity with the Netherlands. The work of the women who first appreciated the significance of their Dutch heirlooms, and who began their systematic study and the creation of Dutch museums cannot be overestimated. The popular writers who brought Irving's conception of the Dutch into the twentieth century and expanded or criticized it in the light of new discoveries certainly increased awareness of the Dutch among their audience. Now the historians, curators, and archaeologists of the present generation are gathering specialized data, which for the first time permits a fully rounded interpretation of the Hudson Valley Dutch. At last it is possible to put them in their proper place in the American heritage.

"A Brisk Gale, Bay of New York," engraving by W. S. Bennett.

CONCLUSION

The Uses of Diversity

AFTER tracing the history of the Dutch tradition in the Hudson Valley, it is possible to inquire further into why it has been so neglected. One reason is certainly that its silent character is at variance with that American tradition of "boosting," in which it sometimes seems that the loudest rather than the fittest survive. In addition, the American tradition created by historians, school-books, and patriotic orations has stressed the achievement of national unity rather than the preservation of individual and local diversity. This traditional framework has made it very difficult to appreciate the contributions of New York and the other Middle Colonies to the American heritage, a problem of which many historians are aware but which they have so far been unable to solve. It is, therefore, possible that understanding the Dutch for their own sake and putting them in their proper place among the founders of American liberty will suggest an angle of vision from which justice can be done to other neglected Americans, and new dimensions can be added to understanding of the American way of life.

The first great American national historians wrote in the nineteenth century, when the principal theme of history throughout the English-speaking world was the epic of the achievement of political liberty through the development of institutions of representative government. In England, the climax of this epic was the Glorious Revolution of 1689, which established the supremacy of Parliament, described in the widely read works of Thomas Babington Macaulay. In America it was the Declaration of Inde-

257

pendence, which cast off the tyranny of royal prerogative and taxation without representation, and paved the way for the assertion of the rights of the common man — the principal theme of the first great American historian, George Bancroft. The place of the Dutch in this story was that assigned to them by Motley; a patient, stubborn people achieving liberty by sheer endurance, which enabled them to survive until their oppressors exhausted themselves. But in the history of the Dutch in America, so far as it was then known, there was no such epic struggle to capture the imagination of either historians or their readers, nor did any of their history contribute directly to the chain of events leading up to "the shot heard round the world."

The next step in the development of the American national tradition involved a change in the audience for whom historians wrote. The generation of Bancroft and Motley considered themselves men of letters writing for literate adults who read history for information and enjoyment; at this time children did not study history in school, except as patriotic selections in prose and verse were included in such widely used textbooks as the McGuffey readers. But about the turn of the twentieth century American education was revolutionized from top to bottom by the Progressives, who organized it for the first time on a truly national basis. They faced the problems created as millions of immigrant children had to learn the English language before they could learn to read, and had to learn how American government worked and what the American heritage was all about so that they could grow up to be good citizens — for which purpose courses in civics and American history came to be required in nearly all schools. To meet the need for great numbers of teachers, the Progressives founded most of the nation's teacher-training institutions and developed a coherent philosophy of education. Then they went on to write textbooks in all subjects, including history, for teachers so trained to use, and publishers developed a system for distributing these books in quantity to schools throughout the nation. It is easy to see why the conception of the American heritage presented by these textbooks emphasized its descent from the English tradition, its homogeneity, and the importance of patriotism. All ethnic groups — including the Dutch — participated in it as elements in the "melting pot" who were most successful as they left behind their distinctive characteristics to adopt those common to all Americans.

As American history thus became first and foremost a subject universally required in schools, and therefore a professional specialty of teachers, a simultaneous revolution in the universities began to produce scholars who considered themselves professional historians, who found in research and teaching about the American past both their life work and their livelihood. Their ideal of scholarship was based upon German models, including the seminar method of research, in which a series of events was reconstructed by close critical scrutiny of original documents, and the literary form of the monograph, an article or book which related in great detail all that could be learned about a very strictly limited subject. On the basis of many such studies, which were believed to be "scientific" accounts of what really happened in the past, scholars constructed wide-ranging "theses" to explain significant patterns they observed in the facts.

The best-known American thesis was that advanced by Frederick Jackson Turner, who asserted that the unique features of American liberty developed from Americans' experience of conflict with the frontier environment, a point of view which had no place for the Dutch, or any ethnic groups, except as they participated in the common lot of pioneers. Another group of historians, led by Charles M. Andrews, impressed by the emergence of worldwide imperialism, approached American colonial history as part of the history of the eighteenth-century British Empire, in which relationships between the governments of the colonies and London were far more important than their relationships with the people they governed. A third group, of whom the best-known was Charles A. Beard, explored economic and social movements, particularly the influence of invested wealth and the protest of the poor against exploitation by great corporations; they therefore had little interest in the Dutch tradition of cooperation between classes for the benefit of everyone in the local community.

It has long been recognized that these national interpretations left out much of American experience, particularly on the regional level; many regional histories have therefore been written. The first such region to achieve an identity of its own was New England, which from the beginning had been unique among the colonies in that its settlers deliberately transplanted a whole way of life all at once, rather than coming to America for many individual reasons and creating a society after they arrived. New England authors dominated American historical writing until the end of the nineteenth century, and took it for granted that the American way of life was that of New England, which the people of other regions ought to adopt. About the turn of the twentieth century a group of historians from the South, considering this attitude an insult added to the injury of their defeat in the Civil War, began to write the history of a Southern way of life derived from that of Virginia, which was as venerable as that of New England and had made as significant contributions to the founding of the American nation. About the same time historians in the West, particularly those who agreed with the Populists that Eastern financial interests were exploiting Western farmers, seized upon Turner's frontier thesis as the basis for a regional interpretation which asserted that the West was the most American part of America.

In all this flood of regionalism there was no place for New York. Since the eighteenth century the expression "Middle Colonies" had been used when it was necessary for some reason to distinguish New York, New Jersey, Pennsylvania, and Delaware from New England and the South, but this area, defined only by the negative attribute of not being one of the others, had developed neither a regional consciousness nor a regional history. A few books were written about it, primarily by historians who, having written one work about colonial New England and another about the South, wished to write a third about the remaining colonies in order to present the result as a trilogy covering the entire colonial period.

The first of these was John Fiske, an ardent New Englander whose *Dutch and Quaker Colonies in America* presented the Dutch period as an era of unrelieved tyranny by the West India Company, which was finally ended by the good fortune of the English conquest. Fiske's Dutch characters were based upon those of Washington Irving, largely because all of Fiske's books originated as lecture series in which audiences enjoyed an element of comedy, but reviewers pointed out that, on the basis of the documents cited in his own footnotes, Fiske should have known that these characterizations were inconsistent with the facts. Another book dealing with the Middle Colonies was written by a Southern historian, Thomas Jefferson Wertenbaker, who after a first volume extolling *The First Gentlemen of Virginia* and a second excoriating *The Puritan Oligarchy*, completed the trilogy with a third bearing the cumbersome title *The Founding of American Civilization: the Middle Colonies.* This book emphasized the ethnic and religious diversity of those colonies, giving careful attention to both the Dutch and the Pennsylvania Germans, with many keen insights based on material culture as well as written documents, but Wertenbaker was unable to draw any conclusion concerning their significance.

It was suggested at a recent conference at the American Philosophical Society in Philadelphia that one reason for this difficulty in interpreting the history of the "Middle" region is that it does not exist. It has never, either by homogeneous transplantation of culture of the necessity of defending itself against military or economic attack, had any reason to develop a regional identity as did New England, the South, and the West. Instead, New York and Philadelphia have become symbols of national identity, and the experience of the people of the Middle States has reflected that of the dominant tradition of the American people. This is certainly partly true, but it leaves out everything in the history of those states which cannot be related to such landmarks as Wall Street and Independence Hall — including again nearly all the history of the Dutch and the Pennsylvania Germans.

Another suggestion at the same conference was that New York and Pennsylvania are at least as different from each other as both are from New England and the South — a fact borne out by the astonishing ignorance of most of the people of each concerning the other. Most New Yorkers are far more familiar with the Yankee tradition, which they acknowledge to be of a different region, than they are with even the basic facts in the history of Pennsylvania, with which New York has a longer common border than any other state; and Pennsylvanians — as the conference papers demonstrate — are at least as unacquainted with the history of New York. Each, in particular, tends to regard the non-English element in the culture of the other as "quaint" and "foreign," even though observers who group the two together do so, as did Wertenbaker, on the basis of their ethnic heterogeneity. A very recent book by John A. Neuenschwinde argues that sectional consciousness was created among the delegates from the Middle Colonies to the Second Continental Congress by their resistance to the movement for independence, which they saw as a New England scheme to dominate the rest of the colonies. He does not, however, show that this consciousness extended to the people of the Middle Colonies, still less to the non-English ethnic groups among them.

But historians of the State of New York have done no better at creating an interpretation which will make room for the Dutch tradition. Brodhead and O'Callaghan, despite their familiarity with the Dutch archives, accepted the nineteenth-century assumptions that the rule of the West India Company was tyrannical and that the history of the Dutch in the Hudson Valley ended in 1664. Carl Becker, whose famous thesis that the American Revolution was less a conflict over home rule than over who should rule at home was based upon a study of the coming of the Revolution in New York, likewise saw that struggle taking place entirely within the framework of British constitutional theory and practice. Even when he later wrote an article comparing the Loyalist and Patriot view of Peter Van Schaack and John Jay, and a brilliant essay entitled "The Spirit of '76" in which these attitudes were embodied in imagined characters named Jeremiah Wynkoop and Nicholas Van Schoickendinck, it apparently never occurred to him that their Dutch inheritance could have had any impact upon their understanding of American liberty. In 1933-37 the State of New York published a history under the editorship of State Historian Alexander C. Flick, whose 10 volumes consisted of 10 essays apiece, each written by a different specialist; the Dutch received their share, but no attempt was made to relate the various chapters to each other or to draw conclusions bringing together their various points of view. Finally, the now-standard *Short History of New York State* by David M. Ellis, James A. Frost, Harold C. Syrett, and Harry J. Carman focuses, like all the rest, upon trends in the history of New York which are also important in national history, and therefore relates the events of the Dutch period as an interesting preface with little connection to the story which follows.

Aware that these interpretations leave out some of the most important aspects of the history of New York, a group of younger scholars has directed attention to the fact of its diversity. Milton M. Klein focuses upon social diversity, pointing out that in the colonial period the peaceful coexistence of numerous mutually exclusive ethnic and religious groups was in itself a hard-won achievement. Patricia U. Bonomi describes the effect of this social diversity upon colonial politics, showing how it contributed to the creation of the factions which were direct precursors of American political parties. Michael G. Kammen shows how social, religious, and political diversity contributed to the creation of an ambiguous state of mind which developed into the characteristic paradox of American intellectual history, the balance between stability and change, visible in many aspects of American experience.

All of these interpretations make much more room for the Dutch than any that have preceded them, but all focus upon that state of mutual tolerance which is the end result of diversity rather than upon the diversity itself. They act upon the advice of Constance Rourke:

> ... it is obvious that many rich variables belonging to the older cultures were absent there . . . the constructive effect upon the cultural forces actually planted here has been neglected. Because they appeared in comparative isolation they reverberated like loud voices in an empty room; and they fell into new relationships . . . Essential patterns of thought, emotion and imagination were freshly twisted, emboldened, pulled into new dimensional forms; and it is the resultant configuration that must concern us rather than the separated parts of their antecedent sources.[1]

But they do not take into consideration that in order to comprehend diversity it is necessary to understand the various elements of which it is composed.

Reinterpreting the American heritage to explain the part the Dutch — and many other ethnic groups — have in fact played in it is, therefore, very important in making the observance of the nation's Bicentennail meaningful to all the people, whatever their ancestry. It requires a number of fundamental shifts in proportion concerning what is important in American history, some of which are suggested by looking from their own point of view at the history of the Dutch in America, which is as long as that of the English and much longer than that of most other ethnic groups in the United States. One such shift in proportion, which helps to explain why it has been so hard to write the history of the Middle Colonies, is that the relationship between local elements and the national tradition have not always been identical. From the New England point of view, the government of the state and even the nation was town meetings writ large; from the point of view of Virginia, the government of county magistrates was that of the House of Burgesses writ small. But in colonial New York the Dutch patrician system in Albany and some smaller towns including Schenectady and Kingston, and the similar structure of society in rural communities, operated almost entirely independently of the struggle for power between the Assembly and the governors. These groups were very much aware of each other and sometimes worked together, but Dutch colonists, even when they possessed enough property to be voters, simply did not share the everyday interest in provincial and imperial affairs widespread among English people in the colonies. They participated actively in their local communities and were most anxious for the preservation of liberties which they understood primarily in terms of commercial privileges, but until those liberties appeared to be threatened they were not much concerned about the abstract rights of Englishmen.

The Dutch tradition was also differently proportioned with respect to the relationship between public and private affairs. Present-day Americans have a keen sense of public responsibility which has grown out of their function as voters and their education for the duties of citizenship; the colonial Dutch did not share this awareness. Patricians recognized that their wealth conferred upon them an obligation to use it for the good of the community, and plebeians recognized an obligation to work for the benefit of the community and to fight for it if it were attacked. But by and large both patricians and plebeians felt that their obligations to the community would take care of themselves if they fulfilled their private responsibilities to advance the interests of their family, their craft or trade, and their church. If they were successful in their efforts to increase the family fortune, expand the market for the goods they made or sold, or contribute to the building of a church or the foundation of a charity, both private and public interests would be served simultaneously — so that as a rule the Dutch felt that they best served the interests of the community by conscientious attention to their own.

A third difference in proportion between Dutch and American traditions was the relationship between words and deeds. As Albany Dutchman Abraham Lansing observed: "You cannot, as a rule, judge a Dutchman by his professions, for he seldom makes them; you must judge him as he always asks to be judged, by the result of his labors."[2] It is, therefore, necessary to go beyond written documents to the actions of Hudson Valley Dutchmen — often as recorded by observers who were not Dutch — to appreciate the silent patterns of behavior which characterized their tradition. These patterns were, of course, not biologically inherited, but learned from parents in childhood — as often from mothers as from fathers, so that it is necessary to observe them not only in individuals who inherited Dutch names, but also in those whose Dutch heritage was on the maternal side. In studying such traditions it is important to remember that since children learn from both of their parents, different traditions may either reinforce each other or clash, in which case some children may adopt that of the dominant parent, others rebel against both, and still others abandon conflicting parental traditions to conform to the standards of their neighbors. It is also possible for newcomers to a community to learn elements of its tradition as adults, as French Huguenots, German Palatines, and individuals from other nations adjusted to the Dutch way of life, and as the Dutch themselves eventually adapted to English and American culture. Evidence from material culture — objects the Dutch made or used — reveal further aspects of their tradition not described in documents, if the historian uses disciplined imagination to envision the part these objects played in the life of the people.

When American history is viewed in the different proportions here suggested, the Dutch tradition — or rather, the combination of diverse traditions of which it is composed — suddenly makes sense as an integral part of it, and its remarkable continuity emerges as a historical fact particularly demonstrable with reference to commerce, religious toleration, human endurance, and political organization. Commercial advantage was the principal motivation of exploration and settlement of the New World by Dutchmen who were at the same time creating a worldwide mercantile empire. After the English conquest, Hudson Valley Dutch merchants rapidly developed a comparable structure of trade within the British Empire. Their descendants in the United States applied the same imperial vision to developing the resources of the American continent, particularly in transportation, communication, and finance.

Religious toleration has been an equally important element of Old and New World Dutch culture. The very intensity of their own convictions helped most Dutchmen to respect similar convictions in others, and merchants realized in addition that sectarian strife interfered with commerce. The Dutch decided most controversial questions by local option, and within localities dissident individuals and groups were seldom persecuted unless they disturbed the peace of the community; this policy of "connivance" was reinforced in New Netherland by the effects of distance, local differences, and the need to encourage immigration. Under English rule the Dutch developed it further as a defense against the Anglican establishment. The extent to which it became a part of the foundation of the Reformed Church in America was revealed in the nineteenth century when the denomination welcomed the Seceders from the established Church of the Netherlands, with the assurance that the denominational organization wished only to protect the particular liberties of individual congregations.

Other features of the Dutch tradition became particularly evident as the Hudson Valley Dutch participated with other ethnic groups in creating the American nation. Endurance had long been required of the Dutch in their struggles against the sea and against Spanish tyranny. In the New World, it sustained them through the hardships of the frontier, and during the Revolution enabled them to withstand the seven-year siege of the Hudson Valley. In subsequent American history, the descendants of the Hudson Valley Dutch were never again so pushed to the wall, but nineteenth-century Dutch immigrants in the Middle West displayed similar resilience in the face of difficult environmental and economic circumstances.

The Dutch also found their inherited political tradition useful in helping to unite the diverse elements in New York, particularly since the political conditions in the Middle States, with their many ethnic groups and strong local traditions, very much resembled those of the Netherlands. His Dutch inheritance, therefore, made essential contributions to Martin Van Buren's construction of the Democratic party in New York State and in the nation. Descendants of the Hudson Valley Dutch and representatives of the Michigan "Colonie" also contributed another Dutch tradition to American politics by their services in the exercise of diplomacy, in promoting cooperation and compromise in domestic affairs, and eventually by supporting organizations for international cooperation.

Therefore, the Dutch tradition is not merely significant as a survival, a sort of curious social fossil embedded in the strata of American history. It is very much alive in America today, and by a sudden and fortuitous chain of circumstances it has been called from its silence to national leadership in a period of crisis as well as of Bicentennial celebration. It just so happens that both the President and the Vice-President of the United States in 1976 will be closely associated with the Dutch tradition, though neither bears a Dutch name. President Ford has for a quarter-century represented the Dutch constituency including Holland, Michigan, and reflects the tradition of Diekema and Vandenberg in his emphasis upon actions that speak louder than words, political compromise, and the application of moral and religious standards in public affairs. Vice-President Rockefeller is descended from an early eighteenth-century German immigrant to the upper Hudson Valley whose family adapted to Dutch culture before that of the English; he himself has followed in the political tradition of Van Buren and two Roosevelts, all governors of New York who went on to national leadership, and also embodies the Dutch tradition of considering a great fortune a public trust to be administered for the benefit of the entire community.

It may thus be recognized, without belaboring an astonishing coincidence, that the plebeian and patrician Dutch traditions are working side by side in the highest offices in the land, at a time which many Americans believe to be quite as critical as the crisis of 200 years ago when for a few crucial weeks, and for seven long years, the fate of American independence rested in the hands of the Hudson Valley Dutch. They saved themselves and helped to save the nation then by using their traditional qualities of individual endurance, taking practical local action to deal with immediate problems, and balancing their diversities to achieve a common denominator of unity sufficient to sustain the survival of the community while respecting the liberties of all its members. Such qualities promise to be at least as useful in dealing with the crises of the 1970s, and perhaps the most significant contribution the Dutch tradition can make to the Bicentennial is to remind the American people of the continuing importance of these qualities in their history and to encourage them to use them again to build solid foundations for their future liberty.

NOTES TO THE CHAPTERS

Chapter 1 — Beaver Skins and Wild Men

1. Robert Juet, "The Third Voyage of Master Henry Hudson," in J. Franklin Jameson, ed., *Narratives of New Netherland* (1909; repr. New York: Barnes and Noble, 1967), 19.

2. *Ibid.*, 23.

3. Van Cleaf Bachman, *Peltries or Plantations* (Baltimore: Johns Hopkins University Press, 1969), 12.

4. Nicholaes Wassenaer, "Historische Verhael," in Jameson, *Narratives*, 75-76.

Chapter 2 — Many Faces of New Netherland

1. Isaac Jogues, "Novum Belgium," in Jameson, *Narratives*, 260.

2. Ellis M. Raesly, *Portrait of New Netherland* (New York: Columbia University Press, 1945), 128.

Chapter 4 — Patricians and Plebeians

1. Quoted in S. G. Nissenson, *The Patroon's Domain* (New York: Columbia University Press, 1936), 304.

2. Jacob Judd, "Frederick Philipse and the Madagascar Trade," *New-York Historical Society Quarterly* 55 (1971): 362.

3. Alexander Hamilton, *Gentleman's Progress* (Chapel Hill, N.C.: University of North Carolina Press, 1948), 87.

4. Anne McVicar Grant, *Memoirs of an American Lady* (London: Longmans, 1808), 83.

5. Hamilton, *Gentleman's Progress*, 89.

6. Raesly, *Portrait*, 163.

7. Leonard Gansevoort (?), "Advice on chusing a wife," August 14, 1771, Gansevoort family letters, Gansevoort-Lansing Collection, New York Public Library (hereafter cited as GLC).

8. Peter Kalm, *Peter Kalm's Travels in North America; the English Version of 1770*, ed. Adolph B. Benson (1937; repr. New York: Dover Publications, 1966), 346-47.

9. Grant, *Memoirs*, 74-75.

10. *Peter Kalm's Travels*, 343.

Chapter 5 — Golden Fields

1. *Peter Kalm's Travels*, 335.

2. Grant, *Memoirs*, 30-31.

Chapter 6 — Faiths of Their Fathers

1. Jogues, in Jameson, *Narratives*, 260.

2. Quoted in Henry E. Kessler and Eugene Rachlis, *Peter Stuyvesant and His New York* (New York: Random House, 1959), 196.

3. Joel Munsell, *Collections on the History of Albany* (Albany, 1865-72), II, 384-85.

4. James Tanis, *Dutch Calvinistic Pietism in the Middle Colonies* (The Hague: Martinus Nijhoff, 1967), 43.

Chapter 7 — The Dutch Revolt

1. William Corry to Sir William Johnson, August 23, 1759, *Sir William Johnson Papers* (Albany: University of the State of New York, 1921-65), III, 129.

2. *The New-York Journal; or, the General Advertiser*, May 10, 1770.

3. Leonard Gansevoort to Peter Gansevoort, August 28, 1775, Peter Gansevoort Military Papers, GLC.

Chapter 8 — The Siege of the Hudson Valley

1. William Smith, Jr., *Historical Memoirs from 12 July 1776 to 25 July 1778*, ed. H. W. Sabine (New York: Colburn and Tegg, 1958), Nov. 5, 1776, p. 35.

2. H. O. H. Vernon-Jackson, "A Loyalist's Wife; Letters of Mrs. Philip Van Cortlandt, December 1776 to February 1777," *History Today* (August 1964): 576-77.

3. Livingston Manor Committee, "Minutes," *New York Genealogical and Biographical Record* 60 (1929): 328.

4. "Examination of John Van den Bergh," in Peter Force, *American Archives* (Washington, D. C.: U.S. Government Printing Office, 1851), 5th Ser., III, 524.

5. Quoted in Staughton Lynd, "The Tenant Rising at Livingston Manor, May 1777," *New-York Historical Society Quarterly* 48 (April 1964): 174.

6. Colonel Peter Gansevoort to Colonel Barry St. Leger, August 9, 1777, Peter Gansevoort Military Papers, GLC.

7. John Adams to Abigail Adams, September 2, 1777, *Adams Family Correspondence* (Cambridge, Mass.: Harvard University Press, 1963), II, 331.

8. Catherine Van Schaick to Peter Gansevoort, July 8, 1777, Gansevoort Family Letters, GLC.

9. General John Burgoyne to Parliament, quoted in Francis P. Kimball, *Capital Region of New York State* (New York: Lavis Historical Publishing Co., 1942), I: 369-70.

10. Peter Gansevoort to Catherine Van Schaick Gansevoort, September 14, 1780, Peter Gansevoort Military Papers, GLC.

11. Simeon Baldwin, "Diary," March 26, 1783, transcript in "Miscellaneous Historical Collections," GLC.

12. *Ibid.*

Chapter 9 — *E PLURIBUS UNUM*

1. Robert Troup to Rufus King, April 4, 1809, in Charles R. King, ed., *The Life and Correspondence of Rufus King* (New York, 1894-1900), V, 148-49.

Chapter 10 — Folklore, Fiction, and Fact

1. Sara P. Rodes, "Washington Irving's Use of Traditional Folklore," *Southern Folklore Quarterly* 20 (September 1956): 146.

2. James Kirke Paulding to Gasherie DeWitt (?), December 28, 1827, in Ralph M. Aderman, ed., *The Letters of James Kirke Paulding* (Madison, Wis.: The University of Wisconsin Press, 1962), 93.

3. Charles E. Fitch, ed., *Recollections: Abraham Lansing* (Albany, N.Y.: Privately printed, 1909), 109,111.

4. Harold Frederic, *In the Valley* (New York: Charles Scribner's Sons, 1890), 189.

5. George William Curtis, ed., *The Correspondence of John Lothrop Motley*, 2nd ed. (London: John Murray, 1889), I, 146.

6. David Levin, *History as Romantic Art* (1959; repr. New York: Harcourt, Brace and World, 1963), 188-89.

Chapter 11 — The Americanization of the Dutch

1. Elizabeth Bleecker of Harmanus Bleecker, May 25, 1812, in Harriet L. P. Rice, *Harmanus Bleecker* (Albany, N.Y.: Privately printed, 1924), 25.

2. A. J. F. Van Laer, quoted in Thomas J. Wertenbaker, *Founding of American Civilization: the Middle Colonies* (New York, 1949), 116-17.

3. Erastus Root, quoted in Jabez D. Hammond, *History of Political Parties in the State of New York* (Albany, N.Y.: Van Benthuysen, 1842), I, 581.

4. James C. Curtis, *The Fox at Bay* (Lexington, Ky.: The University Press of Kentucky, 1970), viii.

5. James Kirke Paulding to Andrew Jackson, October 4, 1843, in Aderman, ed., *Letters of Paulding*, 353.

6. Robert P. Swierenga, "The Ethnic Voter and the First Lincoln Election," *Civil War History* (March 1965), 29-30.

Chapter 12 — Recovering the Dutch Tradition

1. Harmanus Bleecker to John V. L. Pruyn, March 1, 1839, in Rice, *Bleecker*, 111.

2. "Constitution of the Holland Society," Article III, *Holland Society Yearbook* (1916), 106.

3. Hendrik van Laer, quoted in Kenneth Scott and Kenn Stryker-Rodda, "Holland Society Publishes van Laer Translations," *de Halve Maen* 49 (April 1974): 5.

Conclusion — The Uses of Diversity

1. Constance Rourke, *Roots of American Culture* (New York, 1942), 54-55.

2. Fitch, ed., *Recollections: Abraham Lansing*, 111.

Chapter 11 — The Americanization of the Dutch

1. Elizabeth Bleecker of Harmanus Bleecker, May 25, 1812, in Harriet L. P. Rice, *Harmanus Bleecker* (Albany, N.Y.: Privately printed, 1924), 25.

2. A. J. F. Van Laer, quoted in Thomas J. Wertenbaker, *Founding of American Civilization: the Middle Colonies* (New York, 1949), 116-17.

3. Erastus Root, quoted in Jabez D. Hammond, *History of Political Parties in the State of New York* (Albany, N.Y.: Van Benthuysen, 1842), I, 581.

4. James C. Curtis, *The Fox at Bay* (Lexington, Ky.: The University Press of Kentucky, 1970), viii.

5. James Kirke Paulding to Andrew Jackson, October 4, 1843, in Aderman, ed., *Letters of Paulding*, 353.

6. Robert P. Swierenga, "The Ethnic Voter and the First Lincoln Election," *Civil War History* (March 1965), 29-30.

Chapter 12 — Recovering the Dutch Tradition

1. Harmanus Bleecker to John V. L. Pruyn, March 1, 1839, in Rice, *Bleecker*, 111.

2. "Constitution of the Holland Society," Article III, *Holland Society Yearbook* (1916), 106.

3. Hendrik van Laer, quoted in Kenneth Scott and Kenn Stryker-Rodda, "Holland Society Publishes van Laer Translations," *de Halve Maen* 49 (April 1974): 5.

Conclusion — The Uses of Diversity

1. Constance Rourke, *Roots of American Culture* (New York, 1942), 54-55.

2. Fitch, ed., *Recollections: Abraham Lansing*, 111.

NOTES TO THE CHAPTERS

Chapter 1 — Beaver Skins and Wild Men

1. Robert Juet, "The Third Voyage of Master Henry Hudson," in J. Franklin Jameson, ed., *Narratives of New Netherland* (1909; repr. New York: Barnes and Noble, 1967), 19.

2. *Ibid.*, 23.

3. Van Cleaf Bachman, *Peltries or Plantations* (Baltimore: Johns Hopkins University Press, 1969), 12.

4. Nicholaes Wassenaer, "Historische Verhael," in Jameson, *Narratives*, 75-76.

Chapter 2 — Many Faces of New Netherland

1. Isaac Jogues, "Novum Belgium," in Jameson, *Narratives*, 260.

2. Ellis M. Raesly, *Portrait of New Netherland* (New York: Columbia University Press, 1945), 128.

Chapter 4 — Patricians and Plebeians

1. Quoted in S. G. Nissenson, *The Patroon's Domain* (New York: Columbia University Press, 1936), 304.

2. Jacob Judd, "Frederick Philipse and the Madagascar Trade," *New-York Historical Society Quarterly* 55 (1971): 362.

3. Alexander Hamilton, *Gentleman's Progress* (Chapel Hill, N.C.: University of North Carolina Press, 1948), 87.

4. Anne McVicar Grant, *Memoirs of an American Lady* (London: Longmans, 1808), 83.

5. Hamilton, *Gentleman's Progress*, 89.

6. Raesly, *Portrait*, 163.

7. Leonard Gansevoort (?), "Advice on chusing a wife," August 14, 1771, Gansevoort family letters, Gansevoort-Lansing Collection, New York Public Library (hereafter cited as GLC).

8. Peter Kalm, *Peter Kalm's Travels in North America; the English Version of 1770*, ed. Adolph B. Benson (1937; repr. New York: Dover Publications, 1966), 346-47.

9. Grant, *Memoirs*, 74-75.

10. *Peter Kalm's Travels*, 343.

Chapter 5 — Golden Fields

1. *Peter Kalm's Travels*, 335.

2. Grant, *Memoirs*, 30-31.

Chapter 6 — Faiths of Their Fathers

1. Jogues, in Jameson, *Narratives*, 260.

2. Quoted in Henry E. Kessler and Eugene Rachlis, *Peter Stuyvesant and His New York* (New York: Random House, 1959), 196.

3. Joel Munsell, *Collections on the History of Albany* (Albany, 1865-72), II, 384-85.

4. James Tanis, *Dutch Calvinistic Pietism in the Middle Colonies* (The Hague: Martinus Nijhoff, 1967), 43.

Chapter 7 — The Dutch Revolt

1. William Corry to Sir William Johnson, August 23, 1759, *Sir William Johnson Papers* (Albany: University of the State of New York, 1921-65), III, 129.

2. *The New-York Journal; or, the General Advertiser*, May 10, 1770.

3. Leonard Gansevoort to Peter Gansevoort, August 28, 1775, Peter Gansevoort Military Papers, GLC.

Chapter 8 — The Siege of the Hudson Valley

1. William Smith, Jr., *Historical Memoirs from 12 July 1776 to 25 July 1778*, ed. H. W. Sabine (New York: Colburn and Tegg, 1958), Nov. 5, 1776, p. 35.

2. H. O. H. Vernon-Jackson, "A Loyalist's Wife; Letters of Mrs. Philip Van Cortlandt, December 1776 to February 1777," *History Today* (August 1964): 576-77.

3. Livingston Manor Committee, "Minutes," *New York Genealogical and Biographical Record* 60 (1929): 328.

4. "Examination of John Van den Bergh," in Peter Force, *American Archives* (Washington, D. C.: U.S. Government Printing Office, 1851), 5th Ser., III, 524.

5. Quoted in Staughton Lynd, "The Tenant Rising at Livingston Manor, May 1777," *New-York Historical Society Quarterly* 48 (April 1964): 174.

6. Colonel Peter Gansevoort to Colonel Barry St. Leger, August 9, 1777, Peter Gansevoort Military Papers, GLC.

7. John Adams to Abigail Adams, September 2, 1777, *Adams Family Correspondence* (Cambridge, Mass.: Harvard University Press, 1963), II, 331.

8. Catherine Van Schaick to Peter Gansevoort, July 8, 1777, Gansevoort Family Letters, GLC.

9. General John Burgoyne to Parliament, quoted in Francis P. Kimball, *Capital Region of New York State* (New York: Lavis Historical Publishing Co., 1942), I: 369-70.

10. Peter Gansevoort to Catherine Van Schaick Gansevoort, September 14, 1780, Peter Gansevoort Military Papers, GLC.

11. Simeon Baldwin, "Diary," March 26, 1783, transcript in "Miscellaneous Historical Collections," GLC.

12. *Ibid.*

Chapter 9 — *E PLURIBUS UNUM*

1. Robert Troup to Rufus King, April 4, 1809, in Charles R. King, ed., *The Life and Correspondence of Rufus King* (New York, 1894-1900), V, 148-49.

Chapter 10 — Folklore, Fiction, and Fact

1. Sara P. Rodes, "Washington Irving's Use of Traditional Folklore," *Southern Folklore Quarterly* 20 (September 1956): 146.

2. James Kirke Paulding to Gasherie DeWitt (?), December 28, 1827, in Ralph M. Aderman, ed., *The Letters of James Kirke Paulding* (Madison, Wis.: The University of Wisconsin Press, 1962), 93.

3. Charles E. Fitch, ed., *Recollections: Abraham Lansing* (Albany, N.Y.: Privately printed, 1909), 109,111.

4. Harold Frederic, *In the Valley* (New York: Charles Scribner's Sons, 1890), 189.

5. George William Curtis, ed., *The Correspondence of John Lothrop Motley*, 2nd ed. (London: John Murray, 1889), I, 146.

6. David Levin, *History as Romantic Art* (1959; repr. New York: Harcourt, Brace and World, 1963), 188-89.

BIBLIOGRAPHICAL NOTE

Introduction — Silence is Golden

The most complete standard history of the Netherlands in English is still Petrus J. Blok's *History of the People of the Netherlands* (New York: G. P. Putnam's Sons, 1898-1912), 5 volumes. Much of it has been superseded in Dutch by the works of Pieter Geyl, but not all of them have been translated. The volumes which are available include *The Revolt of the Netherlands* (1932; repr. New York: Barnes and Noble, 1958), *The History of the Low Countries* (New York: St. Martin's Press, 1964), and *The Netherlands in the Seventeenth Century* (1936, under the title, *The Netherlands Divided*; repr. New York: Barnes and Noble, 1961, 1964), 2 parts. A few basic works on special subjects available in paperback include Henri Pirenne's *Early Democracies in the Low Countries* (New York: Harper and Row, 1963) on the patrician structure of local government; and Johan John Huizinga's *The Waning of the Middle Ages* (Garden City, N.Y.: Doubleday, 1956) on the cultural base of late medieval Flemish art, literature, and religion. Charles Wilson's *The Dutch Republic* (New York: McGraw-Hill, 1968) is a comprehensive introduction to the Golden Age, and Violet Barbour's *Capitalism in Amsterdam in the Seventeenth Century* (Ann Arbor, Mich.: University of Michigan Press, 1963) describes the complexity of Dutch commerce and finance.

Chapter 1 — Beaver Skins and Wild Men

Juet's diary and a number of other early accounts of the Hudson Valley are in J. Franklin Jameson's *Narratives of New Netherland* (1909; repr. New York: Barnes and Noble, 1967). The story of Hudson's voyage has been repeatedly told; a convenient brief version is Milton W. Hamilton's *Henry*

Hudson and the Dutch in New York (Albany: University of the State of New York, 1964). Simon Hart's "Dutch Records Tell Story of Hudson's Voyage," *de Halve Maen* 36:1-2 (April-July 1961), adds information from Dutch sources. C. R. Boxer's *Dutch Seaborne Empire* (New York: Knopf, 1965) is the standard work in English on the Dutch colonies. D. W. Davies' *A Primer of Dutch Seventeenth-Century Overseas Trade* (The Hague: Martinus Nijhoff, 1961) places them in the total context of trade in the Golden Age. The complex history of early Dutch attempts to exploit the Hudson Valley fur trade is explored in Simon Hart's *The Prehistory of the New Netherlands Company* (Amsterdam: City of Amsterdam Press, 1959) and in Thomas J. Condon's *New York Beginnings* (New York: New York University Press, 1968). Van Cleaf Bachman's *Peltries or Plantations* (Baltimore: John Hopkins University Press, 1969) is a history of the early years of the Dutch West India Company. None of these works, however, concentrates upon establishing the exact sequence of events in the settlement of New Netherland, which is explored in Edwin R. Van Kleeck's "Is Fort Orange Older Than New Amsterdam?" *de Halve Maen* 36:2 (July 1961), in C. A. Weslager's "Did Minuit Buy Manhattan Island from the Indians?" *de Halve Maen* 43:3 (October 1968), and in Weslager's *Dutch Explorers, Traders and Settlers in the Delaware Valley* (Philadelphia: University of Pennsylvania Press, 1961). Exhaustive documentation concerning the founding of New Amsterdam has recently been collected for the Holland Society by George O. Zabriskie; it is to be hoped that it will in time be published. Van den Bogart's journal is in Jameson. The standard history of Dutch relations with the Indians is Allen W. Trelease's *Indian Affairs in Colonial New York* (Ithaca, N.Y.: Cornell University Press, 1960); additional details are offered by C. A. Weslager in "Who Survived the Indian Massacre at Swanendael?" *de Halve Maen* 40:3 (October 1965), and by Reginald McMahon in "Achter Col Colony on the Hackensack," *New Jersey History* (1971).

Chapter 2 — Many Faces of New Netherland

Condon and Bachman are the standard works for the beginning of settlement. George O. Zabriskie's "The Founding Families of New Netherland; No. 4 — The Rapalje-Rapelje Family," *de Halve Maen* 46:4-47:2 (January-July 1972), offers the most authoritative information available about the Walloon colonists. S. G. Nissenson's *The Patroon's Domain* (New York: Columbia University Press, 1936) is the standard work on Rensselaerswyck; important primary sources include *Van Rensselaer Bowier Manuscripts*, trans. A. J. F. Van Laer (Albany: University of the State of New York, 1908) and *Minutes of the Court of Rensselaerswyck*, trans. A. J. F. Van Laer (Albany: University of the State of New York, 1922). Other early settlements are described in Adrian C. Leiby's *The Early Dutch and Swedish Settlers of New Jersey*

(Princeton: D. Van Nostrand, 1964) and in Theodora DuBois and Dorothy Valentine Smith's *Staten Island Patroons* (The Staten Island Historical Society, 1961). Works on Dutch culture in New Netherland include Esther Singleton's *Dutch New York* (1909; repr. New York; Benjamin Blom, 1968), which is in some respects out of date but still valuable. Ellis Lawrence Raesly's *Portrait of New Netherland* (New York: Columbia University Press, 1945) includes the only discussion of New Netherland literature, and Maud Esther Dillard's *An Album of New Netherland* (New York: Bramhall House, 1963) illustrates important aspects of Dutch material culture. There are also numerous valuable articles about the New Netherland way of life in *de Halve Maen*. There is no authoritative life of Peter Stuyvesant, but Henry H. Kessler and Eugene Rachlin's *Peter Stuyvesant and His New York* (New York: Random House, 1959) is adequate in the meantime, and S. J. Fockema Andreae's "Data on the Dutch Background of Peter Stuyvesant," *de Halve Maen* 39:1 (April 1964), adds significant information from the Netherlands. Recently published is Adriaen Van der Donck's *Description of the New Netherland* (Syracuse, N.Y.: Syracuse University Press, 1968). Comments on the Dutch colonial experience include Langdon C. Wright's "Local Government and Central Authority in New Netherland," *New-York Historical Society Quarterly* (January 1973), which tries to detach the history of New Netherland from the English context of American history, but makes no reference to developments in the Netherlands, and C. B. Currey's "Dutch Colonial Failure in New York," *Mankind* (April 1970), which contends that New Netherland demonstrates "the worst possible bastardization of methods available for the establishment of colonies" (p. 18).

Chapter 3 — The Cockpit of America

Dutch and French competition for Indian alliances is described in Trelease and in an exceedingly important article, Bruce G. Trigger's "Mohawk-Mahican War (1624-28): The Establishment of a Pattern," *Canadian Historical Review* (September 1971): 276-86. Isaac de Rasière's journal of his visit to Plymouth is in Jameson. Ronald D. Cohen's "Hartford Treaty of 1650: Anglo-Dutch Cooperation in the Seventeenth Century," *New-York Historical Society Quarterly* (October 1969), illustrates an important aspect of early relations with New England. The conflict with New Sweden is described in C. A. Weslager's *Dutch Explorers*, and his "New Jersey: Site of First Dutch Colony on Delaware," *de Halve Maen* 39:1-2 (April-July 1964); and in Simon Hart's "The City-Colony of New Amstel on the Delaware," *de Halve Maen* 29:4-40:1 (January-April 1965). Of the many descriptions of the English conquest, Raesly and Kessler-Rachlis are effective. Ronald D. Cohen's "New England Colonies and the Dutch Recapture of New York, 1673-74," *New-York Historical Society Quarterly* (January 1972), illuminates a little-known subject. The proprietary system is described in John E. Pomfret's *Province of East New Jersey, 1609-1702* (Princeton: Princeton University Press, 1962). The adjustment of the young Van Rensselaers to English rule is described in Nissenson; in *Correspondence of Jeremias Van Rensselaer*, trans. A. J. F. Van Laer (Albany: University of the State of New York, 1932); in *Correspondence of Maria Van Rensselaer*, trans. A. J. F. Van Laer (Albany: University of the State of New York, 1935); and in Robert G. Wheeler's "House of Jeremias Van Rensselaer, 1658-66," *New-York Historical Society Quarterly* 45 (January 1961): 75-88.

A remarkable imaginative interpretation of life at Rensselaerswyck at the end of the Dutch period is Erick Berry's *Seven Beaver Skins* (Philadelphia: John C. Winston, 1948). The transition from Dutch to English local government is illustrated by A. J. F. Van Laer's translations of the *Minutes of the Court of Fort Orange and Beverwyck* (Albany: University of the State of New York, 1920-23), 2 volumes, and *Minutes of the Court of Albany, Rensselaerswyck, and Schenectady* (Albany: University of the State of New York, 1926-32), 3 volumes. Imperial conflicts and Indian relations in the Dongan period are described in Trelease; Francis Jennings' "Glory, Death, and Transfiguration: The Susquehannock Indians in the Seventeenth Century," *Proceedings of the American Philosophical Society* 112:1 (January 1968): 9-53, adds the dimension of competition from Pennsylvania. Various aspects of Leisler's Rebellion are described in Jerome R. Reich's *Leisler's Rebellion* (Chicago: University of Chicago Press, 1953), and in three works by Lawrence H. Leder: *Robert Livingston and the Politics of Colonial New York* (Chapel Hill, N.C.: University of North Carolina Press, 1961), "The Glorious Revolution and the Pattern of Imperial Relationships," *New York History* (July 1965), and "The Politics of Upheaval in New York," *New-York Historical Society Quarterly* (1960): 413-27. Events in Albany, including the Schenectady massacre, are related in the minutes of the "Albany Convention" in Edmund B. O'Callaghan, ed., *Documentary History of the State of New York* (Albany: State of New York, 1848-52), volume 2. The 1709 and 1711 Canadian expeditions are described in G. M. Waller's *Samuel Vetch* (Chapel Hill, N.C.: University of North Carolina Press, 1960) and in Richmond P. Bond's *Queen Anne's American Kings* (New York: Octagon Press, 1972).

Chapter 4 — Patricians and Plebeians

The patrician system of Hudson Valley Dutch social organization is described in Alice P. Kenney's "Dutch Patricians in Colonial Albany," *New York History* (July 1967). Phyllis Geesey Larmer's "Pieter Schuyler — Albany's First Citizen," *de Halve Maen* 47:1-2 (April-July 1972), relates the life of Peter Schuyler. For the Albany fur trade, see David A. Armour's "Merchants of Albany, N.Y., 1686-1760" (Ph.D. dissertation, Northwestern University,

1965), Cadwallader Colden's *The History of the Five Indian Nations* (Ithaca, N.Y.: Cornell University Press, 1958); and Peter Wraxall's *Abridgement of the Indian Affairs*, ed. Charles McIlwain, Harvard Historical Studies, Volume 21 (Cambridge, Mass.: Harvard University Press, 1915). New York's commerce with pirates is studied in Jacob Judd's "Frederick Philipse and the Madagascar Trade," *New-York Historical Society Quarterly* (October 1971), and in his "Lord Bellomont and Captain Kidd," *New-York Historical Society Quarterly* (January 1963); for the development of legitimate trade see Virginia D. Harrington's *The New York Merchant on the Eve of the Revolution* (1935; repr. Gloucester, Mass.: Peter Smith, 1964). The standard work on colonial urban life is Carl Bridenbaugh's *Cities in the Wilderness* (1938; repr. New York: Capricorn Books, 1955), which studies New York but does not emphasize its Dutch community. For artisans, see Carl Bridenbaugh's *The Colonial Craftsman* (1950; repr. Chicago: University of Chicago Press, 1961); for slaves, Edgar J. McManus' *History of Negro Slavery in New York* (Syracuse University Press, 1966). Dutch houses are described in Rosalie Fellows Bailey's *Pre-Revolutionary Dutch Houses and Families in Northern New Jersey and Southern New York* (1936; repr. New York: Dover Publications, 1968), in Helen Wilkinson Reynolds' *Dutch Houses in the Hudson Valley Before 1776* (1929; repr. New York: Dover Publications, 1965), and in the forthcoming work on urban Dutch houses by Roderick H. Blackburn. Norman S. Rice's *New York Furniture before 1840 in the Collection of the Albany Institute of History and Art* (Albany: Albany Institute of History and Art, 1962) illustrates some Dutch furniture. For the Hudson Valley limners, see Robert G. Wheeler's "The Albany of Magdalena Douw," *Winterthur Portfolio* No. 4 (1968): 63-74; *American Painting to 1776: a Reappraisal*, ed. Ian M. G. Quimby (Charlottesville, Va.: University Press of Virginia, 1971); Bruce Etchison's "The Glen-Sanders Portraits of Scotia, N.Y.," *Antiques* 89 (February 1966): 245-47; and *The Schuyler Limner . . .* (Albany: Albany Institute of History and Art, 1959). Norman S. Rice's *Albany Silver* (Albany: Albany Institute of History and Art, 1964) introduces Hudson Valley silverware; Charles K. Winne, Jr.'s "Colonial Silvermaking and Some Albany Smiths," *de Halve Maen* 35:4-36:2 (January-July 1961), discusses some Dutch silversmiths; and Mrs. M. P. Ferris' "A Chapter on Some Old Spoons," *Harpers Bazar* (September 27, 1890), discusses the special subject of "monkey spoons." Kenneth Scott's "Funeral Customs in Colonial New York," *New York Folklore Quarterly* (Winter 1959), and Wilfred B. Talman's "Death Customs Among the Colonial Dutch," *de Halve Maen* 42:4-43:1 (January-April 1968), detail funeral customs. A primary source for the life of Dutch women is Anne McVicar Grant, *Memoirs of an American Lady* (London: Longmans, 1808). Travelers as Alexander Hamilton (*Gentleman's Progress* [1948; repr. Westport, Conn.: Greenwood, 1973]) and Peter Kalm (*Peter Kalm's Travels in North America*, ed. Adolph B. Benson [1937; repr. New York: Dover Publications, 1966]) made many interesting observations in Dutch towns.

Chapter 5 — Golden Fields

B. H. Slicher van Bath is the leading Dutch agricultural historian, but most of his works have not been translated; the works of G. E. Fussell are very helpful in the meantime, especially "Low Countries' Influence on English Farming," *English Historical Review* (October 1959). Ulysses Prentiss Hedrick's *A History of Agriculture in the State of New York* (1933; repr. New York: Hill and Wang, 1966) is standard for farming in the Hudson Valley. Information about the first farms in New Netherland may be gleaned from Jameson and *Van Rensselaer Bowier Manuscripts.* Cornelius Ackerson's "Agriculture in New Netherland's History," *de Halve Maen* 35:4 (January 1961), draws together some of these materials. Van der Donck is the principal primary source for New Netherland; *Correspondence of Jeremias Van Rensselaer* also adds many details. Peter H. Cousins' *Hog Plow and Sith* (Dearborn, Mich.: Greenfield Village and Henry Ford Museum) describes Dutch tools; Kalm, Dutch crops; and Ruth Johnson Piwonka's "Dutch Gardens in the Hudson Valley," *de Halve Maen* 49:2-3 (July-October 1974), Dutch gardens. John Fitchen's *The New World Dutch Barn* (Syracuse, N.Y.: Syracuse University Press, 1968) explains the construction of Dutch barns. Dutch farms in New Jersey are depicted in McMahon, "Achter Col," and Thomas J. Wertenbaker's *Founding of American Civilization: The Middle Colonies* (New York: Charles Scribner's Sons, 1938). There is considerable description of farm buildings, particularly hay barracks, in Kristin Lunde Gibbons' "The Van bergen Overmantel" (M.A. thesis, Cooperstown Graduate Program, State University of New York, College at Oneonta, 1966). Marvin D. Schwartz's "The Jan Martense Schenck House in the Brooklyn Museum," *Antiques* 85:4 (April 1964): 421-28, depicts boer home life. The way of life of manor lords is described in *Philipsburg Manor* (Tarrytown, N.Y.: Sleepy Hollow Restorations, 1969) in Joseph T. Butler's "The Family Furniture at Van Cortlandt Manor," *A Sleepy Hollow Restorations Portfolio* (Tarrytown, N.Y.: Sleepy Hollow Restorations, n.d.), and in John M. Graham, II's "History in Houses: Van Cortland Manor," *Antiques* 78 (November 1960): 472-77. Alf Evers' *The Catskills* (Garden City, N.Y.: Doubleday, 1972) relates the history of the Hardenbergh Patent, and Sung Bok Kim's "A New Look at the Great Landlords of Eighteenth-Century New York," *William and Mary Quarterly*, 3d ser., 27:4 (October 1970), explores the positive contribution of the leasehold system. Irving Mark's *Agrarian Conflicts in Colonial New York* (Port Washington, N.Y.: Ira Friedman, 1940) is the principal source on tenant unrest. Dutch expansion into New Jersey is related in Leiby, Pomfret, Peter O. Wacker's *Musconetcong Valley of New Jersey: a Historical Geography* (New Brunswick, N.J.: Rutgers University Press, 1968), and in Ruth M. Keesey's "Rivers and Roads in Old Bergen County," *de Halve Maen* 39:3-40:2 (October 1964-July 1965). Martha Keniston Hunt, "Early Settlements in the Minisink Country," *de Halve Maen* 50, no. 1-2, dispels many myths about the old Mini Road region. Kenneth E. Hasbrouck's "The Huguenots of

New Paltz, N.Y.," *de Halve Maen* 36:4 (January 1962), tells the story of some of the Huguenots.

Chapter 6 — Faiths of Their Fathers

The fundamental source for the Dutch Church in New York is *Ecclesiastical Records, State of New York* (Albany: State of New York, 1901-16), 7 volumes; Edward Tanjore Corwin's *A Manual of the Reformed Church in America* (New York: Board of Publication, Reformed Church in America, 1869) brings together valuable biographical information about the ministers. An important religious tradition of the Netherlands is described in Cornelis Reedeijk's "What Is Typically Dutch in Erasmus?" *Delta* (Winter 1959-60): 35-44. Gerald F. DeJong's "Ziekentroosters or Comforters of the Sick in New Netherland," *New-York Historical Society Quarterly* (October 1970), discusses the earliest religious workers in New Netherland. The narratives of Domines Michaelius and Megapolensis are in Jameson; Gerald F. De Jong's "Domine Johannes Megapolensis: Minister to New Netherland," *New-York Historical Society Quarterly* (January 1968), fills out his biography. Frederick J. Zwierlein's *Religion in New Netherland* (1910; repr. New York: Da Capo Press, 1971) depicts the intolerance of the Dutch Reformed Church in New Netherland. Raesly gives many details of religious dissidence, and George L. Smith's *Religion and Trade in New Netherland* (Ithaca, N.Y.: Cornell University Press, 1973) describes the development of toleration with reference to the Netherlands tradition of "connivance." Leisler's suit against Nicholas Van Rensselaer is in *Minutes of the Court of Albany*. The early career of Domine Selyns is recounted by Raesly; Howard C. Hageman's "Henricus Selyns" in *Seminar II on the Cultural Mosaic of New Netherland, October 20-22, 1972* (Rensselaerville, N.Y.: The Institute on Man and Science), relates the events of his second New York pastorate. W. Stanford Reid's "Battle Hymns of the Lord: Calvinist Psalmody of the Sixteenth Century," *Sixteenth Century Journal* 2 (1971), and Alice P. Kenney's "Hudson Valley Dutch Psalmody," *The Hymn* 25:1 (January 1974): 15-26, explore the musical tradition of the Dutch Reformed in the Old World and the New. Robert G. Wheeler's "The Use of Symbolism in Hudson Valley Paintings of the Early Eighteenth Century," *New York History* 36, no. 3, and his "Hudson Valley Religious Paintings," *Antiques* 63 (1953): 346-50, describe the limners' Bible illustrations. James Tanis' *Dutch Calvinistic Pietism in the Middle Colonies* (The Hague: Martinus Nijhoff, 1967) tells the history of Frelinghuysen, and J. J. Mol's *Breaking of Traditions: Theological Convictions in Colonial America* (Berkeley, Calif.: Glendessary Press, 1968) compares adaptation to American circumstances of orthodox and Pietist clergy in sociological terms. The end of the younger Frelinghuysen's career in Albany is recorded by Anne Grant.

Chapter 7 — The Dutch Revolt

Works isolating the role of the Dutch in the American Revolution are almost nonexistent, and it is not the purpose of this essay to provide a general bibliography of the coming of the Revolution in New York; Milton M. Klein's *New York in the American Revolution* (Albany: New York State American Revolution Bicentennial Commission, 1974) is exhaustive. Patricia U. Bonomi's *Factious People* (New York: Columbia University Press, 1971) depicts the role of the Albany "city state" in provincial politics and supersedes Beverly McAnear, "Politics in Provincial New York, 1689-1761" (Ph.D. dissertation, Stanford University, 1935) as a general account of the development of factions in the colonial period. The events of the French and Indian War in Albany are described in detail, with full documentation, in Armour, in Alice P. Kenney's "Dutch Patricians," and in her *The Gansevoorts of Albany* (Syracuse, N.Y.: Syracuse University Press, 1969). Milton M. Klein's "Church, State and Education: Testing the Issue in Colonial New York," *New York History* 45:4 (October 1964): 291-303, tells how the Dutch became involved in that controversy. Imperial crises of the 1760s are analyzed in Carl Lotus Becker's *The History of Political Parties in the Province of New York* (Madison, Wis.: University of Wisconsin Press, 1909); in Harrington; in Beverly McAnear's "The Albany Stamp Act Riots," *William and Mary Quarterly*, 3d ser., 4 (1947): 486-98; in Leopold S. Launitz-Schürer's "Whig-Loyalists: the De Lanceys of New York," *New-York Historical Society Quarterly* 56 (July 1972); in Lawrence H. Leder's "The New York Elections of 1769: an Assault on Privilege," *Mississippi Valley Historical Review* 49 (March 1963): 675-82; and in Don R. Gerlach's *Philip Schuyler and the American Revolution in New York* (Lincoln, Nebr.: University of Nebraska Press, 1964). A forthcoming booklet by Saul Belinsky relates the rise of Abraham Yates. The coming of the Revolution to Albany is recorded in *Minutes of the Albany Committee of Correspondence, 1775-78* (Albany: University of the State of New York, 1923), 2 volumes.

Chapter 8 — The Siege of the Hudson Valley

Don R. Gerlach's book and an article "Philip Schuyler and the New York Frontier in 1781," *New-York Historical Society Quarterly* 53:2 (April 1969): 148-81, and Martin H. Bush's *Revolutionary Enigma* (Port Washington, N.Y.: Ira Friedman, 1969) describe the Canadian invasion and Schuyler's later campaigns; Bruce Bliven, Jr.'s *Battle for Manhattan* (1955; repr. Baltimore: Penquin Books, 1964), describes the fighting around New York City. Adrian C. Leiby's *The Revolutionary War in the Hackensack Valley* (New Brunswick, N.J.: Rutgers University Press, 1962) and H. O. Vernon-Jackson's "Loyalist's Wife: Letters of Mrs. Philip Van Cortlandt, 1776-77," *History Today* (August

1964), relate the ordeal of the New Jersey Dutch. Alice P. Kenney's "The
Albany Dutch: Loyalists and Patriots," *New York History* (October 1961): 1-
20, and Staughton Lynd's "The Tenant Rising at Livingston Manor, May
1777," *New-York Historical Society Quarterly* 48 (April 1964): 163-77, dis-
cuss unrest on the manors. Gerlach and Bush also depict the Burgoyne campaign; Robert W. Venables' "Valley of Nettles: The Revolutionary War in the
Mohawk Valley, Summer, 1777" (M.A. thesis, Vanderbilt University, 1965) is
the principal source for the defense of Fort Stanwix, while Kenney's *Gansevoorts* depicts the state of mind in Albany. The guerilla war in New Jersey is
described in Leiby; in Ruth M. Keesey's "Loyalty and Reprisal: The Loyalists
of Bergen County, New Jersey, and Their Estates" (Ph.D. dissertation,
Columbia University, 1957); in Jared C. Lobdell's "Paramus in the War of the
Revolution," *Proceedings of the New Jersey Historical Society* 78:3 (July
1960): 162-77; in Paul H. Smith's "New Jersey Loyalists and the British
'Provincial' Corps in the War for Independence," *New Jersey History* (Summer
1969); and in Frederick W. Bogert's "[Tory] Marauders in the Minnisink,"
Proceedings of the New Jersey Historical Society 82:4 (October 1964): 271-
82. Barbara Graymont's *The Iroquois in the American Revolution* (Syracuse,
N.Y.: Syracuse University Press, 1972) tells of the war against the Iroquois.

Chapter 9 — *E Pluribus Unum*

Factionalism in Revolutionary New York is described in Becker and in
Bernard Mason's *The Road to Independence* (Lexington, Ky.: University of
Kentucky Press, 1966). The local story of Albany is in *Minutes of the Albany
Committee of Correspondence.* Mason tells the story of the 1777 constitu-
tion; and Don R. Gerlach's *Philip Schuyler and the Growth of New York*
(Albany: University of the State of New York, 1968) and Lynd's "Tenant
Rising" comment on the gubernatorial election. Works on the Tories include
William H. Nelson's *The American Tory* (Oxford: Clarendon Press, 1961);
Ruth M. Keesey's "Loyalism in Bergen County, New Jersey," *William and
Mary Quarterly* (October 1961); and Kenney's "Albany Dutch." Peter Van
Schaack's writings are reprinted extensively in Henry C. Van Schaack's *Life
of Peter Van Schaack* (New York: Appleton, 1842); William A. Benton's
Whig-Loyalism (Cranbury, N.J.: Fairleigh Dickinson University Press, 1969)
discusses their significance. The later career of Philip Schuyler is sketched in
Don R. Gerlach's "Philip Schuyler and the New York Frontier in 1781," and
in his *Philip Schuyler and the Growth of New York*, and postwar political
divisions in Staughton Lynd's *Anti-Federalism in Dutchess County, New York*
(Chicago: Loyola University Press, 1962), and in Ernest Wilder Spaulding's
New York in the Critical Period (1932; repr. Port Washington, N.Y.: Ira J.
Friedman, 1963). The controversy over the United States Constitution is
depicted in Linda G. DePauw's *The Eleventh Pillar* (Ithaca, N.Y.: Cornell

University Press, 1966) and Staughton Lynd's "Abraham Yates's History of the Movement of the United States Constitution," *William and Mary Quarterly* (April 1963). Later political developments are described in Alfred F. Young's *Democratic Republicans of New York* (Chapel Hill, N.C.: University of North Carolina Press, 1967). The history of the Holland Land Company is William Chazanof's *Joseph Ellicott and the Holland Land Company* (Syracuse, N.Y.: Syracuse University Press, 1970).

Chapter 10 — Folklore, Fiction, and Fact

The standard life of Irving is Stanley T. Williams' *Life of Washington Irving* (1935; repr. New York: Octagon Press, 1971), 2 volumes; a definitive edition of his works is being published by the University of Wisconsin Press. *Knickerbocker* is available in paperback — Washington Irving, *Knickerbocker's History of New York* (1848; repr. New York: Capricorn Books, 1965). The real Knickerbocker family is discussed in Chase Viele's "The Knickerbockers of Upstate New York," *de Halve Maen* 47:3-48:1 (October 1972-April 1973). *The Knickerbocker Tradition*, ed. Andrew B. Myers (Tarrytown, N.Y.: Sleepy Hollow Restorations, 1974), Harry Miller Lydenberg's *Irving's Knickerbocker and Some of Its Sources* (New York: New York Public Library, 1953), and Van Wyck Brooks's *The World of Washington Irving* (New York: E. P. Dutton, 1944) add considerable background information. Sara P. Rodes's "Washington Irving's Use of Traditional Folklore," *Southern Folklore Quarterly* 20:3 (September 1956), is valuable for Irving's use of folklore; Lillian Schlissel's "John Quidor in New York," *American Quarterly* 42:4 (Winter 1965): 756-60, discusses John Quidor's illustrations of Irving's works. Robert Charles Wess's *The Image and Use of the Dutch in the Literary Works of Washington Irving* (Ph.D. dissertation, University of Notre Dame, 1970) is disappointing because its knowledge of the Dutch tradition is superficial. Charles H. Roe's "Paulding Family," *Westchester Historian* (Summer 1967), offers information on Paulding's family; and *Letters of James Kirke Paulding*, ed. Ralph M. Aderman (Madison, Wis.: University of Wisconsin Press, 1962) is especially revealing. James Kirke Paulding's *The Dutchman's Fireside* (1831; repr. New York: Somerset Publications, n.d.), 2 volumes; Charles Fenno Hoffman's *Greyslaer* (1840; repr. New York: Scholarly Reprints, 1968), 2 volumes; and James Fenimore Cooper's *Satanstoe* (1845; repr. Lincoln, Nebr.: University of Nebraska Press, 1962) are vivid fictional depictions of the Dutch tradition. Willem J. van Balen's "The Truth About St. Nicholas and Santa Claus," *de Halve Maen* 46:4 (January 1972), considers the development of the Santa Claus tradition; Samuel W. Patterson's "The Centenary of Clement C. Moore, the Poet of Christmas Eve," *Historical Magazine of the Protestant Episcopal Church* (September 1963), discusses Clement C. Moore as an Episcopalian with little reference to "A Visit from Saint Nicholas." Alice P. Kenney's "Dutch Traditions in American Literature," *de Halve Maen* 48:1 (April 1973), summarizes much information in this chapter. Salvatore Mondello's "John Vanderlyn," *New-York Historical Society Quarterly* 52:2 (April 1968): 161-83; Roland Van Zandt's "Catskills and the Rise of American Landscape Painting," *New-York Historical Society Quarterly* (July 1965); James T. Callow's *Kindred Spirits* (Chapel Hill, N.C.: University of North Carolina Press, 1967); and Edward K. Spahn's "Bryant and Verplanck, the Yankee and the Yorker," *New York History* (January 1968), offer insights into the "Knickerbocker" writers and painters. Perry Miller's *The Raven and the Whale* (1956; repr. Westport, Conn.: Greenwood, 1973) tells the story of Evert Duyckinck; and Jacob Landy's *The Architecture of Minard LaFever* (New York: Columbia University Press, 1970), that of Minard LaFever. The standard life of Melville is Leon Howard's *Herman Melville* (Berkeley, Calif.: University of California Press, 1951), and Eleanor M. Metcalf's *Herman Melville* (Cambridge, Mass.: Harvard University Press, 1953) and Jay Leyda's *Melville Log* (New York: Harcourt, Brace, 1951) also provide helpful information; Kenney's *Gansevoorts* expands on his Dutch characteristics. Novels of the Dutch tradition in the Revolution include David Murdoch's *The Dutch Dominie of the Catskills* (New York: Derby and Jackson, 1861), Amelia E. Barr's *The Bow of Orange Ribbon* (New York: Dodd, Mead, 1886), and Harold Frederic's *In the Valley* (New York: Charles Scribner's Sons, 1890); studies of Frederic's works are Thomas F. O'Donnell and Hoyt C. Franchere's *Harold Frederic* (New York: Twayne, 1961) and Austin Briggs, Jr.'s *The Novels of Harold Frederic* (Ithaca, N.Y.: Cornell University Press, 1969). Motley's histories of the Dutch have been reprinted by AMS Press in *The Writings of John Lothrop Motley — The Rise of the Dutch Republic* (vols. 1-5), *The History of the United Netherlands* (vols. 6-11), and *The Life and Death of John van Oldenbarneveld* (vols. 12-14). Motley's interpretation of the Dutch is discussed in David Levin's *History as Romantic Art* (1959; repr. New York: Harcourt, Brace and World, 1963) and Robert Wheaton's "Motley and the Dutch Historians," *New England Quarterly* 35:3 (September 1962): 318-36, and depicted in *The Correspondence of John Lothrop Motley*, ed. George William Curtis, 2d ed. (London: John Murray, 1889), 2 volumes.

Chapter 11 — The Americanization of the Dutch

The transformation of Albany is described in Kenney's *Gansevoorts* and David M. Ellis' "Yankee-Dutch Confrontation in the Albany Area," *New England Quarterly* (June 1972): 262-70. The decline of the Dutch language is detailed in Charles Theodore Gehring's "The Dutch Language in Colonial New York" (Ph.D. dissertation, Indiana University, 1973) and Alice P. Kenney's "Evidences of Regard: Three Generations of American Love Letters," *Bulletin of*

the New York Public Library 76 (1972): 92-119. McManus relates the aboli-
tion of slavery in New York. Westward migration of boers is depicted in David
F. Carmony and Sam K. Swope's "From Lycoming County, Pennsylvania,
to Parke County, Indiana: Recollections of Andrew Ten Brook, 1786-1823,"
Indiana Magazine of History (March 1965). The Dutch in nineteenth-century
New York politics are mentioned in Dixon Ryan Fox's *The Decline of
Aristocracy in the Politics of New York*, ed. Robert V. Remini (1919; repr.
New York: Harper and Row, 1965) and Lee Benson's *The Concept of
Jacksonian Democracy* (1961; repr. New York: Atheneum, 1964), and the
career of Martin Van Buren in his own *Autobiography* (Washington: American
Historical Association, 1919), Robert V. Remini's *Martin Van Buren and
the Making of the Democratic Party* (New York: Columbia University Press,
1959), Frank O. Gatell's "Sober Second Thoughts on Van Buren, the Albany
Regency, and the Wall Street Conspiracy," *Journal of American History* 53:1
(June 1966): 19-40, and James C. Curtis' *Fox at Bay* (Lexington, Ky.: Uni-
versity Press of Kentucky, 1970). The standard history of the Dutch in the
Midwest is Henry S. Lucas' *Netherlanders in America* (Ann Arbor, Mich.:
University of Michigan Press, 1955); Pamela and J. W. Smit's *Dutch in
America, 1609-1970* (Dobbs Ferry, N.Y.: Oceana Publications, 1972) is a
useful short survey. Further details about the Michigan colony are in Enton
J. Bruins' "Holocaust [fire] in Holland [Michigan], 1871," *Michigan History*
(1971), and John A. Jackle and James O. Wheeler's "Changing Residential
Structure of the Dutch Population in Kalamazoo, Michigan," *Annals of the
Association of American Geographers* (September 1969); that in Iowa in
Robert P. Swierenga's "Ethnic Voter and the First Lincoln Elections," *Civil
War History* (March 1965); and "A Dutch Immigrant's View of Frontier
Iowa," *Annals of Iowa* 38:2 (Fall 1965): 81-118; and that in South Dakota
in Gerald F. De Jong's "The Dutch in Emmons County," *North Dakota
History* (July 1962). The later history of the Albany patricians is described in
Alice P. Kenney's *Gansevoorts*; "Kate Gansevoort's Grand Tour," *New York
History* 47:4 (October 1966): 343-61; "Sir Galahad and the Knight of the
Apron String," *New York History* (October 1970); and "The Holland
Society's Compleat Angler," *de Halve Maen* 49:3-4 (October 1974-January
1975); the rise of the Irish is discussed in William E. Rowley's "Irish Aristoc-
racy of Albany, 1798-1878," *New York History* 52 (July 1971). The contri-
bution of members of the Schuyler family are described in Ralph P. Rosen-
berg's "Eugene Schuyler's Doctor of Philosophy Degree," *Journal of Higher
Education* (October 1962), and Walter J. Trattner's "Louisa Lee Schuyler and
the Founding of the State Charities Aid Association," *New-York Historical
Society Quarterly* (July 1967); the Vrooman family in Ross H. Paulson's
Radicalism and Reform (Lexington, Ky.: University Press of Kentucky, 1968).
Works on the Progressives include Edward Bok's *The Americanization of
Edward Bok* (1921; repr. Westport, Conn.: Greenwood, 1972), Maurice M.
Vance's *Charles Richard Van Hise* (Madison, Wis.: Wisconsin State Historical
Society, 1960), and James D. Wilkes's "Claude H. Van Tyne: The Professor

and the Hun," *Michigan History* (February 1971): 183-204. The Michigan Dutch Republicans are discussed in C. Warren Van der Hill's "Representative from Holland: Gerrit John Diekema," *Michigan History* (Winter 1967), "A Dutch-American Returns to the Netherlands," *Michigan History* (Spring 1969), and *Gerrit J. Diekema* (Grand Rapids, Mich.: W. B. Eerdmans, 1970), and in C. David Tompkins' *Senator Arthur H. Vandenberg* (Lansing, Mich.: Michigan State University Press, 1970).

Chapter 12 — Recovering the Dutch Tradition

Many works discussed in this chapter have already been cited and will not be listed again. Harry F. Jackson's *Scholar in the Wilderness: Francis Adrian Van der Kemp* (Syracuse, N.Y.: Syracuse University Press, 1963) discusses the New York Dutch records. Harriet L. P. Rice's *Harmanus Bleecker* (Albany, 1924) and Adriaan J. Barnouw's "John Romeyn Brodhead, 1814-73," *de Halve Maen* 39:3 (October 1964), describe the discovery of the records in the Netherlands. The works of O'Callaghan and Fernow are listed in Peter R. Christoph's "Translators of Dutch Records Evaluated," *de Halve Maen* 49:1 (April 1974). Joel Munsell's *Annals of Albany* (Albany, 1850-69), 10 volumes, and his *Collections on the History of Albany* (Albany, 1865-72), 4 volumes, along with I. N. Phelps Stokes's *Iconography of Manhattan Island* (1915; repr. New York: Arno Press, 1967), 6 volumes, are fundamental primary sources. The Holland Society is described in Frederick W. Bogert's "The Holland Society: As We Were — and Are," *de Halve Maen* 44:3 (October 1969), in its *Yearbooks*, and in correspondence with members. The writings of Mary L. D. Ferris are described in Alice P. Kenney's "Mary L. D. Ferris and the Dutch tradition," *de Halve Maen* 47:4, 48:2 (January, July 1973), and in Mrs. Ferris' own "Poetic Tribute to the Holland Society," *de Halve Maen* 49:1 (April 1974); and Catherine Gansevoort Lansing and the Gansevoort-Lansing Collection in Kenney's *Gansevoorts*. George Olin Zabriskie's "The Founding Families of New Netherland; Nos. 5 and 6 — the Roelofs and Bogardus Families," *de Halve Maen* 47:3-48:3 (October 1972-October 1973), sets the record straight on Anneke Janse. Kenneth Scott and Ken Stryker-Rodda's "Holland Society Publishes Van Laer Translations," *de Halve Maen* 49:1 (April 1974), relates the career of A. J. F. Van Laer. Dutch Folklore is mentioned in Carl Carmer's *The Hudson* (New York: Rinehart, 1939) and Harold W. Thompson's *Body, Boots & Britches* (1939; repr. New York: Dover Publications, 1962); fictional works include Kenneth Lewis Roberts' *Rabble in Arms* (Garden City, N.Y.: Doubleday, 1947), Berry's *Seven Beaver Skins*, and Mary Hun Sears's *Hudson Crossroads* (New York: Exposition Press, 1953). Tulip festivals are described in George Ver Steeg, *et al.*, "Dutch Tulip Festivals in Iowa," *Palimpsest* (April 1964). Sleepy Hollow Restorations (Tarrytown, New York) has been most active in museum publications; a list of those in

286   STUBBORN FOR LIBERTY

print can be obtained from them. Discussion of archaeological "digs" includes
"'Digs' Reveal Dutch Era Traces," *de Halve Maen* 45:3 (October 1970), and
"Find Artifacts at Fort Orange," *de Halve Maen* 45:4 (January 1971). State
archaeology reports include John G. Waite and Paul R. Huey's *Senate House:
an Historic Structure Report* (Albany: State of New York, 1971), Waite and
Huey's *Washington's Headquarters, the Hasbrouck House: an Historic Structure Report* (Albany: State of New York, 1971), Paul R. Huey's *Archeology
at the Schuyler Flatts, 1971-74* (Albany: New York State Division for Historic Preservation, 1974), and John G. Waite, Paul R. Huey, and Geoffrey M.
Stein's *A Compilation of Historical and Architectural Data on the New York
State Maritime Museum Block in New York City* (Albany: State of New York,
1969). Hendrick Edelman's *Dutch-American Bibliography: 1643-1794* (Ithaca,
N.Y.: Spoken Language Services, 1974) has recently been published, as has
Gerald DeLong, *The Dutch in America, 1609-1974* (Boston: Twayne, 1975).
which stresses the immigrant experience of the Dutch.

Conclusion — The Uses of Diversity

Works on the Middle Colonies include John Fiske's *The Dutch and Quaker
Colonies in America* (Boston: Houghton Mifflin, 1899), 2 volumes, Wertenbaker's *Middle Colonies*, John A. Neuenschwander's *The Middle Colonies
and the Coming of the American Revolution* (Port Washington, N.Y.: Kenni-
kat Press, 1973), Milton M. Klein's *Politics of Diversity* (Port Washington,
N.Y.: Kennikat Press, 1974), and Whitfield J. Bell, *et al.*, "Middle States
Tradition in American Historiography," *Proceedings of the American Philo-
sophical Society* (April 15, 1964): 176-61. Two studies of Fiske are Milton
Berman's *John Fiske: The Evolution of a Popularizer* (Cambridge, Mass.:
Harvard University Press, 1961) and George P. Winston's *John Fiske* (New
York: Twayne, 1972). Bernard Mason's "Heritage of Carl Becker," *New-York
Historical Society Quarterly* 53:2 (April 1969): 127-47, comments on
Becker's thesis and his interest in the paradoxes of Revolutionary loyalties;
Flick and Ellis are standard histories of the state. Milton M. Klein's "Cultural
Tyros of Colonial New York," *South Atlantic Quarterly* (Spring 1967), and
"New York in the American Colonies: a New Look," *New York History* 53:2
(April 1972): 132-56; Michael Kammen's *People of Paradox* (New York:
Knopf, 1972), and Bonomi all deal with the concept of diversity. Alice P.
Kenney's "Private Worlds in the Middle Colonies," *New York History* (Janu-
ary 1970): 5-31, develops further the interpretation of diversity here pre-
sented and applies it to the Pennsylvania Germans as well as the Hudson
Valley Dutch.

INDEX

STUBBORN FOR LIBERTY

The Dutch in New York

was composed in 10-point IBM Selectric Century Medium, leaded two points
by Metricomp Studios, Grundy Center, Iowa, with display type
in Century Expanded by J. M. Bundscho, Inc., Chicago, Illinois;
printed offset on Perkins & Squier 55-pound Litho by
by Vicks Lithograph and Printing Corporation, Yorkville, New York;
smyth-sewn and bound over boards in Columbia Colonial Vellum by
Vail-Ballou Press, Inc., Binghamton, New York;
and published by

SYRACUSE UNIVERSITY PRESS

Syracuse, New York 13210